SIMPLE THEORY,
HARD REALITY

SUNY Series in New Directions in Crime and Justice Studies
Austin T. Turk, Editor

SIMPLE THEORY, HARD REALITY

The Impact of Sentencing Reforms on Courts, Prisons, and Crime

Tamasak Wicharaya

STATE UNIVERSITY
OF NEW YORK
PRESS

Published by
State University of New York Press, Albany

© 1995   State University of New York

Production by Susan Geraghty
Marketing by Nancy Farrell

Printed in the United States of America

For information, address State University of New York Press,
State University Plaza, Albany, N.Y., 12246

Library of Congress Cataloging-in-Publication Data

Wicharaya, Tamasak, 1958–
    Simple theory, hard reality : the impact of sentencing reforms on
courts, prisons, and crime / Tamasak Wicharaya.
        p.   cm. — (New directions in crime and justice studies)
    Includes bibliographical references and index.
    ISBN 0–7914–2507–X (hc : acid-free paper). — ISBN 0–7914–2508–8
(pbk. : acid-free paper)
    1. Sentences (Criminal procedure)—United States. 2. Prison
sentences—United States. 3. Prison sentences—United States-
-Evaluation. 4. Mandatory sentences—United States—Evaluation.
I. Title. II. Series: SUNY series, New directions in crime and
justice studies.
KF9685.W53 1995
345.73'0772—dc20   94-31688
                                                                  CIP

10 9 8 7 6 5 4 3 2 1

To Bob and June

CONTENTS

ILLUSTRATION

TABLES

FOREWORD

Crime is the number one concern of Americans as of this writing. With problems of the economy seemingly solved by the second year of the Clinton administration, the nation focuses its attention (and its fears) on the threat of crime. Concerns for rehabilitation and even deterrence appear to have receded for many Americans in favor of simple, retributive justice. The obstacle to achieving this goal seems to be that, in exercising discretion available to the judiciary, the criminal justice system has become "soft on crime."

Because democracy gives people the ability to control their rulers, public inclination is to change all this. Most voters have in their heads any number of simple theories of cause and effect (we call it "conventional wisdom") about public policy issues. In the case of crime, the answer appears to be simple: limit the discretion of the judiciary to impose punishment and insist on mandatory and minimum sentences for those who violate the law.

But the matter is not so simple. In the federal system, as it turns out, criminal justice is one of the very few areas governed almost exclusively under state sovereignty. This means that actions by the federal government will have only marginal effects. Even so, there is a flurry of activity at the national level passing legislation to "get tough on crime." The most recent example is the famous "three strikes and you are out" legislation that dooms an offender to life imprisonment, without parole, upon conviction for a third felony.

State actions, which have far more impact on crime control than actions taken at the federal level, vary widely as legislators rush to show that they are "tougher than thou" on crime. Georgia, ironically following softball rules rather than those of baseball, adopted "two strikes and you are out" legislation. In limiting the discretion of the judiciary, states have adopted "mandatory minimum sentences," as in Massachusetts and Michigan; "mandatory determinate sentencing," in Maine and Illinois; "presumptive determinate sentencing," in California and North Carolina;

and "presumptive sentencing guidelines," in Minnesota and Washington. Other states have adopted "voluntary sentencing guidelines."

What has been the effect of this "get tough on crime" crusade? The relatively few studies to date have been limited to policy outcomes in a single or a few states. Professor Wicharaya's work uses a comparative state framework to compare outcomes across states and over time of these efforts by state legislatures to determine judicial policy. In conducting the research, the author has made use of a wide range of theories, including those relating to institutional adaptation and the prominent "work group" models explaining judicial outcomes.

As important as the substantive findings is the creative extension of techniques for pooled data analysis. In many respects, the methodology confronts several issues that remain largely unresolved in applications of pooled data and extends the techniques beyond those generally employed in the literature of political science. In fact, it is only this methodological sophistication that allows the author to reach generalizable conclusions concerning state efforts to limit discretion and constrain judicial behavior.

The principal finding of the research is that simple theories directing public policy are likely to produce counterintuitive results. Contrary to the presumption that limiting judicial discretion produces less crime, it not only has no significant impact on relevant crime rates, it even results in fewer incarcerations. Simple theories of criminal justice do not account for the hard realities confronting the criminal justice system: fewer prison facilities because the public refuses to pay the price of incarceration, increases in violent crimes, pressures to process cases through plea bargains, and the decriminalization of "recreational" drug use. Faced with these and other harsh realities, the men and women who staff the work groups of the criminal justice system cope by utilizing what discretion they still retain. The results are the outcomes documented persuasively by the author.

Results of the analysis offer cogent explanations why state efforts to control judicial discretion have such unanticipated or even contrary consequences. These findings should be a subject of study for all state policy makers engaged in policies designed to modify state criminal justice systems. If for no other reason, the findings should be taken seriously, as one reader put it, because "they provide strong evidence of just how ill-considered, futile, and counterproductive has been the politics of 'tougher is better' so dominant over past years."

Robert B. Albritton
Northern Illinois University

ACKNOWLEDGMENTS

In writing this book, I am indebted to several scholars at Northern Illinois University: David Luckenbill, who kept me abreast of the literature on sentencing reform and courts and served on my dissertation advisory committee; Paul Calhane, a wonderful advisor whose unrelenting critiques refined many of my undeveloped ideas in the early version of the book; Lettie Wenner, who elucidated my thoughts about a typology of sentencing reform. Much of this book, particularly all the research work that goes into the first draft of the manuscript, took shape when I was a research associate and data analyst at the Center for Governmental Studies at Northern Illinois University in DeKalb. My thanks go to the center's then-director Pete Trott, project coordinator Bob Sheets, and my colleague John Baj for their assistance and support.

I would like to thank both anonymous readers for their valuable comments that led to major revisions on chapters 5 through 7. I am grateful to acknowledge the following publishers who have granted permission to reprint part of the original material that first appeared under their auspices. Excerpt from *Research on Sentencing* by Alfred Blumstein, Jacqueline Cohen, Susan E. Martin, and Michael H. Tonry, eds. Reprinted with permission from *Research on Sentencing: The Search for Reform.* Copyright 1983 by the National Academy of Sciences. Courtesy of the National Academy Press, Washington, D.C. Excerpt from "North Carolina's Determinate Sentencing Legislation" *Judicature* 68:140–52 by Stevens H. Clarke. Reprinted with permission from American Judicature Society. Copyright 1984 by American Judicature Society. Courtesy of American Judicature, Chicago, Illinois.

Writing a book is an enduring endeavor. What makes writing this book rewarding is to learn the process through which it has evolved from just a rough idea about doing evaluation to a uniquely designed policy evaluation that becomes a classic case study to share with students and policy analysts alike. Under his guidance and direction from my first year at Northern Illinois to the day I defended my dissertation, Robert B. Albritton began exposing me to research design and statistical procedures that have been employed in this work. Not only did he continue to feed me with provocatively challenging questions, but he also helped me discover gratifying answers. This book has benefited enormously from his committed and insightful reflection on both substantive and methodological matters.

My sincere thanks and appreciations to all. Despite all this assistance, some inadequacies may remain. It is because I failed to take advice and insisted on going my own way. I alone take responsibility for them. Furthermore, this book appears in this publication series because Ajarn Bob has kindly arranged with the Press for me after I had already returned home. To him, I owe much more than my words can do justice. This book is dedicated to Ajarn Bob, my mentor, and also to my dearest wife, June, who deserves special thanks for the love, understanding, and support she has given me while I worked on this book.

CHAPTER 1

An Introduction to Sentencing Reform

"The punishment should fit the crime."
"The public demands a prison sentence."
"This sentence will be a warning to others."
"Lock them up and throw away the key."
"And nobody can get you out."
"Three strikes and you are out."

These political campaign slogans reflect a popular response to the rise in violent crime during the past several decades. Political campaign oratory, of course, regularly oversimplifies the complex swirl of contending arguments about policy reforms. Beginning in the early 1970s, lawmakers, criminal justice professionals, academic analysts, and prisoners' rights advocacy groups reevaluated the rehabilitative goals of American prisons. The rehabilitative ideal was widely criticized because of disparities in sentences, paroles, and other outcomes of the criminal justice system. This political and academic debate brought to an end the indeterminate sentence system, which, in the name of rehabilitation, had granted judges and parole boards broad sentencing and releasing discretion.

State legislatures began by the mid–1970s to discard the rehabilitative ideal, embrace a punitive response to criminal violence and increasing crime rates, and, in effect, revive the nineteenth-century determinate sentence system. This shift in criminal justice policy was pervasive in scope and debatable in principle. To date, every state has adopted at least one type of sentencing reform. These reforms apply to a wide variety of offenses and offenders. They not only eliminate judicial discretion in many instances, but also set forth a new set of sentencing goals.

In the second half of the 1970s at least sixteen states passed mandatory minimum sentencing laws. In the early 1980s the number of states enacting such laws doubled. By 1983 the criminal codes of forty-nine states had mandatory prison sentences for certain crimes. Today at least ten states prescribe determinate sentences for the majority of criminal offenses, eight states have presumptive sentencing standards, and at least six states implement varied forms of sentencing guidelines.

This study will review the origins of sentencing reforms, explain their features and rationales, and evaluate their impacts on the criminal justice system and violent crime rates in the United States. Three major research questions will be addressed to reveal nationwide consequences of sentencing reforms. First, have criminal sentencing reform policies succeeded in increasing the certainty of punishment? Second, have these sentencing policies increased the size of prison populations? Finally—and perhaps most important—has the implementation of these policies been a deterrent to crime?

A THEORY OF CRIMINAL SENTENCING REFORM

The present study requires a conceptually sound and simplistic model or theoretical framework by which to explain how sentencing reforms have been formulated, implemented, and evaluated in this country. In seeking to explain these hotly debated and often value-laden governmental reactions to the crime problem, we characterize "crime policies" in the United States during the past two decades as "simple theory"—a theory of criminal sentencing reform. It is a simple theory that reduces normally much more complex causal chains among relevant factors to a rather simplistic form that describes and predicts policy consequences, both intended and unintended. This theoretical framework provides us with a conceptual lens through which we can evaluate whether sentencing reform policies have achieved their declared goals and also what unintended consequences of implementing them have been produced.

Crime policies, including criminal sentencing reform policies, are derived from criminology theories that usually possess competing and conflicting policy implications. The fact that there have been so many theories in the field of criminology makes both policy makers and laypersons adhere to criminology theories that are consistent with preferred crime policies. One reason is that "people tend to believe in one or another theory of crime because its policy implications are consistent with what they believe should be done about crime" (Vold and Bernard 1986, 343).

It is also obvious that those who study crime come into the field of criminology from many other disciples that tend to influence and shape their professional views toward human nature and society. Sociologists, for example, tend to see crime as the end result of economic and sociological factors and believe in eradication of its root causes by fighting poverty. Some believe in rehabilitation theories simply because they advocate treatment both in correctional institutions and in the community. Others believe in deterrence theories that prescribe punishment as the appropriate response to crime. These competing crime policies make certain theoretical assumptions about crime that we must hold in order to believe that they will work (Vold and Bernard 1986, 340–57).

In formulating policies, policy makers make "assumptions about what governments can do and what the consequences of their actions will be." In general, public policies imply a simple theory that takes the form "If X exists, then Y will follow." This simple theory will enable us to observe whether a particular policy fails either because the government fails to do X in full (which means that the simple theory may still be operating) or because X fails to produce the consequences as the theory predicts (which means that the simple theory is not operating). In practice, the causal chains on which a policy is based are usually much more complex (Hogwood and Gunn 1984, 18).

We admit that theories underlying policy are inevitably "complex" but we expect policy derived from theory to be "simple." For crime policy, most of us make certain theoretical assumptions about crime that we must hold in order to believe that such policy will work; and we are also willing to believe in the theory that implies what we believe should be done about crime (Vold and Bernard 1986, 348).

The theory of criminal sentencing reform explains the causal chains that link four key policy-relevant variables: sentencing reform policies, sentencing behavior, the size of prison populations, and crime rate, as illustrated in figure 1.1. A set of eight causal relationships logically derived from criminology theories such as deterrence and incapacitation is clearly spelled out in the theory of criminal sentencing reform in order to understand or make sense of sentencing reform policies. It is obvious that some of these relationships attempt to define what appear to have been the policy maker's intentions, both stated and unstated, in formulating criminal sentencing reform policies. Other relationships attempt to

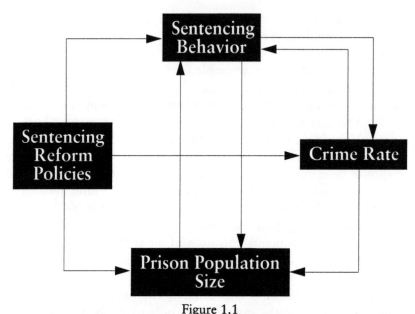

Figure 1.1
A Conceptual Framework for the Evaluation of
the Impacts of Criminal Sentencing Reforms in the United States

explain what consequences reform policies are intended to produce (outputs) and what policy impact they are intended to achieve (outcomes). There are also statements that address some aspects of unintended results policy makers may or may not have foreseen. The following statements refer to this set of relationships:

1. Sentencing behavior influences the crime rate. Getting tough with criminals by increasing the certainty and severity of actually imposed punishment will deter crime. If the rate of imprisonment and the average sentence length increase, then the crime rate will decrease.

2. Sentencing reform policy influences the crime rate. Getting tough with criminals by increasing penalties prescribed in the revised criminal codes will deter crime. If a sentencing reform policy adopted in a given state appears to be tougher, then the crime rate will decrease.

3. Sentencing reform policy influences sentencing behavior. Variation in the rigidity of discretionary control—flat, determinate, mandatory, presumptive, voluntary, and indeterminate sentences—can achieve varying levels of

compliance in case disposition. The greater the rigidity of discretionary control, the higher the degree of uniformity in the certainty and severity of sentencing outcomes (compliance). While we expect this relationship to hold, we should foresee the unintended results in the following form: the greater the rigidity of discretionary control, the higher the degree of internal resistance to change (noncompliance).

4. Sentencing behavior affects the size of prison populations. If the rate of imprisonment and the average sentence length increase, then the size of prison populations will enlarge.

5. Sentencing reform policy affects the size of prison populations. If sentencing reform policy endorses determinate sentences, then the size of prison populations will enlarge.

6. The crime rate affects the size of prison populations. If the crime rate increases, then the number of persons arrested, prosecuted, convicted, and sentenced to prison will increase.

7. The crime rate influences sentencing behavior. A conventional view holds that if the crime rate grows, sentencing behavior will be more punitive. We also foresee the unintended results that can be explained by the system overload hypothesis: If the crime rate increases, then the system will be strained and rates of conviction and imprisonment will decline.

8. The size of prison populations influences sentencing behavior. If the size of prison populations enlarges to the extent that prisons operate beyond their rated capacities, then sentencing behavior will become less punitive and imprisonment rates and average sentence lengths will decrease.

The theory of criminal sentencing reform will be used to guide this evaluation study in explaining criminal sentencing reform policies as crime policies. The objective of the present study is to observe whether sentencing reforms have been capable of doing what policy makers believe should be done and to determine whether there are problems with theories underlying criminal sentencing reform policies, the internal consistency of the "simple theory" (policy theories), and the apparent validity of its theoretical assumptions (criminology theories).

An Overview of Sentencing Reform

Criminal sentencing laws over the past two centuries have oscillated between two extremes: determinate and indeterminate sanctions. The development of these laws can be divided into three phases: criminal law reform around the end of the eighteenth century, correctional reform since the 1870s, and sentencing reform since the early 1970s. In the first phase, states revised their criminal codes to substitute incarceration for capital and corporal punishment for noncapital crimes. The principle of equal punishment for the same crime, proposed by classical criminologist Cesare Beccaria in *On Crimes and Punishments* (1777), gave rise to the definite or flat sentence. The statutes prescribed penalties of fixed terms, and the function of judges was to determine guilt or innocence. The intent was to increase the certainty of proportionate (neither overly lenient nor overly harsh) punishment to achieve deterrence. The view toward crime and punishment inherent in criminal laws was articulated by English philosopher Jeremy Bentham's utilitarian principle (Cullen and Gilbert 1982, 46–58; Tappan 1960, 430–37; Twentieth Century Fund Task Force on Criminal Sentencing [hereafter cited as Twentieth Century Fund], 1976, 85–89; Vold and Bernard 1986, 18–34).

At the end of the nineteenth century, judges could impose indefinite sentences, incarcerating criminals with both minimum and maximum terms. The duration of a sentence was conditioned on the behavior of the imprisoned offender. The enactment of good-time laws and a parole system as part of correctional reform from the 1870s through the 1920s led to the emergence of indeterminate sentences in America. Imposing indeterminate or open-ended sentences without minimum or maximum limits, judges left to experts in determining when to release inmates back to society. State criminal codes granted parole boards broad discretionary power in discerning individualized treatment for rehabilitation of the offender and deciding when the treated offender was rehabilitated or perhaps cured, no longer dangerous, and thus ready to be released. The assumption that criminals were sick and in need of professional help was derived from the positivistic school of criminology's argument that crime was caused by forces beyond the control of the individual (Cullen and Gilbert 1982, 64–83; Dershowitz 1976, 89–98; Tappan 1960, 433–37).

Criminal justice policy today has several primary goals: deterrence and incapacitation for the protection of the general public as well as retributive sanctions commensurate with the gravity of crimes. The determinate sentencing reforms in the past fifteen years revised the early-nineteenth-century strategy of overcoming disparities and discrimination in sentencing. Reasons for advocating such reforms varied among individuals and groups. From the conservative perspective, determinate sentences ensure certain and severe punishment. The restoration of law and order can be achieved through deterrence and incapacitation. The conservative idea of promoting determinate sentencing reform to achieve law and order gained popular support, leading to the adoption of mandatory minimum sentences for the most severe offenses in forty-nine states. Liberals regard the determinate sentence as a fairer system, with equal punishment for similar crimes, proportionate to the gravity of crimes committed. The liberal "just deserts" approach to sentencing reform, outlined in von Hirsch's *Doing Justice* (1976), was widely endorsed by lawmakers, who passed presumptive sentencing laws in eight states.

Various forms of determinate sentencing have been in place in the United States for several years. Evaluative studies have reported on the effects on the system operation of the following reform types: mandatory minimum sentencing laws, mandatory determinate sentencing laws, presumptive determinate sentencing laws, presumptive sentencing guidelines, and voluntary sentencing guidelines. Most of these studies reveal that these types of reform received inconsistent support from criminal justice professionals. Previous evaluations found some evidence of behavioral adaptation by judges, prosecutors, and defense attorneys in the implementation process. However, given the kinds of data analyzed and the research designs employed, any conclusions about the success or failure of sentencing reforms must await further research.

Major problems encountered in this research involve design issues. Several methodological shortcomings inherent in these single-state case studies leave the reader wondering about the plausibility of many rival explanations not accounted for by research designs of these studies. Despite this problem with research validity, researchers tend to overstate their generalized conclusions by drawing inferences that the data and research design cannot support (Cohen and Tonry 1983; Tonry 1987). Further research with a better design and sufficient data is clearly needed. Unlike prior evaluation research on this topic, this study takes a national perspective in its analysis of longitudinal data from forty-seven states before and after their sentencing reforms. This study will compare the effects of the five types of reform on the three major areas of policy interest: courts, prisons, and crime rates.

In this chapter, both sentencing reform models and the court community model will be discussed. The theoretical foundations of sentencing reform models have two major components: legislative control over sentencing decisions and the deterrent and incapacitative effects of the determinate sentence. The court community model provides a set of rival arguments based on the application of modern organization theories to the study of criminal courts. This study proposes an alternative view of criminal courts to help explain the absence of reform impact in the United States. The discussion then turns to one of the most crucial problems in evaluation research: how to define policy success criteria. These criteria should discern both intended and unintended consequences of sentencing reform.

Models of Sentencing Reform

Sentencing reform models posit a relationship among sentencing policy, sentencing behavior, and crime rates. Five sentencing reform models share the proposition that legislative control over sentencing decisions is the key to achieving desired changes in sentencing behavior, which are expected in turn to reduce crime rates.

Mandatory sentencing laws incorporate the principles of deterrence and incapacitation into their implementation process by mandating lengthy imprisonment for offenders convicted of designated crimes. These mandatory prison sentences promise punishment that is both certain and severe. The theory is to ensure that the costs of prohibited acts outweigh their benefits. In plain language, crime does not pay. Many revised criminal codes specify mandatory minimum prison terms as an additional deterrent. From the deterrence perspective, rational, calculating, potential criminals who perceive that the cost of punishment outweighs the benefit of a crime will refrain from prohibited acts. In addition, incarcerative sentences have a preventive effect on crime by incapacitating offenders, thus preventing them from committing other crimes.

This line of argument is not new to the study of crime and punishment. Deterrence theory is rooted in the works of eighteenth-century penologists Beccaria and Bentham (Vold and Bernard 1986). Criminals are assumed to be rational, calculating individuals free to determine their own actions, legal or illegal. In this view, punishment in general and imprisonment in particular is a main instrument for creating fear and thus controlling behavior. Attention was refocused on this classical approach in the late 1960s, when both theoretical and empirical questions about deterrence were reconsidered more thoroughly in the light of modern behavioral sciences and quantitative methods (Andenaes 1974; Becker 1968; Ehrlich 1973; Gibbs 1975; Phillips and Votey 1972; van den Haag 1975; Wilson 1975; Zimring and Hawkins 1973).

Since the adoption of sentencing reform for crime control, researchers have developed and tested deterrence models with empirical data (Silberman 1976; Tittle and Rowe 1973; Waldo and Chiricos 1972). Modern deterrence theory focuses on the potential criminal's perception of sanction threats, rather than the quality of the sanctions imposed (Grasmick and Bryjak 1980; Paternoster et al. 1983a; Teevan 1976; Tittle 1977; Williams and Hawkins 1986). While deterrence is a complex psychological phenomenon, the recent determinate sentencing reform relies on an oversimplified relationship between criminal acts and penalty schedules.

In their book *Deterrence*, Zimring and Hawkins (1973, 72) draw attention to several theoretical concepts that distinguish between general deterrence and individual or special deterrence. Determinate sentencing contains several features intended to produce both general and individual deterrent effects. Prescription of lengthy imprisonment in the mandatory sentencing laws is consistent with the idea of punishment as a threatened consequence of serious crimes. At the same time, it alerts the general public to the fact that serious crimes will not be tolerated, and it reinforces and builds respect for law and social order. "To get tough with criminals" draws support from the process of general deterrence briefly discussed above. Individual deterrence aims at reducing recidivism through punishment.

Adherents of deterrence view sentencing reform as a way to maximize the efficacy of legal sanction by increasing both certainty and severity of punishment. Mandatory minimum sentences are based on the deterrent effects of lengthy imprisonment for violent crimes. This element of sentencing reform relies on the argument that while both certainty and severity of sanction are important, neither alone is sufficient. Lengthy imprisonment imposed sparingly would have limited effects on crime, and consistency in the use of lenient sanctions is unlikely to produce any deterrent effects at all. Certainty and severity are interdependent and can reinforce one another synergistically (van den Haag 1975, 115).

Sentencing reform policy stands mainly for deterrence. The popular endorsement of mandatory sentencing laws throughout the United States emphasizes this goal. The law-and-order sentiment overrides the demand for justice in guiding criminal justice policy today in most states. The means to this political end is legislative control over judicial discretion in sentencing. The focus on sentencing decisions rests on the notion that sentencing behavior plays a vital role in determining the type and nature of legal sanctions for those convicted of crimes. To guarantee certainty and severity of punishment, changes in criminal laws and procedures are necessary to eliminate sentencing discretion regarding type of sentence and prison terms. Here the criminal court is charged with converting reform intentions into action, and the sentencing judge is the most important implementing agent.

Sentencing discretion exists in three major areas: (1) determining when incarcerative sentences are necessary; (2) if necessary, determining the appropriate lengths of sentence; and (3) determining when to release offenders. The first includes the certainty of severe punishment, given that imprisonment is considered harsher than other alternatives. The second involves the decision to set prison terms when imprisonment is used, and defines the degree of sanction severity. The third deals with the termination of prison terms for early release.

Various sentencing reforms, which will be reviewed more thoroughly in chapter 3, are designed to eliminate or reduce judicial discretion in these three areas. The ranges within which judges can exercise their discretion vary within these reform types, though the rigidity of restrictions on sentencing discretion does not necessarily vary to the same extent.

For instance, some new state laws seek to increase the certainty of imprisonment by mandating nonsuspendable prison terms to be served prior to parole eligibility. In most cases, judicial discretion to impose prison terms below mandated minimums is eliminated. This reform strategy was imposed to ensure a minimum level of punishment for target crimes. At the same time, there is a tendency in state laws to grant judges broad discretion above mandated minimums.

Reduction of judicial sentencing discretion has obviously been developed by legislatures to shape sentencing behavior. The objective of sentencing reforms is uniform application of imprisonment for serious offenses such as felonies involving firearms and repeat or habitual offenders. Uniformity in sentencing decisions presumably raises the expectation of imprisonment, at least among convicts. However, this is a reasonable presumption only when conviction is certain for real offenses as charged and indicted (Coffee and Tonry 1983). Uniform use of incarcerative sentences based on convictions does not necessarily mean that imprisonment is uniformly imposed for real offenses.

An assumption of determinate sentencing reform is that certain and severe punishment can be achieved by specific sentencing standards. Proponents argue that individualization of punishment often leads to capricious use of imprisonment, particularly when it is negotiated in exchange for guilty pleas, and extensive use of early parole release. To be more specific, the indeterminate sentence system makes punishment uncertain. Reformers are convinced that sentencing reforms are needed to overcome abuses of discretionary power (Dershowitz 1976; Fogel 1975; Frankel 1972; Gaylin 1974; Hart 1968; Morris 1974; van den Haag 1975; Wilson 1975). The conviction shared by advocates of determinate sentencing laws is that restrictions on sentencing and releasing discretion are essential to foster both certainty and severity of punishment, among other things (Feeley 1983, 117).

The individualization/standardization dichotomy is a key to understanding the fundamental difference between indeterminacy and determinacy in sentencing. While the indeterminate sentence system is based on individualized judgment, the determinate sentence system relies on standardized rules. A purely indeterminate system is characterized by individualization of punishments and vast discretionary power. A purely determinate system of definite or flat sentences requires standardization of punishments. Although determinate sentencing reforms vary in their rigidity, they endorse standardization, which is at the heart of the current sentencing policy. The higher the degree of standardization, the greater the rigidity of control and the more predictable the sentencing behavior that should result. A preference for strict sentencing rules, with some variation among the five sentencing models, reflects the pessimistic view of determinate sentencing advocates, who regard judges as prone to abuse their discretionary powers in the sentencing process.

A basic assumption about the effect of control on judicial behavior is that judges will comply with the reform goals when strict rules are imposed. In principle, judges and lawyers must follow criminal procedures in handling cases. But in practice, this fundamental assumption does not necessarily hold because formal compliance with rules tends to follow adjustment of facts to justify decisions reached in advance. If this is the case, adjustment to circumvent rules is difficult to regulate.

Another assumption by advocates of appellate sentence review about the role of criminal procedures is that decisions inconsistent with the rules are subject to checks and balances. Either the prosecutor or the defense counsel can appeal decisions inconsistent with the law. However, such appellate review exists more in theory than in practice because most sentencing decisions are made outside the adversarial system of checks and balances (Nimmer 1978, 22–24).

To a large extent, the mandatory sentencing reform model emphasizes control over sentencing behavior to increase the certainty and severity of punishment. The likelihood of policy success rests heavily on the effect of such control mechanisms on actual sentencing outcomes. Compliance with the standardization principle, not only in form but also in substance, should lead to a system in which incarcerative punishment is more certain, particularly for offenders of violent crimes eligible for mandatory prison terms.

Theoretical issues and empirical evidence of deterrence have been reviewed since the mid–1970s (Anderson 1979; Blumstein et al. 1978; Fattah 1977; Gibbs 1975). Thus far, it remains unclear that punishment deters criminals, under what circumstances it deters criminals, and what kinds of punishment have deterrent effects. There is no consistent evidence that legal sanctions have significant effects on criminal behavior.

THE COURT COMMUNITY MODEL

It is important to understand how criminal courts operate because what happens at courthouses determines the outcomes of cases.

Courts do not merely apply the law to specific criminal cases coming before them. Most cases are not tried; they are settled. Their outcomes are either directly or indirectly negotiated in the plea process. It is not the content of criminal laws and procedures that generally matters, but the way these cases are handled. Understanding how cases are processed can help explain how courts determine the outcomes of cases.

An organizational approach to the study of criminal courts is a product of empirical research begun in the late 1960s by analysts including Blumberg (1967), Carter (1974), Cole (1973), Eisenstein and Jacob (1977), Eisenstein et al. (1988), and Packer (1968).[1] Among many concepts widely employed in explaining the actions of criminal courts, three merit special attention. Courts can be viewed as case processors because of their specialized functions performed by "courtroom work groups" (Eisenstein and Jacob 1977; Nardulli et al. 1988, 17–18). Alternatively, courts can be viewed as political institutions. Not only are members of court personnel recruited in a political process, but they also interact with one another politically. What happens in courts determines "who gets what" in the play of power (Eisenstein et al. 1988, 10–11; Nardulli et al. 1988, 18–20). In addition, courts can be conceptualized as communities in which judges, lawyers, and clerks (inhabitants) depend on each other to get their jobs done (occupational interdependence) at courthouses (common workplace). People working there develop a common set of values, perceptions, attitudes, language (verbal and nonverbal), and tradition. These factors affect inhabitants' interpersonal relations and work techniques (Eisenstein et al. 1988, 22–33).

The concept of courts as communities draws support from a sociological approach to a study of complex human institutions in the field of modern organization theory. The court community model integrates several organizational concepts: organizations as open systems, informal relationships within organizations, power and politics in and around organizations, and organizational culture. Thus, the metaphor of courts as communities provides a sociological approach to understanding how they actually run their everyday business.

---

1. For a review of the organizational study of criminal courts, see Nardulli (1979).

Modern Organization Theories

The concepts of cooperation and adaptation reflect Simon's (1947) and Selznick's (1949) view of organizations as cooperative systems that maintain their internal stability by adapting to environmental influences. Cyert and March (1963) explain the process by which coalitions are formed to derive decisions through bargaining and side payments. Agreements within coalitions depend on the values of these side payments shaped by organizations' external environments and prior experience.

The adaptive system concept originated in contemporary organization theory literature, rooted in the works of Katz and Kahn (1966), Thompson (1967), von Bertalanffy (1951), and Weiner (1948). Both Weiner's cybernetics and von Bertalanffy's general systems theory emphasize the input-output-feedback iterative process of self-regulating behavior. In a social system, people in organizations tend to compensate for external forces exerting pressure at one location by adjusting their behavior at another location. This adaptive response to outside influences is called "homeostatic resistance." The principle of "equifinality" suggests that an adaptive system tends to develop multiple paths to reach the same final outcomes (Katz and Kahn 1966). This adaptive behavior is learned from prior experience and develops into organizational culture, norms, and values (Schein 1985).

Courts as Communities

The court community model rests on a set of underlying assumptions about the legal culture. The first is that a sense of community exists among people working at courthouses. Having a common workplace, courthouse officials share certain beliefs about their interpersonal relationships, certain attitudes about how cases should be processed, a special language for their verbal and nonverbal communication, and a sense of tradition in running courthouse business (Eisenstein et al. 1988, 28–33). Members of a court community interact with one another in performing their occupational duties as they adapt to external forces. Court communities adjust constantly as they respond to changes in the larger communities they serve.

As noted above, courtroom work groups and courthouse personnel can be regarded as belonging to a court community. Each work group has at least three principal actors: a judge, a prosecutor, and a defense counsel. They are highly specialized professionals representing the interests of their sponsoring organizations, who must work together to determine the outcomes of defendants' cases. Having to work together on a case teaches members of a work group how to cooperate and compromise. Their familiarity can increase their cooperative interactions in disposing of cases. Courtroom work groups share four major goals: to handle cases expeditiously, to reduce uncertainty in the outcomes of cases, to maintain group cohesion, and to do justice (Eisenstein and Jacob 1977). These shared goals influence how a particular case is handled and resolved.

Doing justice is what courtroom work groups think they do. Problems arise when members of work groups have different criteria for justice. The concept of "equal justice under law" means that defendants pleading guilty or going to trial should receive equal treatment according to their offenses (Eisenstein et al. 1988, 5; Zimring 1976). Thus, applying the law to specific circumstances of a case requires no discretionary adjustment for offenders' characteristics. But in practice, work groups exercise their discretion in what they see as appropriate in a given case and to a given offender. In a sense, certain adjustments are made to achieve proper punishment in plea negotiations and circumvent rules work groups see as inappropriate (Rosett and Cressey 1976, 7). Discretionary adjustments are not necessarily concessions in exchange for guilty pleas (Rosett and Cressey 1976, 163), and the exercise of discretion in settling cases is not strictly free from rules or norms (Heumann 1978; Mather 1974, 1979). These adjustments are influenced by a "legal culture" shared by members of the court community (Eisenstein and Jacob 1977; Eisenstein et al. 1988; Heumann 1978; Mather 1979; Rosett and Cressey 1976; Utz 1978).

Guilty Plea Models

The argument that sentencing outcomes are largely a product of plea negotiation is pertinent to the reform issue. First, *charge bargaining* can lead to conviction on reduced or substituted charges that can circumvent reformed sentencing standards. Second, *fact bargaining* can mitigate the severity of original offenses and lead to conviction of lesser charges. Third, *sentence bargaining* can influence the choice between incarceration and alternatives and, if incarceration is used, the length of the selected sentence.

Two models of plea bargaining are used to explain the types of disposition outcome it produces. In the concession model, increased certainty of conviction is a major objective that drives prosecutors to exchange concessions for guilty pleas. In accepting these offers, defendants and defense counsels waive their right to a fair trial and enter a guilty plea on charges the prosecutors might not have proven beyond a reasonable doubt. This type of plea negotiation can lead to conviction on reduced charges (charge bargaining), omission of key facts involved (fact bargaining), or adjustment or suspension of sentence length (sentence bargaining). Each type of plea bargaining can make the difference between imprisonment and nonincarcerative sentences or suspension of imprisonment. Deliberate manipulation of evidentiary facts is possible to secure certainty of negotiated sentencing outcomes (Alschuler 1979; Church 1976; Cole 1973; Friedman 1979; Krislov 1979). These explicit forms of plea bargaining have been criticized for their differential, perhaps unjust, results, accompanied by an ad hoc, irregular, and unpredictable pattern of punishment (Krislov 1979, 575–76).

The consensus model suggests that work groups follow some unwritten rules in selecting appropriate punishments for particular cases (Heumann 1978; Mather 1974; Rosett and Cressey 1976; Utz 1978). This model explains plea negotiations in which deals are not made explicit. The emphasis on "the social and cultural experience of the courtroom" leads to the contention that the plea process is more orderly than critics of the concessions model have thought. Plea negotiation is structured by guiding principles and rules (Mather 1979). Rosett and Cressey, for example, argue that work group norms exist at all courthouses and play a vital role in determining when to impose incarcerative sentences and how long sentences should be (1976, 90–91).

Some sociologists view criminal courts as akin to modern supermarkets, where the price tags (prison or probation, and, if prison, how long) for various commodities (classes of felonies, prior conviction records, use of firearms, and other aggravating factors) are posted in advance (Feeley 1979, 462; Rosett and Cressey 1976). In a sense, plea negotiation ensures that judges follow these norms. As students of criminal courts note: "Going rates, like supermarket prices, reduce the uncertainty and the need to bargain over what every case is worth" (Nardulli et al. 1988, 208–9).

In conclusion, the metaphor of courts as communities provides a useful tool for explaining how courts run their everyday business. It is essential to understand courts' everyday operations from this organizational perspective in order to explore ways they respond to changes imposed from outside.

DEFINITION OF POLICY SUCCESS

Evaluating public programs is difficult for several reasons. Determining policy success requires criteria for evaluation that reflect policy goals. Social scientists agree that the difficulty in defining policy success lies in problems encountered in determining policy goals (Rutman 1980). Defining policy success is more problematic when policy goals are vague or conflicting. It is even more difficult when the policy produces negative side effects or unintended consequences in implementation. How these conceptual problems are treated in this study raises several issues.

Problems with Policy Goals

This study considers policy goals in two related areas: sentencing behavior and crime. The first involves the outcomes of cases, whereas the second concerns the effects of these case outcomes on crime rates.

To determine whether public programs attain their goals is difficult from either a substantive or methodological perspective (Bingham and Felbinger 1989; Bowler 1974; Langbein 1980; Rossi and Freeman 1985; Rutman 1980). The term "success" is a vague concept that requires knowledge about policy goals. One faces problems with developing success criteria particularly when "the intent of the policy itself is difficult to ascertain" (Casper and Brereton 1984, 122). It is essential first to identify the goals and then to select those goals that are of policy interest for evaluation.

Not all goals are clearly stated in statutes. Some goals emerge during the course of policy debate. Defining these goals requires analysis of policy formulation and key elements that constitute policy. Evaluating goal attainment requires identifying criteria of success that recognize not only explicitly stated goals, or manifest goals, but also those inherent in policy arguments, or latent goals (Casper and Brereton 1984, 123).

During the policy debate in states concerning more use of determinate sentences, law-and-order adherents advocated the automatically applied severe penalties of the mandatory minimum sentencing schemes. At the same time, liberals suggested limited use of incarceration and shorter but determinate sentences under presumptive sentencing systems (Cullen and Gilbert 1982, 127–31). To broaden the base of political support for policy adoption, state legislatures built coalitions and compromised to avoid conflict, which always produced vague policies. Coalitions between law-and-order conservatives and "doing justice" liberals in Illinois and Minnesota, for example, incorporated their conflicting interests in sentencing reform into the negotiated policy formulation (Casper and Brereton 1984, 126; Shane-DuBow et al. 1985, 159; Zimring 1983, 101–16).

There are significant differences between conservative and liberal advocates of determinate sentencing in terms of emphases and goals (Feeley 1983, 117). Conservatives emphasize that punishment through deterrence and incapacitation through lengthy imprisonment reduce domestic violence and restore societal order (Newman 1978; van den Haag 1975; Wilson 1975). Liberals stress the promotion of prisoners' rights, reductions in sentencing disparity and discrimination, and increased accountability in criminal justice decision making. Liberals are less interested in crime control, but take a stand for fairness and equality in sentencing. Their dissatisfaction with indeterminate sentences leaves them no other options but to advocate determinate sentences (American Friends Service Committee 1971; Fogel 1975; Frankel 1972; Twentieth Century Fund 1976).

Another problem in identifying policy goals emanates from an abstraction of policy concepts and symbolic uses of political rhetoric (Edelman 1967) that obscure the relationship between means and ends (Braybrooke and Lindblom 1985; Hogwood and Gunn 1984; Lindblom 1959). This relationship involves the extent to which reform features are instrumental in attaining policy goals. The concepts of equality, equity, and fairness in sentencing practices are abstract and difficult to define, and even more difficult to measure and evaluate.

Measuring deterrent and incapacitative effects of legal sanctions is also problematic because of problems with deterrence theories themselves (Greenberg 1975; Nagin 1978). Deterrence theorists argue that potential criminals act rationally, calculating the risk of being caught and the costs to themselves of punishment (Grasmick and Bryjak 1980; Paternoster et al. 1983a; Waldo and Chiricos 1972; Williams and Hawkins 1986). These theorists provide no explanation of how to define potential would-be criminals and how to measure whether they refrain from criminal acts or are deterred by fear of punishment or other confounding social control factors (Paternoster et al. 1983b; Thomas and Bishop 1984; Tittle and Rowe 1973).

Despite such problems with the definition of policy goals for evaluation, there is some agreement about what the reforms should achieve. Both conservative and liberal reformers agree that "punishment means prison" and that sentences should be administered consistently (Zimring 1983, 107). While conservatives favor the certainty of "severe" punishment, liberals call for the certainty of "fair" punishment.

The criminal sentencing reforms in the United States are broad, complex, and diverse. Mandatory minimum sentencing laws are identified with certain and severe punishment for deterrent and incapacitative effects. Presumptive sentencing laws and sentencing guidelines share the goal of promoting justice through fair and certain punishment. This study is not intended to evaluate all policy success criteria. Rather, it is limited to analyzing the goal of promoting certainty of imprisonment agreed on by both conservatives and liberals.

Crime control was the underlying goal of many who voted for more determinate sentences in state legislatures. The certainty of severe punishment was directed toward controlling crime, even when it was not stated explicitly in the statutes. This study is not designed to test deterrence theory or explain crime phenomena, but rather to evaluate whether the sentencing reforms served as an effective deterrent to crime.

Within the scope of this study, only two indicators of policy success were selected for evaluation. First, successful implementation will be measured by an increase in the probability of prison commitment per adult arrest, that is, the use rate of incarcerative sentences. Second, if sentencing reforms serve as an effective deterrent to crime, crime rates should drop during the period of implementation. Therefore, crime rates are also measured to evaluate policy consequences on potential criminals after an appropriate lag time for deterrence to have an effect.

Problems with Unintended Consequences

In addition to the two criteria for policy success, this study will also attend to policy impacts that were not intended by the sentencing reformers. The National Research Council Panel on Sentencing Research acknowledges that sentencing reforms can produce heavy financial and administrative burdens on the corrections sector. In particular, they can lead to crowding in state institutions (Blumstein et al. 1983, 225). This policy concern has stimulated research on the relationship between sentencing reforms and prison crowding (Casper 1984; Hepburn and Goodstein 1986; Mullen et al. 1980). In 1979 about 40 percent of inmates were housed in local jails in Mississippi and about 25 percent in Alabama (Blumstein et al. 1983, 230). Seven years later, many states continued to house a substantial portion of their prisoners in local jails, particularly in New Jersey (16%), Kentucky (14%), Louisiana (22%), Mississippi (17%), and Tennessee (14%) (Flanagan and Jamieson 1988, 483).

The growth in prison populations, however, cannot be attributed solely to changes in sentencing policies. Other factors influence the size of prison populations, such as changes in the composition of the civilian population and changes in crime rates. In this study, attention will be paid to the impact of sentencing reform policies on the size of prison populations in state institutions relative to the civilian population in the states.

PLAN OF THE STUDY

This chapter has explained the theory of sentencing reform, the features of sentencing reforms, and problems confronting definitions of policy success. Both intended and unintended consequences of the reforms were considered for evaluation. Sentencing reforms were analyzed with regard to their theoretical foundations and strategic instruments for achieving desired behavioral changes. The court community model advanced by contemporary students of criminal courts was examined to provide an organizational context for sentencing reforms.

Chapter 2 traces the evolution of the American criminal justice system from colonial times to the present. This historical analysis focuses on how changes in values and theories of crime and punishment moved from a punitive model to a rehabiliative one and back to deterrence.

Criminal justice reformers since the 1970s have sought to determine legal sanctions by controlling judicial behavior and discretion in sentencing. Criminal sentencing reforms have led to alterations in criminal procedures in the United States. These reforms vary from state to state but fall into five major types, which will be defined and explained in chapter 3.

A series of single-case studies has evaluated early experiences with reform implementation and their impacts on sentencing outcomes and crime rates. These evaluations, which will be reviewed in chapter 4, reveal several substantive findings of implementation difficulties. The generalizability of these findings is limited by the research designs employed. The discussion will also cover methodological issues in the sentencing reform evaluation literature.

Methodological issues related to research design and statistical procedures will be discussed more thoroughly in appendixes A and B. Evaluation models will be specified, one for each research question. The discussion will center on the development of research methodologies particularly designed for a study of comparative public policy in the American states.

Chapter 5 will explore the context and dynamics of the criminal court process that explain what happens at courthouses and how it affects the dispositional outcomes of criminal cases. In chapter 6, both pooled time-series and interrupted time-series analyses will be used to document the wide variance in the consequences of sentencing reforms nationwide. The period under study covers at least fourteen years. Major substantive findings will be discussed with reference to the five types of sentencing reform strategies. Chapter 7 will summarize major research findings and their policy implications. Finally, both the sentencing reform theory and the court community explanation will be reevaluated in light of the results of this evaluation study.

CHAPTER 2

The Origins of Sentencing Reforms

From a sociological perspective, societal values and other social forces have a crucial role in shaping public policy in response to social problems, including crime. Penal policy, one important area of governmental response to crime, determines how to handle those accused of committing a crime. Whether to rehabilitate or merely to punish the offender in pursuit of reduction in crime relies mainly on crime theories and their underlying assumptions about criminal behavior. Theories of punishment also play a part in guiding penal policy. To a certain extent, public policy mirrors the competing views and theories of crime and punishment as well as proposed solutions to the crime problem. Some theories, however, provide no pragmatic solutions that can be translated into realistic policy. But sometimes, public policy attempts to address problems for which theorists do not have policy solutions. Thus, theories are often used only to justify governmental actions.

This chapter reviews penal policy in America from colonial times to the present. Attention will be given to the changing views of crime and punishment that shaped societal responses to crime in general and public policy that guided official sanctioning procedures and practices in particular. Criminal laws and procedures in the United States have changed to accommodate changes in sentencing policy during the past two centuries. In retrospect, Americans have experienced criminal law reform, correctional reform, and, recently, court reform. As the discussion in the following pages will demonstrate, the concept of the therapeutic state played a vital role in guiding rehabilitative policy throughout the longest period of American history. The mid–1970s sentencing reform represents a marked shift in policy back to many elements of the criminal law reform that preceded rehabilitative policy.

This chapter is divided into three major sections. The first section surveys the emergence of criminal law reform in the United States. The American Revolution brought about the modernization of state criminal codes and procedures that eliminated primitive sanctions, including corporal punishment. The second section explains the rise and fall of the therapeutic state. What are major elements of the therapeutic state? What are major reasons for its rise and fall? The third section is devoted to the analysis of the origins of the recent sentencing reform. It will explore social and political forces being brought into play during the course of the reform movement.

CRIMINAL LAW REFORM

Criminal law reform at the turn of the eighteenth century was largely a product of a broader social reform movement taking place in Europe. This social reform was influenced by European civilization forces, including intellectual and cultural revolution, political thoughts, classical economic theories, and legal philosophy. As a result of the American Revolution, state laws were drafted in accord with the political values and principles of the United States Constitution. Criminal codes replaced the cruel and primitive sanctions of colonial codes with more humane and modernized punishments. This period of American history can be described as an initial phase of penal policy reform (1770s–1870s). This section will discuss the criminal law reform in comparison with the colonists' reactions to crime. The objective is to focus on the view of crime, types of punishment, and sanctioning goals.

Colonial Penology

Prior to the American Revolution, criminals were viewed as depraved and incorrigible by nature. This view toward crime reflects the Calvinist doctrine of the natural depravity of humankind (Cullen and Gilbert 1982; Dershowitz 1976). In viewing crime as sin, the colonists reacted to crime by punishing offenders swiftly, publicly, and harshly. The goal of criminal sanctions was punitive and retributive. The colonial sense of justice was "an eye for an eye" reaction to crime. The goal of punishment was to secure public safety and to revenge the victims by infliction of pain and public humiliation on the offenders (Barnes 1968; Inverarity et al. 1983, 126–48; Rothman 1971; Sutherland and Cressey 1978; Walker 1980).

There were several forms of harsh punishment, including capital and corporal punishment, public humiliation, banishment, and fines. The death penalty was prescribed much less often for criminal offenses other than murder in colonial America than in England or France. However, colonial criminal codes contained a number of crimes punishable by execution. There were, for instance, a total of eleven capital offenses in Pennsylvania and fourteen in Connecticut during the seventeenth century (Barnes 1968, 29–30; Walker 1980, 12–13). In eighteenth-century Massachusetts, third-time offenders of such minor crimes as stealing or burglary were subject to the death penalty (Rothman 1971, 52).

Corporal punishment, particularly whipping, was widely used both in conjunction with, and frequently in place of, a fine for an indigent offender. The intent of the stocks or the pillory was to humiliate those guilty of unlawful misconduct. Branding was another form of public humiliation for those committing first-time, less serious offenses. Banishment served the purpose of isolating offenders from the community for public protection. Other types of isolation were strictly applied for pretrial detention and not for sanction purposes.

The wide range of capital offenses in colonial criminal codes had to do with the role of religion. Offenses against God were frequently harsh; many carried the death penalty. Following the church fathers, the colonists equated crime with sin and, thus, envisioned a criminal as a depraved creature (Walker 1980, 13). Any third-time offender was believed to be incorrigible. In order to cope with the hardened and vicious criminals, the colonists were left only with capital punishment, devised to promote their own safety (Rothman 1971, 52).

Incarcerative Reform

The advent of Enlightenment ideas as in the notable works of Montesquieu, Voltaire, Beccaria, Bentham, and others played a vital role in bringing about law reform during the decades following the Revolution. The theology of the church fathers and the doctrine of the divine right of kings were discredited and finally fell into a state of disuse. The pessimistic outlook of criminal sentences was cast aside and superseded by the intellectualism and rationalism of these social contract and utilitarian philosophers.

The classical school of criminology then emerged (Barnes 1968, 75; Cullen and Gilbert 1982, 51–64).

In *On Crimes and Punishments*, Cesare Beccaria elaborated his ideas for penal reform (Hagan 1985, 12–14; Tappan 1960, 586; Vold and Bernard 1986, 18–26). Capital punishment was said to be excessively harsh and unnecessary. Deprivation of liberty via imprisonment was considered a more fruitful mechanism for deterrence. As Beccaria suggested, incarceration could be more easily carried out than the death penalty. In his *The Principles of Morals and Legislation*, Jeremy Bentham laid the groundwork for the notion of deterrence in line with Beccaria's reform proposal (Hagan 1985, 14–16; Tappan 1960, 586–87).

As a result of criminal law reform, criminal codes in many states prescribed lengthy and legislatively fixed prison terms. For instance, a criminal served forty years in prison for murder, twenty years for arson, and ten years for burglary (Blumstein et al. 1983, 58). This kind of penalty schedule was a flat system. Judges were charged with determining the offenders' guilt or innocence and applying laws. Under this flat sentencing, there was no room for discretion in selecting prison sentences.

Penal reform was tried by the Quakers in Pennsylvania. In the late seventeenth century they adopted the "Great Law," which prescribed prison sentences in lieu of corporal and capital punishment. The death penalty was abolished for all crimes except murder. Most serious crimes carried prison sentences under the law. From the Quakers' point of view, incarceration was used for the reformation of the offender. As they argued, solitary cells would allow for penitence on the part of the offender. To reflect this humanitarian outlook, prisons were called penitentiaries (Barnes 1968, 32; Walker 1980, 33).

As the history of criminal law reform indicates, the evolution of penal policy was a movement from the pessimistic view of human nature justifying the need for cruel, unusual, and retributive punishment at one end of the spectrum to the optimistic, humane, and utilitarian punishment at the other end. Capital and corporal punishment as well as banishment diminished. Imprisonment was justified by deterrence theory and its utilitarian function. Another competing goal was to reform the offender while he or she was incarcerated in the penitentiary. It was this latter goal of incarceration that became a crucial element of the therapeutic state.

THE RISE AND FALL OF THE THERAPEUTIC STATE

The term "therapeutic state" here refers to penal policy in the United States since the Declaration of Principles by the National Congress on Penitentiary and Reformatory Discipline at the October 1870 meetings in Cincinnati, Ohio. The National Congress Principles embraced rehabilitation as a primary goal directed toward reduction in crime (Cullen and Gilbert 1982, 68). The therapeutic state or rehabilitative policy had enjoyed wide acceptance for many decades.

Rehabilitation was guided by a scientific view of criminal behavior and appropriate solutions derived from it. In his *The Borderland of Criminal Justice*, Francis A. Allen identifies three major assumptions of the rehabilitative ideal: (1) human behavior is the product of antecedent causes that can be discovered and explained through scientific methods; (2) such scientific knowledge about the antecedents of human behavior can be used to achieve the scientific control of human behavior; and (3) scientific treatment should serve the therapeutic function of promoting changes in the behavior of the convicted offender in the interest of his own happiness, health, and satisfactions and in the interest of social defense (1964, 26).

The Roots of the Therapeutic State

The transition from the flat sentence system to the indeterminate sentence system took place gradually. A major reason for indeterminate sentencing was to improve prison conditions associated with prison crowding, brutality, and disorder due to lengthy flat sentences. Attention was paid to the prison design suitable to increase custodial control of inmate behavior. Solitary cells, for example, were designed to isolate convicts in order to enhance their reformation (Blumstein et al. 1983, 59; Cullen and Gilbert 1982, 61–64).

Another important factor influencing the creation of indeterminate sentences was the emergence of several new concepts in treating prisoners. Flat sentences were regarded as inconsistent with reformatory principles. Appropriate treatment required both reward for cooperation and penalty for disobedience as incentives for the process of reforming the offender. Thus, imprisonment was no longer necessary once the offender was reformed. But in reality, convicts still had to serve their sentences in full, regardless of their behavior (Rothman 1971, 250–51). This idea led to the creation of a good-time system, the commutation of sentences for prisoners' good behavior, in New York during the 1820s (Barnes 1968, 311–15).

In 1870 the National Congress on Penitentiary and Reformatory Discipline promulgated the tenets of a new penology. Crime was viewed as a moral disease. Thus, treatment should effect moral regeneration by "doing good" for the criminals, not by merely punishing them. Unlike the scientific argument for rehabilitation, advocates of the new penology drew support from a nonscientific belief. As Zebulon Brockway, then the superintendent of the Detroit House of Correction, explicitly stated: "evil is to be overcome with good" (Cullen and Gilbert 1982, 71). Another argument rested on "the curative powers of the indeterminate sentence" and regulated treatment for the prisoner's self-interest (Cullen and Gilbert 1982, 72). In 1877 a parole system, one of the most crucial elements of the indeterminate sentence system, was adopted at the Elmira Reformatory in New York (Blumstein et al. 1983, 60; Dershowitz 1976, 94; Rothman 1980, 32).

During the early years of parole, a sentence was neither flat nor completely open-ended. It was long enough for reformation to occur but not in excess of the maximum term prescribed by legislation (Barnes 1968, 317; Rothman 1980, 33). Using Tappan's (1960) terminology, it was indefinite. An administrative scheme was devised with reward and penalty marks for inmate behavior that determined when the inmate would earn his or her "ticket-of-leave" for parole release (Cullen and Gilbert 1982, 73). Indeterminate sentencing was in widespread use after the opening decade of the twentieth century (Barnes 1968, 315). In order to facilitate the administration of the prison system and to enhance the implementation of individualized treatment, parole boards, supervision programs, and the practice of probation were established and expanded considerably. By 1922 all but four states had either one or more of thirteen forms of indeterminate sentencing (Dershowitz 1976, 95). The therapeutic state had penetrated every aspect of penal policy, and continued for more than half a century.

The Structure of the Therapeutic State

Individualized treatment drew support from European positivist criminologists Cesare Lombroso (1835–1909), Enrico Ferri

(1856–1928), and Raffaele Garofalo (1852–1934). These criminologists studied criminality by application of scientific methods in search of causal theories. Contemporary American positivists engaged in formulating theories related to physical characteristics, biological factors, intelligence, personality, and social and economic determinants of the offender (Vold and Bernard 1986).

These positivistic theories share a set of fundamental assumptions that contradict those of deterrence and retribution theories. Under the first basic assumption, criminal behavior is determined by numerous forces beyond the control of the individual. Further, the causes of criminal behavior tend to vary greatly from one offender to another (Vold and Bernard 1986, 36–142). In light of this theoretical conception and with the view of the offender as sick, and thus in need of treatment to be prescribed by the expert on a case-by-case basis, penal reformers sought to individualize criminal justice procedures to expedite rehabilitation programs (Blumstein et al. 1983, 60; Cullen and Gilbert 1982, 76; Rothman 1980, 43–81).

Advocates of indeterminate sentences agreed on the necessity of individualization. Thus, attention was paid not to the crime committed but to the criminal. Implementing individualized treatment under a indeterminate sentence system requires that discretionary powers be granted to those involved in sentencing decisions of the legal process (American Friends Service Committee 1971, 84). The Progressives' optimistic rehabilitation theories endorsed the therapeutic state with trust in its agents and their adherence to the principle of doing good for the offender. Since these professionals took the responsibility of carrying out treatment programs in "good faith," there were no compelling reasons to withhold from them the basic requirement of rehabilitation: the exercise of discretionary powers (Cullen and Gilbert 1982, 78–79).

To do good was to prescribe the most appropriate treatments for the offender on a case-by-case basis. The prescription of treatment was contingent on the offender's potential for rehabilitation according to the experts' judgments. Who would receive probation; when to release the offender on parole supervision; who was hardened and incorrigible or remained dangerous to society if set free— all of these questions require administrative and judicial discretion.

In his *Conscience and Convenience*, David Rothman argues that the Progressives enlarged the primary actors' discretionary authority to promote social justice and individual well-being. As he observes, "reformers saw no reason to circumscribe narrowly the discretion of the state" and "the state was not a behemoth to be chained and fettered" (1980, 60–61).

Penal policy in the therapeutic state was even endorsed by the United States Supreme Court. In his opinion rendered in *Williams v. New York* (1949), Justice Hugo Black was quoted for his reference to "a prevalent modern philosophy of penology that the punishment should fit the offender and not merely the crime" (Allen 1981, 5). By the 1950s the speculation one could make regarding the future of the therapeutic state was that the dominance of the rehabilitative ideal in directing criminal justice policy in the United States would continue for decades. By the late 1960s, however, the therapeutic state was overwhelmed with many anomalies. Repeated failure of rehabilitative programs was manifested by high rates of recidivism among released convicts, deterioration of prison conditions, official brutality, and inmate revolts.

The Decline of the Therapeutic State

In his *The Decline of the Rehabilitative Ideal*, Francis Allen writes that "the central fact appears inescapable: the rehabilitative ideal has declined in the United States; the decline has been substantial, and it has been precipitous" (1981, 10). For one reason, the academic advocacy of the therapeutic approach has diminished. The erosion of such theoretical support together with the debilitating effect of domestic turmoil and other unfavorable situations gave rise to attacks on rehabilitation by conservative professors as well as liberal academics and practitioners who were once its advocates (Blumstein et al. 1983; Cullen and Gilbert 1982; Tonry 1987; Zimring 1983). A series of publications that emerged after a number of prison uprisings (American Friends Service Committee 1971; Frankel 1972; Fogel 1975; Gaylin 1974; Twentieth Century Fund 1972; van den Haag 1975; Wilson 1975) demonstrate that the theoretical foundation of the therapeutic state has been eroded (Allen 1981, 9).

Social factors that weakened the therapeutic state antedated the 1970s, when most of the major reform conditions occurred (Allen 1981, 29). Widespread fear of violent crime, political unrest and hostility toward authority in the course of the civil rights movement and the Vietnam War demonstrations, political corruption and scandals, and a growing public pessimism—all affected the rehabilitative ideal unfavorably in the 1960s. As a result, progressive optimism diminished sharply (Allen 1981, 30; Cullen and Gilbert 1982, 82; Dershowitz 1976, 98).

Major legal criticisms of the therapeutic state appeared during the late 1960s and the early 1970s. Among these are the writings of Allen (1964), Davis (1969), Hart (1968), and Rawls (1971), who are cited frequently in the determinate sentencing reform literature. This literature was effective in bringing about widespread reform efforts after the mid–1970s. Liberal criminologists cried for elimination of disparities and discrimination through sentencing reform.

THE SENTENCING REFORM MOVEMENT:
A RETURN TO THE DETERMINATE SENTENCE SYSTEM

The sentencing reform movement of the 1960s and 1970s is a historical event of considerable significance for its impact on the criminal justice system. A decline in indeterminate sentencing, Allen argues, is a product of the concomitant decline of social purpose that brings about an increased public pessimism and hostility toward authority (1981, 30). Ghetto violence as well as antiwar and civil rights turbulence generated a hostile, often brutal, response, which in turn led to greater awareness of political oppression with demands for societal amelioration. Strengthening of social welfare and the restoration of law and order became two major political issues.

During the Johnson administration, the quest for social justice and a more efficient criminal justice system, expressed in *The Challenge of Crime in a Free Society* by the President's Commission on Law Enforcement and Administration of Justice (1967a), initiated an emphasis on crime prevention through improved social welfare. The war on poverty as the war on crime viewed inadequate housing and unemployment as root causes of the crime problem (Winslow 1973). But many politicians came to believe that social welfare programs were expensive to run and their effects on crime difficult to assess.

Despite this welfare strategy, crime became the nation's most urgent urban problem during the Nixon administration. Moreover, the Watergate cover-up scandal eroded the public's confidence in the government (Inciardi 1987, 9–30). This legitimacy crisis and loss of trust in public officials intensified the demand for accountability in governmental action (Cullen and Gilbert 1982, 109). In addition, prison uprisings demonstrated prisoners' discontent with indeterminate sentences accompanied by disparity and discrimination in sentencing and prison brutality. Another line of theoretical development based on the concepts of individual rights, justice, criminal responsibility, and punishment evolved into a coherent theme. In part influenced by this development, theorists began to probe whether rehabilitation theory itself was flawed (Blumstein et al. 1983, 2–3).

Crime Control

The crime control issue was a major component of the intense political debate over domestic policy during the 1960s. According to officially reported crime statistics, the murder rate rose sharply from 4.5 per 100,000 population in 1962 to 9.4 per 100,000 in 1972, more than double and the highest rate since 1936. The same pattern was reported for robbery, which rose from 60 per 100,000 in 1960 to 131 per 100,000 in 1968 (Wilson 1975, 5–6). The fear of victimization was pervasive in cities and, during 1965–73, national surveys reported that crime was perceived as the number one urban problem (Inciardi 1987, 21, 28). James Q. Wilson, the author of *Thinking about Crime*, observes: "During the 1960s we were becoming two societies—one affluent and worried, the other pathological and predatory" (1975, 5).

The war-on-crime mentality influenced federal intervention in the areas of welfare programs and criminal justice education and law enforcement hardware. Despite these efforts, rising crime rates seemed to be unaffected. One observer pointed out that this strategy for crime reduction failed to realize its promise (Walker 1980, 252). The failure of the criminal justice system to control crime was a frustrating experience for everyone (Jacob 1986). Conservatives turned to the only attractive alternative: a move toward greater respect for law and restoration of societal order. In his speech before a Yale Law School audience in 1976, President Gerald Ford endorsed a mandatory minimum sentencing model to increase the certainty of criminal sanctions as a means to "insure domestic tranquility" and restore a sense of law and order (Cullen and Gilbert 1982, 102). "Law and order," once presidential candidate Goldwater's slogan in 1964, was taken by Richard Nixon in 1968, reiterated by Gerald Ford in 1976, and repeated by Ronald Reagan in 1980.

The emphasis on law and order was a call to get tough with criminals for the protection of millions of innocent American victims of crime. A general complaint from law and order advocates focused on leniency in previous rehabilitative policy responses to street crime. As they argued, more punishment, not less, should be imposed not only to deter future criminals but also to incapacitate (with lengthy imprisonment) habitual perpetrators of violent crimes. For more certain and severe punishment, criminal sentences should be fixed and their minimum terms made mandatory for selected violent offenses and categories of habitual offenders.

Because of the growing fear of "career criminals" or frequent offenders, Wilson argued that "increasing the certainty of a prison sentence is valuable both for its deterrent as well as for its incapacitative effect" (1975, 178). He explicitly stated his argument: "it would be better to improve the ability of police and prosecutors to identify and arrest high-rate offenders than to improve the ability of judges to sentence convicted offenders.... Judges now incarcerate selectively and always will; the central problem is whether we can improve on the basis for that selectivity" (1983, 155–56). Wilson's position represents the conservative view of sentencing reform from a crime control perspective based on deterrence and incapacitation theories.

Prison Uprisings and the Civil Rights Movement

Prison uprisings played a vital role in sentencing reform of the mid–1970s. In a sense, the civil rights movement in the 1950s and 1960s had reached inside prison walls. In the late 1960s there was a series of inmate riots in a number of state prisons and jails, including those in California, Florida, Indiana, and particularly New York. The prisoners' rights issue became part of the civil rights campaign. One reason was that prisoners had long been disproportionately minorities, particularly blacks. In addition, officials' brutality was identified with frequent reference to racism on the part of white guards against nonwhite inmates, and other poor prison conditions such as denial of some basic constitutional rights and lack of human dignity in prisons. Indeterminate sentencing only added to the problem by giving inmates a sense of injustice due to the inequity they perceived after comparing sentences.

Liberal reformers concluded that indeterminate sentencing did more harm than good for the reasons mentioned above. Based on the liberal interpretation of prisoner revolts during this period, prisoners' discontent with indeterminate sentences was widespread and profound (Blumstein et al. 1983, 61). Following the aftermath of the July 1970 riot at Holmesburg Prison in Philadelphia, ninety-six individuals were reported injured. Commenting on the incident, three Philadelphia judges described the prison as "a cruel, degrading and disgusting place, likely to bring out the worst in man" or "a place ruled by cold-blooded terror" (American Friends Service Committee1971, 1). In the three months that followed, thousands of prisoners in the Tombs of New York City and other city jails rioted in pursuit of prisoners' rights as well as just and humane treatment.

In 1971 the American Friends Service Committee, a body of individuals devoted to the promotion of civil rights in prisons, published its Working Party's report on crime and punishment in America, entitled *Struggle for Justice*. The Working Party preface claims: "These upheavals warn the public that prisoners will no longer submit to whatever is done to them in the name of 'treatment' or 'rehabilitation'" (1971, vi). A list of grievances of the Tombs inmates to the mayor of New York appeared in the report's introductory pages. The list was intended to make several points: plea bargaining contradicts due process of law because the offender is assumed guilty until proved innocent; rehabilitation in prisons is "threat, coercion and intimidation disguised as law and justice"; unnecessary brutality is a standard strategy for custodial control (1971, 2–6). In the same year this volume was published, prisoners at New York's Attica Correctional Facilities rebelled. This resulted in a massacre of twenty-nine inmates and ten hostage guards, with hundreds more wounded when police retook the prison.

In his analysis of this case study, Inciardi described the prison conditions at Attica as embedded with racism: "Above all, for both inmates and officers, 'correction' meant an atmosphere charged with racism" (1987, 588). In his *Criminal Sentences*, Judge Marvin Frankel sees it somewhat differently. Apart from racism, poor communication channels between the two sides created a worsening climate, leading to "the growth of fierce inmate governments" (1972, 46). For Frankel, the abuse of discretionary power is one of the major problems with the indeterminate sentence system. David Fogel agrees with this line of argument. As he points out, "Legislatively prescribed procedures are practically non-existent. Regardless of what the judge finally selects as a sentence, the process itself, with rare exception, is inscrutable" (1975, 195).

Disparity and Discrimination in Sentencing

The question of disparity and discrimination associated with criminal sentencing served as an impetus to sentencing reform, particularly after the Attica incident. Social scientists began to pay increasing attention to this issue in an attempt to examine whether these kinds of unintended consequences existed under the indeterminate sentence system. The extent to which criminal sentences are imposed with several kinds of judicial bias was increasingly subjected to rigorous statistical analysis (Blumstein et al. 1983, 64).

In their *Lawless Judges*, originally published in 1935 and reprinted in 1970, Goldberg and Levenson attribute disparity in sentencing to what they call "lawless trials." By lawless, they mean a "lack of adherence to law" (p. i). "The prevalence of unfair trials," they wrote, "has reached the proportions of a national scandal" (p. 186). There were a number of empirical studies dealing with the subject in the 1940s to 1960s and even more after Attica. In general, black defendants tended to receive harsher sentences than did white defendants. In particular, discrimination existed due to a racial difference between offenders and victims, specifically black violence against white victims (Paternoster 1984; Spohn et al. 1981).

As Gaylin's data suggest, "One of the most glaring and provocative of inequities in a world not known for fairness is a disparity in punishment: when like individuals, committing like offenses, are treated differently" (1974, 3). Gaylin's definition of disparity and Goldberg and Levenson's concept of lawlessness stimulated concerted efforts to develop new measures to overcome disparities in sentencing. Judge Marvin Frankel (1972) proposed a sentencing commission model; David Fogel (1975) opted for a flat sentencing model; the Committee for the Study of Incarceration in *Doing Justice* (von Hirsch 1976), the Twentieth Century

Fund Task Force on Criminal Sentencing in *Fair and Certain Punishment* (1976), and Richard Singer (1979) in *Just Deserts* supported a presumptive sentencing model; and Don Gottfredson et al. (1978) recommended development and adoption of guidelines for sentencing and paroling.

The problem here arises from the intrusion of bias (which can be found almost as much in judges as in any lay group) into the sentencing process. Bias grows, particularly in areas that permit discretion to be exercised freely (American Friends Service Committee 1971, 134–43; Frankel 1972, chapter 2; Goldberg and Levenson 1970, 186–229; Hogarth 1971). In light of this argument, Gaylin believes "Discretion in sentencing, at least, is not an essential to a system of justice and was not always a fundamental part of our judicial system" (1974, 191). It appears inflexible and thus impractical to eliminate judicial discretion for many reasons given by presumptive sentencing advocates. Contrary to Gaylin's position is the conviction that "Discretion is a tool, indispensable for individualization of justice [but] only when properly used." And the leading critic of discretionary justice, Davis, writes: "Let us not oppose individualization of justice through discretion; let us oppose individualization when rules should control. . . . Let us not oppose discretionary justice that is properly confined, structured, and checked; let us oppose discretionary justice that is improperly unconfined, unstructured, and unchecked" (1969, 26).

Restriction of Sentencing Discretion

Determinacy in sentencing has been seen as a solution to the disparity and discrimination issue in the legal process. It is a system under which discretionary power would be either entirely eliminated or severely restricted. In a strict sense, determinacy means flat sentencing without judicial discretion. This is similar to what Beccaria proposed several hundred years ago. The penalty structure should be prescribed by the legislatures and judges should have only the responsibility to determine innocence or guilt and to apply the laws accordingly. This legislative model allocates no authority for judicial discretion to impose sentences other than those prescribed by law (Dershowitz 1976). The penalties are legislatively fixed and should be imposed as such—nothing more and nothing less.

For those in favor of a presumptive structure, a determinate sentence system is one in which some judicial discretion should be preserved but confined within a very narrow range. This judicial model allocates some degree of authority to a permanent body of experts to develop sentencing standards or guidelines for judges. Some degree of flexibility remains for future adjustment without any necessity to enact new laws. The sentences imposed may deviate from the guidelines within an acceptable limit.

Restriction of sentencing discretion is consistent with the emphasis on fairness in sentencing. The principle of "doing justice," which emphasizes fair sentencing procedures, replaces the principle of "doing good," which focuses on rehabilitation of the offender. This line of argument rests on legal values in the administration of criminal justice.

The indeterminate sentence system conflicts with the principles of rights, justice, and proportionality in the application of laws. In his *The Concept of Law*, Hart expresses the idea of justice in terms of equality and proportionality. According to Hart, justice means not only "treat like cases alike" but also "treat different cases differently" (1961, 155). There are two basic elements involved: uniformity in handling like cases and a set of necessary criteria to determine whether cases are alike or different. In light of this theory, individualization of criminal sentences either to punish or rehabilitate runs counter to the principles of justice and proportionality (Hart 1968, 25).

Drawing on social contract philosophers, Locke and Rousseau as well as Kant, John Rawls sees justice as fairness "arising from an original agreement in a situation of equality . . . equality in the assignment of basic rights and duties" (1971, 14). The term "fairness" involves a "rational and mutually disinterested" situation (p. 13). There exists a basic contradiction with the philosophy of utilitarianism. Acknowledged by Rawls himself, as well as by liberal reformers, this contradiction lies in the conviction that "[e]ach person possesses an inviolability founded on justice that even the welfare of society as a whole cannot override. For this reason justice denies that the loss of freedom for some is made right by a greater good shared by others. It does not allow that the sacrifices imposed on a few are outweighed by the larger sum of advantages enjoyed by many" (pp. 3–4). Influenced by this view of justice and fairness, many liberals endorsed "just deserts" rather than deterrence (Singer 1979; Twentieth Century Fund

1976; von Hirsch 1976, 49–52) and more recently "justice as fairness" (Fogel and Hudson 1981; von Hirsch et al. 1987).

A coherent theme has emerged in the literature: discretion threatens justice through discrimination and it breeds injustice in the administration of laws. According to Davis, the exercise of discretionary power "has a deceptive quality that is dangerous to justice. The discretionary power to be lenient is an impossibility without a concomitant discretionary power not to be lenient, and injustice from the discretionary power not to be lenient is especially frequent; the power to be lenient is the power to discriminate" (1969, 170).

This philosophical development evolved into the mainstream of sentencing reform literature. Doing justice in the legal process encompasses concerted efforts to realize at least these two primary elements: "the rights of individuals and the constraints that those rights place on the assertion of state power" (Blumstein et al. 1983, 62). This principle depends on the basic constitutional right to be treated fairly or on the concept of equality that constitutes the due process of law. Adoption of this idea suggests that plea bargaining should be abolished or controlled. At the end of the process, parole should also be abolished if a sentence is to be fair and determinate.

In pursuit of justice and proportionality in sentencing, researchers have been devoted to the development of a set of criteria such as sentencing guidelines with mitigation and aggravation and other factors involved in determining the degree of gravity of offenses. Constraints imposed on sentencing discretion through this strategy should promote a central commitment to treating like cases alike and different cases proportionately with respect to the gravity of offenses (Gottfredson et al. 1978; Singer 1979; von Hirsch 1976).

Along with the development toward limiting discretionary power in sentencing, there has been a tendency toward increased accountability in official decisions in parole release. In a sense, prison administrators and parole boards have a role in the sentencing process by determination of release dates under indeterminate sentencing. Steps have been taken and research studies undertaken to improve administrative accountability through parole standards and guidelines. The initiatives were soon followed by an attempt to develop sentencing guidelines for judges (Gottfredson et al. 1978; Wilkins et al. 1978). Social scientists offered an impetus for control of judicial discretion. It seems evident that "[t]he effect of research on the development of sentencing guidelines has been direct and instrumental" (Blumstein et al. 1983, 66).

CONCLUSION

Before the American Revolution, the concepts of crime and punishment were generally influenced by religious beliefs and were primarily corporal and capital. American optimism and belief in the likelihood of humankind to reform created incarcerative reform. It is conceptually sound to mark the inception of this therapeutic state when the National Congress on Penitentiary and Reformatory Discipline declared its principles of doing good for the offender. The indeterminate sentence system has been an essential element of these therapeutic state principles, which include the rehabilitative ideal, individualization of treatment, and indeterminate sentence.

Most of American history has been a period of the therapeutic state. In the mid–1970s, however, the therapeutic state came under serious criticisms. For more than half a century prior to the recent reform movement, criminal codes and procedures from coast to coast all embodied a penalty structure in which sentences imposed were indeterminate. Whether the convicts received alternative dispositions other than imprisonment or how long they actually served prison terms depended largely on their potential for rehabilitation. Under indeterminate sentencing, prison terms were not specified at the time of conviction, but a minimum term before the convicts become eligible for parole could be imposed. Sentencing authority and responsibility were unevenly allocated, with judicial and administrative discretionary powers varying in large measure across jurisdictions. The key elements of the indeterminate sentence system—the rehabilitative ideal, indeterminacy in sentencing, and individualization of treatment—were bitterly criticized and critics proposed elimination or at best restricted control.

In the mid–1970s states moved toward determinate sentencing, although not all of the elements mentioned above were eliminated. The politics of determinate sentencing reforms centered around reallocation of discretionary power, determination of appropriate penalty structure, and degree of flexibility involved.

Political considerations involved unavoidable trade-offs among flat, mandatory, and presumptive alternative models, which will be discussed in chapter 3.

There was also a shift in public opinion leading to the sudden decline of the therapeutic state. The new criminal justice system has moved toward a determinate sentence system. There are several conceptual arguments for this policy innovation. In terms of sentencing schemes, the idea is to impose restrictions on those who exercise discretionary power in the sentencing process. Fair and certain legal sanctions are part of the reform goals. Another goal is crime control through certainty of punishment achieved through mandatory sentencing systems.

The analysis of penal policy in the United States reveals three major phases of criminal justice history: retribution and deterrence, then rehabilitation, and today back to deterrence and just deserts. Determinate sentencing policy embraces both deterrence and just deserts, even though their major tenets are quite contradictory. Its mandatory version, advocated by the conservatives, reflects the emphasis on deterrence and incapacitation emanating from the public's fear of crime. At the same time, the presumptive version, proposed by the liberals, underscores just deserts and fairness in order to eradicate disparity and discrimination among prisoners.

CHAPTER 3

Sentencing Reforms in Practice

Sentencing reform policy today involves an effort to impose legislative control over official decisions in determining the use of confinement, the period of confinement, and the termination of confinement in the sanctioning process for a wide variety of offenses committed by different types of offenders under varying circumstances. State legislatures have taken several approaches toward a set of shared goals accompanied by several guiding principles. Students of sentencing reform policy in the United States present several sentencing models as a means to describe these basic approaches toward legislative control over sentencing decisions.

In this chapter, a sentencing reform typology will be developed to differentiate various types of sentencing reforms. To accomplish this task, three variables are used: the rigidity of control over judicial discretion, type of legislative control devised, and type of sentence employed. This chapter will analyze five sentencing reform types: mandatory minimum sentencing laws, mandatory determinate sentencing laws, presumptive determinate sentencing laws, presumptive sentencing guidelines, and voluntary sentencing guidelines. Each reform type will be considered separately regarding its characteristics of legislative control over judicial discretion at three crucial decision points in the sentencing process.

LEGISLATIVE CONTROL OVER JUDICIAL DECISIONS: WHEN TO INCARCERATE? FOR HOW LONG? WHEN TO RELEASE?

Sentencing reform targets three decision points: the decision to incarcerate, the selection of sentence length, and the decision to release (Goodstein and Hepburn 1985, 51–82). The decision to incarcerate involves deciding whether to impose prison or jail terms. This in/out decision, the choice between incarceration and its alternatives (i.e., probation, suspended sentence), relies mainly on three considerations: the seriousness of offenses; involvement of a firearm in committing certain offenses; and offender characteristics, especially prior conviction record. When the court decides to incarcerate, a sentence length must be determined. Determination of sentence length can affect the decision to release, particularly when a sentence is determinate.

The first dimension that distinguishes sentencing reform models involves the rigidity of control over the decision to incarcerate and the decision on sentence length. Any reform model lies somewhere on this nondiscretionary/discretionary continuum:

FLAT—Determinate—Mandatory—Presumptive—
Voluntary—INDETERMINATE

At one extreme, a flat sentence is an invariable term of certain years to be served in full, no more and no less. The flat system is too rigid because it eliminates all discretionary power in setting prison terms for any persons convicted of the same designated crime. The incarceration decision is automatic. By this definition, all sentencing decisions are nondiscretionary and predetermined by the legislature (Singer 1978, 404; Twentieth Century Fund 1976, 16).

At the other extreme, an indeterminate sentence is an open-ended term with neither minimum nor maximum limits such as one day to life. Most sentencing reforms lean toward the flat system. There are two types of determinate sentence: definite (flat) and indefinite (nonflat). Tappan defines an indefinite sentence as "a term with a fixed maximum and usually a fixed minimum," such as from five to ten years (1960, 430). Parole is possible within this minimum and maximum range. Thus, a mandatory sentence is a form of indefinite sentence with a discretionary parole regulated by its minimum term requirement. Another form of indefinite sentence, a statutory determinate sentence, eliminates parole release discretion (Singer 1978, 404; Tonry 1987, 101).

There are three types of mandatory reforms: mandatory prison term, mandatory minimum sentence, and mandatory supervision after incarceration. When a prison term is mandatory, the use of incarceration is automatic on conviction of target offenses. This provision eliminates entirely the discretionary power in making the in/out decision. A mandatory minimum sentence dictates that a prison sentence imposed must be at least a certain number of months as specified by law. In some states, the judge can decide not to impose incarceration, that is, the in/out decision is not automatic, but the minimum is required when a prison term is chosen (Galvin 1983, 3; Shane-DuBow et al. 1985). A mandatory reform also exists at the release stage. Many states, including Arkansas, California, Delaware, Illinois, South Carolina, Texas, and West Virginia, mandate certain minimum prison time served minus good-time credit before becoming eligible for early release on parole or mandatory supervision. After release, the ex-convict must be supervised by parole authorities for at least a statutorily specified minimum term (Aspen 1978; Carlson 1982; Lagoy et al. 1978; Shane-DuBow et al. 1985; Tonry 1987; Twentieth Century Fund 1976, 16).

Presumptive sentencing is less rigid than the mandatory reform. This presumptive reform is usually applied to the decision to incarcerate and the decision on sentence length. A presumptive sentence should be imposed on conviction of offenses committed in the typical fashion by typical first-time offenders (Singer 1979, 406). When an offense involves specific aggravating or mitigating factors, the judge may impose a sentence above or below the presumptive sentence (middle term) within predetermined upper or lower limits. Any deviation from this permissible range and from the recommended dispositional criteria for incarceration requires reasoned justification (Tonry 1987, 46; Twentieth Century Fund 1976, 20–21; von Hirsch et al. 1987, 17).

Another distinction among presumptive reforms rests on whether the legislature outlined sentencing standards in the revised statutes or in the more articulated guidelines by its delegated rule-making bodies, usually called sentencing commissions. California's presumptive sentencing scheme was written into law (Lagoy et al. 1978, 388). Unlike the presumptive sentencing laws in California, Indiana, and New Mexico, Minnesota's presumptive sentencing system was developed by the Minnesota Sentencing Guidelines Commission in the form of a sentencing grid (Hamline Law Review 1982; Knapp 1982; Tonry 1987; von Hirsch et al. 1987, 9). Since a sentencing commission is usually composed of a body of experts in the field, some observers believe that sentencing guidelines are more specific and better articulated than sentencing standards as written into law by the legislature (Frankel 1972; von Hirsch et al. 1987, 18). It is reasonable to distinguish presumptive sentencing laws and presumptive sentencing guidelines.

Unlike both mandatory and presumptive reform, the voluntary reform lacks binding legal authority that requires compliance with it. The effectiveness of the guidelines rely solely on voluntary cooperation by the judge. The intent of this reform type is to give judges past sentencing norms as guidelines with regard to the use of incarceration and its length on various respects. The guidelines are developed to provide a description of prevailing practices in particular jurisdictions as a standard for individual judges to adjust their individual pattern toward the norms. The cooperation of those deviating from the norms helps increase consistency and uniformity in sentencing among judges. The voluntary reform is therefore descriptive rather than prescriptive (Cohen and Tonry 1983; Gottfredson et al. 1978; Tonry 1987; Wilkins et al. 1978).

A third dimension for classification of reform types is whether prison terms become determinate sentences in the sense that parole release discretion is eliminated. Among the ten states that made parole decision a nondiscretionary matter, the term of imprisonment is more difficult to change. Early release criteria are rigid and the supervision period after incarceration is subject to more rules (Lagoy et al. 1978). This dimension distinguishes sentencing reform types on the basis of their control over release discretion.

By 1983 the criminal codes of forty-nine states provided mandatory minimum sentences for certain violent offenses. At the same time, thirty-three states revised their statutes to increase penalties for repeat or habitual offenders (Shane-DuBow et al. 1985, 286–88; Tonry 1987, 25). These mandatory prison term statutes removed judicial discretion in selecting incarceration or its alternatives, that is, probation, fines, or suspended sentence. The decision to incarcerate is usually automatic. In some cases, the laws also specify mandatory minimum sentences to control both the in/out decision and the length of sentence.

Mandatory prison terms are most often specified for four categories of offense or offender: violent crimes, habitual or repeat offenders, narcotics violations, and crimes involving the use or carrying of a firearm. Table 3.1 summarizes the extent to which states vary in their use of mandatory prison terms in this respect. Violent crime, a category including murder, is the general target of these laws in forty-four states. In thirty-five states, violent offenses

Table 3.1
Mandatory Minimum Prison Sentences and Their Target Violent
Offense and Offender in the United States

| State | Effective Date[a] | Types of Offense and Offender Affected | | | |
		Violent Crime	Habitual Offender	Drugs	Firearm
a) Mandatory Minimum Sentencing Laws					
Alabama	1980	X	X	X	—
Alaska	1980	X	X	X	X
Arizona	1978	X	X	X	X
Arkansas	1981	X	X	—	X
Delaware	1982	X	X	X	X
Florida	1976	X	—	X	X
Georgia	1980	X	X	X	X
Hawaii	1976	X	X	X	X
Idaho	1979	X	X	X	X
Iowa	1978	X	—	X	X
Kansas	1976	—	—	—	X
Kentucky	1975	—	X	—	X
Louisiana	1978	X	X	X	X
Maryland	1976	X	X	—	X
Massachusetts	1974	X	X	X	X
Michigan	1977	X	—	X	X
Mississippi	1977	X	X	—	X
Missouri	1979	X	—	X	X
Montana	NA	X	—	X	X
Nebraska	1977	X	X	—	—
Nevada	1973	X	X	X	X
New Hampshire	1981	X	—	—	X
New Jersey	1979	X	—	—	X
New York	1978	X	X	X	X

Table 3.1 (continued)

State	Effective Date[a]	Types of Offense and Offender Affected			
		Violent Crime	Habitual Offender	Drugs	Firearm
North Dakota	1975	X	—	—	X
Ohio	1974	X	X	X	X
Oklahoma	1976	—	X	X	X
Oregon	1977	X	—	—	X
South Carolina	1975	X	X	X	—
South Dakota	1978	X	—	X	—
Tennessee	1982	X	X	X	—
Texas	1977	X	X	—	—
Vermont	NA	X	—	—	—
Virginia	1975	—	—	—	X
West Virginia	1981	X	X	—	X
Wyoming	1973	X	X	X	X

b) Mandatory Determinate Sentencing Laws

State	Effective Date[a]	Violent Crime	Habitual Offender	Drugs	Firearm
Connecticut	1981	X	—	X	X
Illinois	1978	X	X	X	X
Maine	1976	X	—	—	X

c) Presumptive Determinate Sentencing Laws

State	Effective Date[a]	Violent Crime	Habitual Offender	Drugs	Firearm
California	1977	X	X	X	X
Colorado	1976	X	X	—	X
Indiana	1977	X	X	X	X
New Mexico	1979	X	X	—	X
North Carolina	1977	X	—	X	X

d) Presumptive Sentencing Guidelines

State	Effective Date[a]	Violent Crime	Habitual Offender	Drugs	Firearm
Minnesota	1980	X	—	—	X
Washington	1984	X	—	X	X

State	Effective Date[a]	Types of Offense and Offender Affected			
		Violent Crime	Habitual Offender	Drugs	Firearm
e) Voluntary Sentencing Guidelines					
Pennsylvania	1981	X	X	—	X
Rhode Island	1982	—	X	X	X
Utah	1978	—	—	—	—
Wisconsin	1982	X	—	—	—
Total		44	30	29	41

[a]These four categories have different effective dates in the following states: violent crime (1973 and 1982) and firearm (1982) in Delaware; firearm (1972), violent crime (1976), and habitual offender (1982) in Maryland; violent crime (1979 and 1982) and habitual offender (1982) in Missouri; firearm (1976) and habitual offender (1982) in Oklahoma; habitual offender (1973) and firearm (1979) in Wyoming.

Legend: NA, date not available; X, yes; —, no.

Source: Jim Galvin, "Setting Prison Terms," *Bureau of Justice Statistics Bulletin,* U.S. Department of Justice, Bureau of Justice Statistics, August 1983, for information on types of offense subject to mandatory prison term statutes; Shane-DuBow et al. (1985) for updated information.

involving the use of a firearm carry mandatory prison terms of varying length. About three fifths of the states have adopted mandatory sentencing laws for habitual offenders or drug offenses. The criminal codes of at least fifteen states prescribe mandatory sentences for all four categories (Galvin 1983). Within the same category of mandatory sentence offenses listed here, the number of offenses carrying mandatory minimum sentences also vary across states. Thus, it is difficult to generalize about the number of these eligible offenses by comparing the number of categories.

In addition to mandatory prison terms, state legislatures have restricted the release discretion for those serving their mandatory prison terms. Many revised codes impose rigid parole eligibility on these inmates, while others make prison terms determinate sentences. Ten states—California, Colorado, Connecticut, Illinois,

Indiana, Maine, Minnesota, New Mexico, North Carolina, and Washington—have adopted statutory determinate sentencing laws. Another six states—Minnesota, Pennsylvania, Rhode Island, Utah, Wisconsin, and Wyoming—have developed sentencing guidelines.

It is obvious that many states adopted more than one type of sentencing reform. Mandatory sentencing laws have been the most popular model ever implemented in the United States in response to serious crimes, particularly those involving drugs and the use of a firearm and repeat offenders considered habitual criminals. In general, mandatory sentences lead to restricted parole eligibility in most states. In Illinois, for example, mandatory sentences are also determinate in the sense that parole was replaced by mandatory supervised release (Aspen 1978; Lagoy et al. 1978). Sentencing guidelines were developed in several states for offenses other than those carrying mandatory sentences.

The in/out decision is subject to rigid control under mandatory sentencing laws. But, in the majority of the states, judicial discretion in determining sentence length and parole release discretion remains broad. In 1983 Galvin analyzed the status of sentencing reform policy in the United States with regard to discretionary power left to the criminal court and parole boards. He defines the range of judicial discretion as narrow when available options to set prison terms are confined within the range of less than one-third of the statutory maximum.

According to Galvin's analysis (shown in table 3.2), thirty-four states and the District of Columbia in category D provide broad discretionary ranges in setting prison terms and release dates. Among ten determinate sentencing states (categories A and B) where there is no parole release discretion, the revised codes provide the judge with broad discretionary power in determining prison terms in Connecticut, Illinois, Indiana, and Maine (category B). Only six states in category A (California, Colorado, Minnesota, New Mexico, North Carolina, and Washington) and six in category C (Arizona, Iowa, Ohio, Pennsylvania, Utah, and West Virginia) have revised their statutes to limit judicial discretion to a narrow range. Parole release discretion is also severely restricted in the category C states.

In summary, the incarceration decision has been mandated by most state legislatures for serious crimes, drug violations, habitual offenders, and crimes involving the use of a firearm. However, dis-

Table 3.2
Legislative Control over Judicial and Administrative
Discretionary Power in Determining Sentence Length and
Parole Release in the United States

No Parole Release Discretion	*Restricted Parole Release Discretion*	
a) Narrow Court Discretion and No Discretionary Parole Board Release (6)	c) Narrow Court Discretion and Discretionary Parole Board Release (6)	
California	Arizona	
Colorado	Iowa	
Minnesota	Ohio	
New Mexico	Pennsylvania	
North Carolina	Utah	
Washington	West Virginia	
b) Broad Court Discretion and No Discretionary Parole Board Release (4)	d) Broad Court Discretion and Discretionary Parole Board Release (35)	
Connecticut	Alabama	Nebraska
Illinois	Alaska	Nevada
Indiana	Arkansas	New Hampshire
Maine	Delaware	New Jersey
	Dist. Columbia	New York
	Florida	North Dakota
	Georgia	Oklahoma
	Hawaii	Oregon
	Idaho	Rhode Island
	Kansas	South Carolina
	Kentucky	South Dakota
	Louisiana	Tennessee
	Maryland	Texas
	Massachusetts	Vermont

Table 3.2 (continued)

No Parole Release Discretion	Restricted Parole Release Discretion	
	Michigan	Virginia
	Mississippi	Wisconsin
	Missouri	Wyoming
	Montana	

Source: Adapted from Jim Galvin, "Setting Prison Terms," Bureau of Justice Statistics Bulletin, U.S. Department of Justice, Bureau of Justice Statistics, August 1983.

cretionary power in determining sentence length and release dates remains broad. In some states, there are also presumptive sentences for all other classes of felony offense. In these and other states, prison sentences were also made determinate, thereby eliminating parole release discretion.

MANDATORY MINIMUM SENTENCING LAWS

In the mid–1950s the idea of mandatory penalties was employed by the Connecticut legislature to increase the certainty of stringent sanctions for traffic violations (Campbell and Ross 1968; Ross 1976). The renewed interest in the use of mandatory penalties emerged in the early 1970s in a more refined and articulated form for drug violations and rapidly extended to cover a wide variety of criminal offenses. This broadened use of mandatory sanctions, particularly mandatory prison terms, was popularized by the 1973 New York Rockefeller Drug Law, the 1974 Massachusetts Bartley–Fox Amendment, and the 1977 Michigan Felony Firearms Statute. In the second half of the 1970s alone mandatory sentences of varied length were listed as penalties for many felony offenses in the revised codes of sixteen states. Mandatory prison sentences for criminal offenses other than murder and drunk driving are today in effect in forty-nine states and the District of Columbia (Shane-DuBow et al. 1985; Tonry 1987).

Mandatory sentencing reform is a legislative response to several political interests and forces: (1) the alarming threats of criminal violence involving the use of a firearm and other deadly weapons that lead to victim death; (2) the belief that drug addiction is an important factor in generating more crimes; (3) the desire to control illegal use of a firearm; and (4) public criticism of government reaction to violent crimes as too lenient and inconsistent. Crime statistics show that the homicide rate doubled in eleven years between 1963 and 1973 and the rate for gun homicide rose nearly 150 percent during the same period (Zimring 1985, 137). The growing public interest in the relationship between firearms and criminal violence gave rise to more research on the subject. It was argued that offenses involving the use of a handgun would lead to victim death far more frequently than those involving other common weapons such as knives (Cook 1983; Luckenbill 1984, 187; Zimring 1985, 138). A review of research done in this area indicates that the credibility of a gun as a weapon may encourage more robberies. Using a gun as a threat can reduce victim resistance, thereby increasing the likelihood of success in committing a crime. Guns also increase the rate of victim death in armed robbery incidents (Zimring 1985, 139).

In the 1960s criminal violence became a national issue (Feeley and Sarat 1980; Finckenauer 1978; Walker 1978). The majority of Americans in opinion surveys perceived the courts as too lenient and inconsistent in punishing criminals (Carlson 1982). In the early 1970s nearly half of armed robbers arrested had prior felony conviction records, but less than half of those convicted received prison sentences (Petersilia and Greenwood 1978, 605). Government reaction to crime and gun control policy could not be separated as an important item on the national agenda at that time.

Mandatory prison sentences for violent offenses involving the use of a firearm provide the middle ground where the two sides of the gun control issue can meet. The procontrol view is that lack of gun control leads to more criminal violence and victim death. This view suggests tighter regulation of handguns and reduction in the number of handguns available in the interstate market. This policy faces opposition from the anticontrol group, who favors hunting and self-protection (Pierce and Bowers 1981). For the latter, mandatory lengthy penalties for the use of a firearm in conjunction with criminal offenses is preferable to strict gun regulation policy (Zimring 1985, 142). For these and other reasons, mandatory sentencing laws were passed by the legislature in one state after another. A general description of these laws with respect to legislative control over sentencing decision is the subject of discussion below.

Mandatory sentencing laws refer to statutes that specify prison sentences required to be imposed and served on conviction of designated offenders (Tonry 1987; Twentieth Century Fund 1976, 16). By definition of the term, no circumstances permit the judge to impose other alternatives; therefore, probation is prohibited and prison terms cannot be suspended. It is a system with a broad range of legislatively mandated sentencing procedures governing the determination of the use of incarcerative sentences, their sentence length, and expiration of such prison terms for release.

Variation exists among states in these procedures with respect to target offenses and prior conviction record, as discussed above. Mandatory minimum sentences are almost always prescribed for the capital crime of murder when the death penalty is not imposed, frequently for serious offenses such as armed robbery and rape, particulary when these offenses involve the use of a gun or offenders with prior conviction records. For instance, armed robbery carries mandatory prison terms in at least eight states: Hawaii, Idaho, Massachusetts, Michigan, Nebraska, Nevada, North Carolina, and Texas. A general pattern of mandatory minimum laws that exist in the United States is that legislative control over the decision to incarcerate varies with type of crimes and offenders (Shane-DuBow et al. 1985).

Legislative control over the decision on sentence length is another important component of mandatory minimum sentencing laws. The new procedures reduce judicial discretion to determine prison terms in two general ways. First, the revised codes specify minimum prison terms for specific target offenses or serious classes of felonies. These minimum prison terms are usually extended when these offenses involve the use of a firearm or when the offenders have a prior conviction record. These minimum sentences vary substantially from one state to another. For instance, any felony committed with a firearm carries a mandatory minimum prison sentence of five years in Iowa and Oregon, and ten years minimum in Hawaii. Gun robbery carries a mandatory minimum of three years in Mississippi, five years in Massachusetts, ten years in South Carolina, and fourteen years in North Carolina (Shane-DuBow et al. 1985).

Mandatory minimum sentences are also specified in the form of extended terms, particularly when the offender used or had in his or her possession a firearm while committing a felony or when the offender had prior conviction record relating to the same offense or any felony. In Massachusetts, for example, a mandatory minimum term of five years was extended to ten years for armed robbers with prior conviction of the same offense. Likewise, a minimum of ten years is mandated for a second conviction of a gun-related offense and also for a third conviction of armed robbery in Oklahoma. According to the Michigan statute, a gun-related felony carries an extended term of thirty years for a third conviction. In Hawaii, mandatory minimum sentences were raised to five years for the use of a firearm while committing any felony of class B, and to ten years for class A. In North Dakota, the offender with a prior conviction record faces a mandatory minimum of ten years for class C, twenty years for class B, and life for class A. Any felony involving the use of a gun is punishable as the next higher class of felony in Texas (Shane-DuBow et al. 1985).

A consecutive sentence strategy is another form of control over determination of sentence length employed in more than ten states. For instance, the laws mandate two years of a separate sentence for the use of a gun in committing any felony in Massachusetts, Michigan, and Virginia and raise to five years for a first conviction in Delaware and Tennessee and for a second conviction in Maryland and Michigan. This example illustrates that the consecutive term varies among these states. Moreover, the term also varies with felonies of different classes. The North Dakota code increases the length of such consecutive terms when a gun was used in more serious classes of offenses. In North Dakota, a consecutive term for the use of a gun in committing a class C felony is two years and this consecutive term doubles for any felony of class A or B (Shane-DuBow et al. 1985).

Parole release discretion is substantially reduced under mandatory minimum sentencing laws for several reasons. A cursory analysis of mandatory minimum sentencing laws indicates that determination of parole release is no longer free from restricted eligibility criteria when mandatory minimum terms are imposed. These mandatory minimum sentences, less good-time credit rewarded for good behavior, must be served in full or in part before parole release can be considered. Reduction of prison terms via good-time credit is now more difficult to earn (Galvin 1983). In general, a discretionary range in granting parole release remains broad in the majority of the states (listed in table 3.2). However, granted with sentencing authority to impose a mandatory minimum prison sentence, the judge also shares some degree of discretionary power to restrict parole eligibility for release consideration.

Legislative control over the decision to release varies with the length of legislatively fixed mandatory minimum prison terms for designated offenses and offenders. A general form of restriction on parole release is that the codes require mandatory minimum prison terms be completed before parole can be considered. This strategy was adopted by the state legislatures in Massachusetts, Michigan, Ohio, and Kansas. Mandatory minimum parole eligibility terms for an offense committed with the use of a firearm and armed robbery vary widely among states. These terms range from a minimum of three years in West Virginia to ten years in Arkansas and Mississippi, with several other states such as Delaware, North Carolina, and South Carolina lying somewhere between the two extremes. A different strategy can be found in the Texas statute. Inmates sentenced to mandatory prison terms for such offenses as murder, robbery, rape, and kidnapping are not eligible for parole until half of the maximum terms or twenty years (whichever is less) have expired (Shane-DuBow et al. 1985).

Overall, the use of incarceration, sentence length, and parole release criteria are now subject to legislative control in the majority of the states adopting mandatory minimum sentencing laws. The scope of legislative control over the exercise of discretion at these three sentencing decision points varies with type of offenses and offenders. The rigidity of control covaries with the floor level of minimum terms, but judicial discretion and parole release discretion remain broad. Finally, mandatory minimum sentencing laws reduce much of the discretion to grant parole release once free from review, by shifting such discretionary power to the judge.

MANDATORY DETERMINATE SENTENCING LAWS

In the majority of states discussed above, restricted parole eligibility criteria do not eliminate entirely parole release discretion and, therefore, release remains discretionary beyond the expiration of mandatory minimum prison terms. Adoption of nondiscretionary parole release in ten states makes their codes widely known as statutory determinate sentencing laws. This determinate system can increase the predictability of release decision because release is no longer a discretionary matter. In general, inmates serving their determinate sentences also have a rough idea about release date from calculation of good-time reduction for good behavior.

In Connecticut, Illinois, and Maine, state legislators have adopted broad sentencing standards. As the term implies, mandatory determinate sentencing laws in these three states combine both mandatory sentencing and determinate sentencing schemes. As in many other mandatory minimum sentencing states, serious crimes committed with the use of a firearm or by a frequent offender carry mandatory minimum prison terms. Judicial discretion in setting prison terms is limited by a broad statutory minimum and maximum range because there are no specific sentencing standards binding selection of prison terms. Prison terms become determinate and relatively free from further discretionary adjustment while prisoners are serving their sentences. However, modification of determinate sentences exists and varies widely due to different methods of calculating good-time reduction for good behavior. Parole release is nondiscretionary and often called mandatory supervised release. This nondiscretionary parole release distinguishes mandatory determinate sentencing states from mandatory minimum sentencing states.

As in other mandatory minimum sentencing states, the incarceration discretion was entirely removed for serious felony classes designated in the statutes of these mandatory determinate sentencing states. The legislatures in these three states share the assumption that judges cannot make good in/out decisions regarding more serious offenses requiring mandatory imprisonment. As a result of sentencing reform in the respective states, mandatory minimum prison sentences are instituted for the most serious class of offenses: Class A in Connecticut, Class X in Illinois, and Murder and Class A felonies in Maine. Felonies committed with the use of a firearm and by offenders with a prior conviction record also carry mandatory minimum prison sentences in these three states. In Illinois, for example, a felony involving the use of a firearm is classified as Class X felony. A Class 2 or greater felony with a prior conviction in the past ten years for a Class 2 or greater felony, like Class X felonies, carries mandatory minimum prison sentences (Aspen 1978; Goodstein and Hepburn 1985; Lagoy et al. 1978; Schuwerk 1984; Shane-DuBow et al. 1985; Tonry 1987; von Hirsch and Hanrahan 1981; Zimring 1983).

The Illinois Class X felonies include the forcible felonies of treason, attempted murder, rape, deviant sexual assault, armed robbery, aggravated arson, and aggravated arson for ransom. This class of X felonies carries a mandatory minimum sentence of six years. With two or subsequent convictions of this class, the mandatory term is life imprisonment. A sentence for Class X with aggravating circumstances must be imposed with a minimum term of thirty years. The regular term for murder is a life sentence of twenty to forty years. Under the extended schedule, the term is life or forty to eighty years (Shane-DuBow et al. 1985, 81–86).

Setting prison terms, in Connecticut as well as in Illinois, is regulated by the legislature within broad ranges of statutory minima and maxima. In Illinois, penalty schedules were substantially reduced in their sentence ranges, but only moderately reduced for more serious felonies. In addition, the minimum limits were raised much higher for Class X felonies (Aspen 1978; Legoy et al. 1978). In comparison with the Illinois revised code, the Connecticut statute prescribes much lower mandatory minima of prison terms for most felony classes with determinate ranges relatively narrower (Goodstein and Hepburn 1985).

Maine is a unique case with broad judicial discretion on sentence length. The Maine code does not provide the statutory minima with a few exceptions of serious offenses (Tonry 1987, 78). Similar to Illinois and Maine, these judicially fixed sentences are relatively free from further modification (Lagoy et al. 1978; Shane-DuBow et al. 1985; Tonry 1987).

With nondiscretionary release in these mandatory determinate sentencing states, release decision is governed by good-time policy. Termination of prison terms is a function of judicially fixed determinate sentences minus good-time credits earned in meritorious service of these sentences. Good-time rewards counted toward reduction of determinate sentences vary widely. The good-time system allows for reduction of determinate sentences by one-half in Illinois and by one-third in Connecticut (Goodstein and Hepburn 1985). A more generous good-time reward policy in Illinois offsets lengthier minimum prison terms than those prescribed by the Connecticut statute. By the same token, shorter determinate sentences are more difficult to reduce via good-time reward in Connecticut.

In summary, mandatory determinate sentencing laws differ in several aspects from mandatory minimum sentencing laws and presumptive determinate sentencing laws. Sentencing reform policy in Connecticut, Illinois, and Maine instituted the use of the mandatory minimum sentencing model for the most serious class of felonies and persistent offenders. These states provide broad sentencing standards for judges to impose determinate sentences selected from within broad statutory ranges. Further change of these determinate terms is no longer discretionary but strictly regulated by the good-time provisions.

PRESUMPTIVE DETERMINATE SENTENCING LAWS

There are five determinate sentencing states that have adopted the presumptive sentencing model advocated by the Twentieth Century Fund Task Force on Criminal Sentencing (1976), the author of *Fair and Certain Punishment*. Unlike the mandatory determinate sentencing states (Connecticut, Illinois, and Maine), which adopt broad sentencing schedules, these presumptive determinate sentencing states have adopted relatively more specific sentencing standards. The presumptive sentencing model seeks to reduce judicial discretion in determining sentence length, when prison is chosen, by providing presumptive sentences for typical offenses committed under typical circumstances by typical offenders with no prior conviction. In general, presumptive sentences are middle terms between lower and upper limits of relatively narrow ranges that vary with classes of offenses. The width of these statutory ranges, however, varies greatly from state to state.

Using this definition, the presumptive determinate sentencing states include California, Colorado, Indiana, North Carolina, and New Mexico. The revised statutes of these five states eliminate parole release discretion, thereby shifting to the sentencing judge discretionary power once granted to parole boards. In fact, four of these states have entirely removed parole release discretion. Colorado is an exception in this regard. The Colorado statute requires judges to impose a period of parole release after incarceration for most classes of offenses (Shane-DuBow et al. 1985, 44). With this judicial parole release, discretionary power once granted to the parole board was shifted to judges.

The Colorado code prescribes presumptive sentence ranges for firearm-related offenses. In this instance, the lower limits of these presumptive ranges are also mandatory. In New Mexico, the existing statute requires mandatory prison sentences for firearm-related offenders with a prior firearm-related conviction. The second or greater conviction of firearm offenses adds three years to presumptive sentences (Shane-DuBow et al. 1985).

One can divide these presumptive determinate sentencing states into two groups. Judicial discretion on sentence length is much narrower in California and Colorado than in Indiana, New Mexico, and North Carolina. A relationship between these ranges and their middle terms exists: the broader the sentence ranges, the longer the presumptive terms. In California, presumptive sentences for Classes A, B, C, and D are seven, six, three, and three years, respectively. The lower-upper prison sentence ranges are as narrow as two to four years in California and Colorado. The Indiana statute prescribes much longer presumptive sentences of five years for Class C, ten years for Class B, and thirty years for Class A. In Indiana, lower and upper limits of prison terms are as broad as six, twenty, and forty years for felonies of Classes C, B, and A, respectively. In general, deviations beyond statutory lower or upper limits for mitigating or aggravating factors require a written justification that is subject to appellate sentence review.

In summary, presumptive determinate sentencing laws provide relatively more specific and articulated sentencing standards, particularly in California and Colorado. The incarceration decision remains unregulated for most typical nonfirearm offenses. The sentencing judge can exercise discretion to set determinate sentences as selected within legislatively prescribed permissible ranges. Setting prison terms outside these ranges generally requires written justification. These determinate sentences are subject to no further modification on a discretionary basis. The release decision is based on the termination of a determinate sentence with good-time reduction.

PRESUMPTIVE SENTENCING GUIDELINES

A presumptive sentencing guidelines system is one in which the legislature empowers a body of experts delegated to develop presumptive sentencing standards and oversee sentencing practices that can lead to revision of such standards. The sentencing standards as implemented in Minnesota and Washington contain the two major elements of this system. First, both established sentencing guidelines commissions to function as rule-making bodies in charge of developing and monitoring the sentencing guidelines. Second, their guidelines prescribe presumptive sentences that require written justification when selected sentences deviate from permissible guidelines ranges.

Instead of writing presumptive sentencing standards into statutes, the legislatures in Minnesota and Washington took a two-step approach. In the first step, a sentencing commission was formed and empowered to draft and monitor guidelines. The development of the guidelines occurred in the second step. There are several advantages in adopting this sentencing commission approach.

First, the sentencing commission approach, initially proposed by Frankel in 1972, can overcome difficulty in writing specific sentencing standards into law. Responsible lawmakers lack professional expertise and time to draft specific standards. Lack of expertise and time is no longer a problem when the drafting responsibility is delegated to a sentencing commission consisting of experts in the field. Second, presumptive sentencing laws would be difficult to change. In this regard, revision of the guidelines is a much easier task through the rule-making process (Singer 1978; von Hirsch and Hanrahan 1981; von Hirsch et al. 1987).

Minnesota

Minnesota's presumptive sentencing guidelines system has three components: (1) the sentencing commission has the capacity to develop specific sentencing standards; (2) presumptive sentences are less rigid than mandatory standards but more specific and within narrower ranges (only plus or minus 15 percent of presumptive sentences for aggravating or mitigating circumstances) than normally specified in most statutes; and (3) appellate sentence review can assure judicial compliance with the guidelines when reasoned justification of imposing sentences deviating from guidelines is subject to external review (Shane-DuBow et al. 1985; Singer 1978, 408; Tonry 1987, 46; von Hirsch and Hanrahan 1981).

More specifically, the Minnesota sentencing guidelines grid consists of a ten-category scale of conviction offense severity on the vertical axis and a seven-point scale of criminal history score on the horizontal axis, making a seventy-cell matrix. Each cell contains a presumptive sentence with a narrow range, where incarceration is presumed, corresponding to the severity of conviction offense and prior conviction record. The bold diagonal line demarcates the use of incarceration and its alternatives. The cells in the area above this dispositional line provide probationary sentences (out); those in the area below the line, incarcerative sentences (in). The dispositional line and presumptive sentence ranges presume the in/out decision and choice of sentence length (von Hirsch et al. 1987, 177–82). Written justification of both dispositional and durational departures from the guidelines is subject to appeal by the defense and the state. The Minnesota statute also creates a class of a few offenses requiring mandatory prison sentences. In general, Minnesota's guidelines recommend the use of incarceration for most serious violent crimes and nonincarceration for less serious property crimes (Goodstein and Hepburn 1985; *Hamline Law Review* 1982; Shane-DuBow et al. 1985; Tonry 1987).

Minnesota's parole guidelines took effect in 1976. This can be viewed as an initial step toward determinacy in sentencing. In 1978 Minnesota abolished parole and the Minnesota Guidelines Commission was established (Shane-DuBow et al. 1985, 159–60; Tonry 1987, 77). Because presumptive sentences imposed by the judge are determinate, calculation of the release date is nondiscretionary. These judicially fixed sentences can be modified only by good-time reduction earned at the rate of one day for every two days of good-time served. This good-time calculation, as in Connecticut, allows actual prison time served to diminish by up to one-third of determinate sentences imposed. The good-time earned is vested and cannot be taken away. Only up to ninety days of good-time not yet vested may be lost due to disciplinary violation. Thus, the judge can predict quite accurately when the offender will be released. At the expiration of sentences less good-time earned, supervised release will be granted with conditions and, if revoked due to violation of such conditions, reincarceration cannot exceed the remaining period of the original sentences. The new structure of Minnesota's presumptive sentencing guidelines shows the likelihood for greater predictability of release and increased equity in sentencing (Goodstein and Hepburn 1985, 79–80; Shane-DuBow et al. 1985, 163).

Washington

A similar reform was pursued in Washington with the passage of the Sentencing Reform Act of 1981. This act mandated the development of presumptive sentencing guidelines and abolished parole (Shane-DuBow et al. 1985, 262–64). Presumptive guidelines, similar to Minnesota's, took effect on July 1, 1984 (Tonry 1987, 57). Washington's guidelines specify much narrower sentence ranges than those of Pennsylvania but slightly wider than those of Minnesota. The Washington guidelines also permit dispositional and durational departures only under "substantial and compelling" circumstances. Following Minnesota, the Washington legislature embraced just deserts and proportionality in principle as manifested by reduction of incarceration for less serious property crimes and recommendations of more incarceration for more serious violent crimes (Tonry 1987, 57).

In summary, Minnesota's and Washington's presumptive sentencing guidelines contain more features than presumptive determinate sentencing laws in California and Colorado. Both guidelines recommend more articulated dispositional and durational decisions. The presumptive determinate sentencing laws in California and Colorado provide no presumption of incarceration for the majority of typical offenses with a few exceptions. Since presumptive sentences are also determinate in Minnesota and Washington, one can reasonably regard them as presumptive determinate sentencing states.

VOLUNTARY SENTENCING GUIDELINES

Sentencing reform policy has developed at a much slower pace in Pennsylvania than in Minnesota. The Philadelphia experiment in using sentencing guidelines began in 1979. The statewide implementation of Pennsylvania's sentencing guidelines became effective in July 1982. The drafting of the guidelines encountered critical opposition from inside and outside the Pennsylvania Sentencing Commission. As a result of subsequent revisions, the list of mitigating and aggravating factors was eliminated from the final draft of the adopted guidelines and guideline sentence ranges widened. Guideline specificity was jeopardized for that reason. The implementation of the guidelines is seen as supplementary to the mandatory minimum sentencing scheme (Shane-DuBow et al. 1985, 227).

Without the binding character explicitly stated in the enabling legislation, the Pennsylvania guidelines can be regarded as voluntary. According to the Pennsylvania statute, the sentencing judge "shall consider" the guidelines (von Hirsch et al. 1987, 196). In Pennsylvania, the guidelines are based on sentencing norms. Sentences imposed that departure from guideline ranges require an accompanying written explanation (Shane-DuBow et al. 1985, 227; Tonry 1987, 56).

In general, judicial discretion remains broad. The guidelines specify three sentence ranges: a normal minimum range, an aggravated minimum range, and a mitigated minimum range. Within a list of aggravating and mitigating factors, the judge is free to select a minimum sentence within any of these three minimum ranges with written reasons. The judge may impose a maximum sentence. The parole board retains most of its discretionary power over parole release. Even though the implementation of the guidelines is not entirely voluntary, determination of incarceration, duration, and termination lacks much of specific sentencing standards expected to be found under presumptive sentencing. Pennsylvania's system falls under voluntary sentencing guidelines.

Several other states adopting similar voluntary sentencing guidelines include, with effective date in parentheses, Rhode Island (1982), Utah (1978), Vermont (1982), and Wisconsin (1983). Rhode Island's benchmark sentencing guidelines, for example, provide no standards for the in/out decision. In general, the decision to impose nonincarcerative sentences is discretionary (Shane-DuBow et al. 1985, 229–31). Still, both judicial and parole release discretion are not substantially curtailed, particularly for nonfirearm and first conviction offenses.

CONCLUSION

Five major sentencing reform types have been reviewed in this chapter. Mandatory minimum sentencing laws eliminate most judicial discretion over the use of incarceration. It reduces the discretionary range for sentence length and parole release, and the overall discretionary power of the judge and parole board is somewhat diminished.

In Illinois, Connecticut, and Maine, mandatory determinate sentencing laws also eliminate parole release discretion. Judicial discretion in selecting appropriate prison terms is still broad, even among mandatory minimum offenses. Since determinate sentences rest on judicial discretion, disparity in sentence length seems unaffected by the reform. At the final point of sentencing decision, calculation of release date is regulated by good-time policy.

Presumptive determinate sentencing laws in California and Colorado, and to a lesser extent, Indiana, New Mexico, and North Carolina, specify much shorter presumptive prison terms within much narrower sentence ranges for most crimes than those specified in the revised statutes of mandatory determinate sentencing states—Connecticut, Illinois, and Maine.

Finally, there are two types of sentencing guidelines: presumptive and voluntary. Presumptive sentencing guidelines in Minnesota and Washington provide more articulated sentencing standards than those written into the revised statutes of presumptive determinate sentencing states. Presumptive sentences are determinate in Minnesota and Washington because termination of time served is nondiscretionary and only affected by good-time reduction. Appellate sentence review is another form of control over judicial discretion. Voluntary sentencing guidelines have no legal binding effects on sentencing decisions. There remain broad judicial discretion and parole release discretion. The voluntary guidelines can be viewed as supplementary to the existing mandatory minimum sentence provisions.

CHAPTER 4

Evaluations of Sentencing Reform Impacts

This chapter reviews prior research on the impacts of sentencing reforms. The purpose is to highlight research findings of courts' output affected by these new sentencing policies. A review of the literature on this topic will be structured by using a typology of sentencing reforms developed in chapter 3. This literature will be summarized to provide a sense of where we are and what can be done to improve the research design of future evaluation studies.

MANDATORY MINIMUM SENTENCING LAWS

Massachusetts' 1974 Bartley–Fox Amendment and Michigan's 1977 Felony Firearms Statute represent two case studies of mandatory minimum sentencing laws. There are a few studies evaluating the impacts of these two revised statutes. Attention will be paid to how courts adapted their ways of handling defendants' cases and how their adaptive responses to the new laws influenced disposition outcomes.

Massachusetts

Massachusetts' Bartley–Fox Amendment requires imposition of mandatory minimum sentences for certain firearm offenses and some violent felony offenses that involve the use of a firearm. After the amendment went into effect in 1974, it was evaluated by several funded research projects. The Massachusetts code attracted researchers because of its intense publicity and promise that punishment under this law would be swift and certain, and that once caught "nobody can get you out" (Beha 1977, 98). Beha (1977) and Rossman et al. (1979) conducted major evaluation studies in Boston.

The Beha study includes all cases of illegal possession, carrying, and use of firearms, which amounted to 615 in 1974 (before) and 467 cases in 1975 (after). Based on these data, prosecutors routinely screened out eligible cases by charging possession offenses in many carrying cases (Beha 1977, 135–37; Cohen and Tonry 1983, 344–46). The proportion of acquittals among all dispositions, however, rose sharply for robbery (from 6% to 31%), assault with a deadly weapon (from 8% to 12%), and firearm-only offenses (from 16% to 36%). The opposite effect was found among no-gun-involved cases, with the acquittal rate dropping from 25 percent to 11 percent (Cohen and Tonry 1983, 346). These increased acquittal rates are in part due to greater efforts made by defense attorneys to avoid mandatory sentences.

In all probability, defendants facing a mandatory minimum sentence would make all-out efforts to avoid conviction. Instead of pleading guilty in exchange for probation or suspended sentences, those who choose not to plead guilty are more likely to get away with no conviction. According to the National Institute of Justice report of Rossman et al.'s findings, dismissal rates went up 4 percent during the first year of implementation (from 18% in 1974 to 22% in 1975) and even much more during the second year (38% in 1976).

The higher prison risk on conviction on the mandatory carrying charge reduced incentives for guilty pleas in exchange for lenient sentences. The mandatory sentence became one key element to consider in plea negotiations based on charge, sentence, or facts of the case. The probability for the court to convict and issue mandatory sentences for carrying offenders is at a low level. The statistics show a sharp drop from 41 percent convicted of total dispositions in 1974, to 25 percent in 1975, and to 17 percent in 1976 (Carlson 1982, 8–10; Rossman et al. 1979, 352–62).

Michigan

In evaluating effects of the Michigan Felony Firearm Statute on judicial dispositions, Heumann and Loftin (1979) conducted a statistical analysis based on case processing and disposition data. This study was designed to measure post-implementation changes in case disposition outcomes. The data studied covered the period of six months before and six months after January 1, 1977, the date the law went into effect. Wayne County, where the prosecutor also forbade dismissal of firearms charges pursuant to charge bargaining, was the site for this research evaluation.

The pre-implementation sample of crimes committed while a firearm was being carried included 145 felonious assault, 240 other assault, and 471 armed robbery cases. In the post-implementation sample, there were 39 felonious assault, 53 other assault, and 164 armed robbery cases. Each subsample for both time periods was analyzed in a tabular form. Comparison was made between before and after periods in order to detect changes in dispositional outcomes. In order to supplement these data, the authors completed a series of personal interviews with judges, prosecutors, and lawyers.

The PROMIS database from which the samples were drawn included only cases warranted for prosecution. The data on cases not warranted for prosecution are not available for analysis. Clearly, there was a tendency toward increased prosecutorial discretion in case screening earlier in the process by not warranting certain types of cases for prosecution. This is somewhat problematic because adaptive behavior by screening out cases from coming to the courts cannot be tested and controlled.

Given this major reservation, the Heumann and Loftin study shows a considerable change in firearm-involved case processing in Wayne County. Felonious assault had a 2 percent increase in the rate of early dismissal. The rate of other assault cases dismissed before the pretrial conference was 26 percent after the law went into effect as opposed to 12 percent before the law. Likewise, the rate for armed robbery increased from 13 percent to 22 percent. This kind of decision not to continue the case can increase the overall nonconviction rate. Thus, more cases got away with armed robbery and other assault charges. For armed robbery, the chance of being dismissed and acquitted combined rose from 32 percent to 39 percent. The figure for other assault charges increased from 36 percent to 50 percent.

Thus, the reduction in the rate of incarceration advantaged the more serious offenders the most. In particular, offenders convicted of robbery using a firearm were less likely to be imprisoned after the 1977 law. The imprisonment rate dropped from 64 percent to 60 percent. The conviction rate with no incarcerative sentence remained low for armed robbery. By contrast, those convicted of less serious offenses received incarcerative sentences more frequently after the law became effective. The imprisonment rates for both felonious and other assault each increased by 4 percent.

According to the data from Wayne County, there was an overall lower probability of imposing criminal sanctions following the 1977 revisions. More than half of defendants charged either with felonious assault (52%) or with other assault (50%) were released without prison sentences. The primary mode of disposition for these defendants was dismissal and acquittal combined. This pattern holds true for armed robbery as well. Many defendants charged with carrying a firearm in armed robbery incidents—slightly over one-third of each sample—were either dismissed or acquitted, thereby avoiding mandatory or other sentences (Heumann and Loftin 1979, tab. 3).

Sentences of two years or more for felonious assault rose from 30 percent to 71 percent, for other assault from 59 percent to 81 percent, and for armed robbery from 87 percent to 93 percent (Cohen and Tonry 1983, 343). Apparently, these figures indicate that two-year minimum sentences were imposed. But it is not certain that the two-year mandatory minimum was added to the typical incarcerative term for the primary offense. Charge reduction from a felony to a misdemeanor for the primary offense is an available option that makes the law inoperative. Also prevalent among judges interviewed was the tendency to reduce the sentence imposed on the primary felony before adding the two-year mandatory term for gun involvement, thereby preserving the prior "going rates" level (Heumann and Loftin 1979, 422). These authors, as well as other observers, acknowledge the existence of adaptive responses to the law (Cohen and Tonry 1983; Heumann and Loftin 1979). The use of a "waiver" trial to dismiss gun charges at trial makes it "a mechanism to circumvent both the mandatory gun law and the prosecutor's ban on charge bargaining" (Cohen and Tonry 1983, 344).

Also in Michigan, Loftin and McDowall (1981) used a database that covered all cases disposed of in the Detroit Recorders Court from 1976 through 1978. In evaluating the impact of the law, they applied Tobit analysis to court dispositions of 8,414 cases originally charged with a violent felony. Upon completion of this project, the authors found no substantial effect on the severity of sentences imposed on felonies involving firearms. The expected time served (the length of time to first possible release) for offenders charged with murder or armed robbery remained unaffected. But there did appear to be some increase in the expected time served for felonious assault and other assaults involving a firearm (Cohen and Tonry 1983, 343; Loftin and McDowall 1981, 154–56).

With advanced statistical analysis, the authors took into account both gun involvement and the time period in which the offenses were committed before or after passage of the law. They concluded that the law made no substantial difference in the probability of imprisonment on conviction of almost all offenses committed with the use of a gun. Only felonious assault offenders experienced significantly higher risk of being incarcerated after the law took effect (Loftin et al. 1983, 295).

Only the felonious assault category had a significant reduction in the conviction rate under the new law. Among offenders who received incarcerative sentences, minimum sentences went up significantly. The only two exceptions to this general increase were among serious offenders, who received longer incarcerative sentences. In fact, the minimum sentences for first- and second-degree murder as well as first-degree criminal sexual conduct experienced some minimal, but not significant, decline (Loftin et al. 1983, 296–97).

In summary, the data from Massachusetts and Michigan indicated a similar pattern of officials' adaptive responses to the new rules. Adjustments to defendants' cases were made during prosecution and plea negotiation. These adjustments in pursuit of guilty pleas shaped the outcome of cases, which in turn can undermine the goals of mandatory minimum sentences.

MANDATORY DETERMINATE SENTENCING LAWS

Maine and Illinois are two pioneering states that adopted mandatory determinate sentences for the majority of offenses (Lagoy et al. 1978). Evaluation studies of the impacts of mandatory determinate sentencing laws in these two states are available for review. The discussion begins with a summary of the results of Maine's study, followed by a review of the Illinois study.

Maine

In 1976 Maine created probationary supervision to replace parole. Sentences were divided between an initial period of incarceration accompanied by a term of probationary supervision. Under "split sentence" provisions, prison sentences imposed became determinate. The judge retains much discretion in determining the length of probationary supervision, which is equivalent to "judicial parole" (Tonry 1987, 84). In addition, the range of fixed sentences remained up to judicial determination, even when minimum unsuspendable sentences were specified for certain offenses.

Maine's determinate sentencing scheme contains various elements that are internally inconsistent with one another. As experts observe, it is "a code which deplores disparities while encouraging individualized sentences, eliminates parole while retaining the possibility of sentence reductions, and requires flat sentences while providing judges with immense discretionary powers" (Shane-DuBow et al. 1985, 127).

Because of the ambiguity of the reform initiated in Maine, little or no impact was expected to take place. A major evaluation was carried out and completed recently by Anspach et al. (1983). These authors report no substantial reform effects attributable to the new laws, noting that:

> Overall, there is little indication that the reform had a substantial, systematic, or consistent effect on the criteria used in the decision as to the type of sentence to impose. Although there is clearly a great deal of variation in criteria used, there is no indication this variation is different either in magnitude or form before and after the reform. The reform has neither resulted in an overall increase in the consistency in the basis of decisions about sentence types, nor has it resulted in an overall increase in the predictability of sentence types. (Anspach et al. 1983, 103)

A lack of sentencing reform impacts in Maine is not surprising. An important reason is that Maine's law did not create a system of specific sentencing standards (Tonry 1987, 85).

Illinois

In an attempt to assess the effects of the determinate sentencing law on patterns of felony dispositions in Illinois, Schuwerk (1984) compared guilty pleas, bench trials, and jury trials that resulted in conviction during 1974–81. The data indicate that guilty pleas remain the prevalent mode of disposition statewide. The majority of all convicted defendants pled guilty to the offenses of which they were convicted. There was no discernible change in heavy reliance of the court system on guilty pleas as a way to convict a defendant.

There was a tendency toward Class X offenders pleading to a lesser charge (Class 1 or lower). According to police arrest statistics, Class 1 felony arrests amounted to only about 3 percent of Class X felony arrests statewide each year during 1979–81. But there were a large number of offenders convicted of a Class 1 felony who were not charged with a Class 1 felony at arrest during the same period.

Plausible explanations for this increase in convictions of Class 1 offense are twofold. First, "defendants are being routinely overcharged and then those charges are reduced to more appropriate ones during the bargaining process." Second, "prosecutors are filing appropriate charges initially, but then are abandoning proveable and appropriate offenses in favor of lesser, factually inappropriate ones" (Schuwerk 1984, 631).

Another study applied interrupted time-series analysis to the Illinois data on felony conviction during 1965–84 (Witayapanyanon 1992). The findings are consistent with Schuwerk's conclusion. Among cases disposed of with a felony charge, the conviction rate dropped by 16 percent statewide. This decreased conviction rate attributed to about a 7 percent reduction in incarcerative sentences as a mode of disposition. The rate of guilty pleas among felony defendants decreased by 14 percent.

The statistics for Cook County Circuit Court show that the effects of the law have been much greater in Cook County than in the rest of the state. Case dispositions without conviction (both dismissals and acquittals combined) increased under the Class X law. The available data suggest a tendency toward screening out unsuccessfully negotiated cases through greater use of dismissals and acquittals.

In summary, Illinois' mandatory determinate sentencing law experienced a similar pattern of implementation problems found in mandatory minimum sentencing states. Heavy reliance for court conviction decisions on guilty pleas resulted in excessive charge reduction of Class X to Class 1 offenses on felony conviction. Reduction in guilty pleas in general led to a substantial decline in conviction and imprisonment rates. These unintended consequences can be attributed to implementation problems most mandatory minimum sentencing laws have encountered.

PRESUMPTIVE DETERMINATE SENTENCING LAWS

Unlike mandatory determinate sentencing laws, the revised statutes of presumptive determinate sentencing states offer more specific sentencing standards. Two of the five such laws selected for review are California's and North Carolina's.

California

A series of major research projects has been completed that assess the impacts of California's presumptive determinate sentencing law (Brewer et al. 1980; Casper et al. 1982; Ku 1980; Lipson and Peterson 1980; Sparks 1981; Utz 1981). Two major studies addressed judicial compliance with presumptive terms (Brewer et al. 1980; California Board of Prison Terms 1981). Drawing on the results of these studies, Cohen and Tonry present distributions of sentences for all offenses with individual statutorily defined breakdown for crimes against persons, property, and drug offenses (360, tab. 7–16). The data indicate that presumptive terms were imposed on most convicted defendants, particularly among most defendants charged with property offenses. However, the use of presumptive terms in general experienced modest decline (from 61 percent in 1977–78 to 54 percent in 1979). A drop in the rate of presumptive sentences was offset by a rise in the proportion of lower limit sentences selected for convicted defendants (from 20 percent in 1977–78 to 27 percent in 1979). This tendency toward greater use of lower limit terms (from 18 percent in 1977–78 to 27 percent in 1979) was found among property offenses, which are generally conceived as less severe than those against persons.

Within the presumptive structure, sentence enhancements have been applied unevenly. Firearm enhancement, for example, tends to be charged, pled to or proved, and imposed more frequently than are body injury and prior criminal history enhancements. In most cases, robbery with the use of a firearm receives enhanced sentences more consistently than do other offenses.

According to the California's Board of Prison Terms data, more than four out of five eligible cases for firearm enhancement were charged as such (Cohen and Tonry 1983, 362). The charging pattern seems to be consistent in applying firearm enhancement across eligible cases. By contrast, application of other enhancements was more inconsistent at the charging stage. This inconsistency suggests that prosecutorial discretion has been more frequently exercised. Less than half the number of eligible offenders with prior criminal history were actually charged with such enhancement. It is also evident that less than one-third of eligible offenders with victim injury involved were charged with such enhancement.

A similar pattern holds for all offenses being pled to or proved among charged cases. Half of eligible cases received sentences with firearm enhancement. Offenders with prior records as well as those involving victim injury, however, received enhanced sentences in less than 20 percent of the eligible cases.

Casper et al. (1982) and Utz (1981) found the proportion of imposed sentence enhancements was even less than that reported above. There was a tendency for cases eligible for application of mandatory sentencing enhancements to be dropped or dismissed during the course of charge negotiations. Prosecutors can drop enhanced charges in exchange for guilty pleas to the primary offenses. Given this adjustment, the rate of compliance on conviction fails to account for the number of cases screened out from the eligible pool (Cohen and Tonry 1983, 364).

Drawing on the Casper et al. and Utz studies, Cohen and Tonry found that plea bargaining remained active under the new law as an effective mechanism for circumventing the new rules. As they remark, "sufficient prison time could usually be obtained with conviction for the basic offense charge, and [enhancement] allegations were often dropped as part of a prison plea" (1983, 378).

The prison use rate, whether measured as court commitments to state prison per one hundred thousand residents or as prison sentences on conviction, continued to rise during the post-reform period across jurisdictions statewide. But the observed increase in sanction severity in California is attributable to persistent trends toward more use of incarcerative sentences established long before the law (Cohen and Tonry 1983, 380–409).

North Carolina

The implementation of the Fair Sentencing Act of 1981 in North Carolina faced several patterns of adaptive behavior among criminal justice officials similar to what has been found in California. In his review of research findings from studies by a research team at the University of North Carolina (Clarke et al. 1983; Clarke 1984), Tonry (1987) reveals that trial rates, which were expected to rise when sentencing outcomes became more predictable, remained stable after passage of the act. In fact, jury trials were reduced substantially. The increased predictability of sentencing decisions did not eliminate offenders' incentive to plead guilty. Neither did sentence bargains increase in the jurisdictions studied. Charge negotiation became more frequently used, particularly when sentences other than presumptive terms were to be imposed.

Increased formal compliance in sentencing practices should come as no surprise. After charge screening processes, remaining cases received sentences largely consistent with presumptive terms specified. Taking into account those cases screened out earlier, it remains doubtful that consistency in application of presumptive terms on conviction by any means has been achieved. Overall, sentences became shorter but, as Clarke reported, the chance of convicted felons receiving incarcerative sentences rose from 55 percent in 1979 to 63 percent in 1981–82 (1984, 148).

Generally speaking, North Carolina has attained some of the impacts the act was intended to accomplish. As frequently found in most jurisdictions, adaptive reactions to the act occurred around the loopholes of reform requirements. As Clarke observes:

> Perhaps the major defect of the FSA was that it attempted to regulate only the lengths of active prison terms. It did not limit in any way the judges' complete discretion to suspend the prison sentence. . . . [W]hile a judge must make written findings to support any active prison term different from the presumptive [unless there was a plea bargain], he need not make any written findings to suspend the prison term altogether. (1984, 142)

Presumptive determinate sentencing laws are not immune from similar implementation problems. Although some degree of intended effects has been achieved among cases receiving presumptive terms, compliance with sentence enhancement provisions has been minimal. The majority of eligible cases were screened out at various stages prior to conviction decisions. As a result, only a small proportion of eligible offenders actually received enhanced sentences as prescribed by the statute.

PRESUMPTIVE SENTENCING GUIDELINES

This section summarizes the results of evaluation studies of presumptive sentencing guidelines in Minnesota and Washington.

These presumptive guidelines became effective on May 1, 1980, in Minnesota and on July 1, 1984, in Washington. Unlike all other reform efforts, observers agree that presumptive guidelines, particularly as implemented in Minnesota, produced substantial improvement in sentencing practices (Tonry 1987, 45). In Minnesota and Washington, sentencing patterns shifted toward the direction contemplated by the legislatures. However, the guidelines in both jurisdictions appear to have encountered some adaptive responses to evade the new sentencing rules, particularly in the plea process.

Minnesota

The Minnesota guidelines view crimes against persons as more severe than crimes against property and, therefore, prescribe more presumptive prison sentences for person offenses than for property offenses. The guidelines provide specific sentencing standards based on severity levels that reflect both seriousness of offense and criminal history record. Cases receiving severity levels located below the dispositional line of the guidelines grid become eligible for presumptive prison sentences. To clarify the guidelines' terminology, a "dispositional departure" means either when a prison sentence is imposed (upward departure) in lieu of a presumptive "out" sentence according to the guidelines, or when a nonprison sentence is imposed (downward departure) in lieu of a presumptive "in" sentence (Tonry 1987, 61). Within the judge's discretion and statutory limits, a nonprison sanction may include "a jail term of up to one year, or else probation, fine, or other community disposition" (von Hirsch et al. 1987, 178). A "durational departure" occurs when a sentence is imposed outside an applicable guideline range (Tonry 1987, 61).

Studies show that the rate of total dispositional departures in Minnesota went down from 19.4 percent in 1978 to 6.2 percent in 1981, 7.2 percent in 1982, 8.9 percent in 1983, and 9.9 percent in 1984 (Knapp 1987, 130; Tonry 1987, 62). There has been an increase in property offenders receiving a prison sentence combined with a decrease in person offenders receiving a nonprison sentence. The former situation can lead to upward departures and the latter to downward departures. However, the rates of both upward and downward dispositional departures were distributed evenly during the first three years of implementation (Tonry 1987,

62). Among eligible "in" cases, 77 percent were imprisoned as recommended in 1981 and 1982, as opposed to only about 40 percent of similar cases convicted in 1978. There is a significant shift toward more imprisonment for person offenses consistent with the guidelines.

The rates of compliance with presumptive sentence ranges were also high. In 1981, 76.4 percent of 827 convictions received prison terms within presumptive ranges. The compliance rate was higher in 1982 (79.6 percent) as well as in 1983 (77.1 percent). For those receiving prison terms outside presumptive ranges in 1981–83, there is a tendency toward imposition of shorter sentences below lower limits of their presumptive ranges (Cohen and Tonry 1983, 419; Tonry 1987, 62).

Under the Minnesota guidelines, plea negotiations were used to circumvent the new rules. As expected, charge negotiations were used more frequently to obtain conviction and also to evade the guidelines than were sentence negotiations. A study explains these two possible ways in which defendants can avoid or reduce presumptive prison sentences (Tonry 1987, 72–73). First, concessions may be offered in charge negotiations that can move cases across offense severity levels. Negotiated charge reductions across offense severity levels increased substantially from 12 percent in 1978 to 27 percent in 1983 (Tonry 1987, 72). This method will have a significant impact on defendants' sentences, particularly when it moves cases across the dispositional line from the area of presumptive imprisonment (below) to the area of presumptive nonimprisonment (above). Second, sentence negotiations were also devised to evade the guidelines. Despite the Minnesota Supreme Court's rulings that a sentence negotiation provides no "substantial and compelling circumstances" under which the judge may depart from guidelines, it remains the most commonly reasoned justification for such departures (Tonry 1987, 73).

Washington

The Washington legislature endorsed a presumptive sentencing guidelines system that has most of Minnesota's ingredients. In Washington, presumptive sentence ranges within which the judge may select without having to give reasons are relatively narrow. As in Minnesota, departures from these presumptive ranges are permissible under "substantial and compelling" circumstances. The guidelines also provide a nonexclusive list of "illustrative" aggravating and mitigating circumstances (von Hirsch et al. 1987, 182–85). Sentencing policy was shifted toward more incarceration for violent offenses and less incarceration for property offenses (Tonry 1987, 57–58).

An in-house preliminary evaluation study by the Washington Sentencing Guidelines Commission (1985), reviewed by Tonry (1987), claimed apparent success in the guidelines' first six months of implementation. In Washington, judges complied with the guidelines by moving toward incarcerating more violent offenders and less property offenders (Tonry 1987, 59). During the first half of 1985 under the guidelines, 63.5 percent of violent offense convictees were imprisoned. This figure represents a significant rise from 46 percent of those convicted of violent offenses in 1982 (Tonry 1987, 69).

In Washington, first-time offenders committing crimes of levels 6 to 14 are subject to presumptive prison terms. According to the commission's data, the percentage distribution of conviction offenses by seriousness levels shows an interesting pattern. The proportion of serious offenders convicted of crimes carrying presumptive prison sentences during the first six months of 1985 was lower than it would have been in 1982. This systematic reduction in the percentage distribution is consistent across presumptive incarceration levels (6 to 14). To the extent that this consistent pattern reflects charge reductions moving cases downward across seriousness levels, charge negotiations were probably employed to evade the guidelines.

In general, presumptive sentencing guidelines have been successfully institutionalized and implemented in Minnesota and Washington (Tonry 1987; von Hirsch et al. 1987). It appears that judges have complied with the guidelines and, therefore, sentencing outcomes became more consistent and uniform than before in both jurisdictions. In Minnesota, disparities in sentencing were substantially reduced with regard to the incarceration decision and, to a lesser extent, sentence length. However, sentence negotiations were often given as "substantial and compelling" circumstances for departing from the guidelines. As another form of circumvention, prosecutors in Minnesota have been engaged in charge negotiations by accepting guilty pleas on less serious charges, thereby moving cases across severity levels. This form of evasion may also be taking place in Washington.

VOLUNTARY SENTENCING GUIDELINES

Voluntary sentencing guidelines are intended to achieve only incremental change from previous sentencing patterns. A primary goal is to articulate prevailing norms in a particular jurisdiction to assist judges in making appropriate sentencing decisions. In order to achieve consistency and uniformity in sentencing, voluntary guidelines provide appropriate sentences for particular offenses and circumstances that reflect the prevailing norms. Thus, only judges who deviate widely from norms would be the target of voluntary guidelines (Cohen and Tonry 1983, 413–15).

Voluntary guidelines were small-scale experimental projects in search of reform in many states and were quickly replaced by other types of statewide sentencing reforms. It is not surprising that voluntary guidelines have had little or no impact on sentencing outcomes. Several available evaluation studies (Carrow et al. 1985; Cohen and Helland 1982; Rich et al. 1981), reviewed by Tonry (1987, 40–43) and others (Cohen and Tonry 1983), conclude that voluntary guidelines did not have a significant impact on the exercise of sentencing discretion by judges in Denver, Newark, and Philadelphia. As a recent study (Carrow et al. 1985) reveals, judges admitted during personal interviews either that voluntary guidelines were often ignored, particularly in plea negotiations, or that guidelines were considered after decisions had already been made (Tonry 1987, 41).

PRIOR EVALUATIONS OF SENTENCING REFORM IMPACTS AND THEIR METHODOLOGICAL LIMITATIONS

There has been a series of major research evaluations of effects of sentencing innovations implemented in this country. Only some of the studies that received national attention have been reviewed in this chapter. Those reviewed reveal little evidence of sentencing reform impact. But our interpretation of research findings should not be limited to these illustrative case studies. There are a number of policy relevant variables to consider in evaluating sentencing reforms. At least three important concepts are of special concern to criminal justice experts in the field: adaptive behavior by personnel in the criminal justice system, changes in patterns of case flow, and their effects on sentence severity and disparity. The literature on reform impacts will be summarized, with particular attention given to these three concepts.

The Panel on Sentencing Research acknowledged the broad scope of sentencing policy concerns. The panel's report concentrates on how the behavior of key criminal justice actors has been affected and to what extent their behavioral responses to reform implementation have had an impact on the defendants. Drawing on the empirical findings of major impact evaluations, the panel has reached the following substantive conclusions:

1. Compliance with procedural requirements of sentencing innovations has been widespread, but such behavioral changes have often represented compliance in form rather than in substance.

2. The extent of compliance with reforms has varied with (a) the level of organizational or political support for the reform; (b) the existence of statutory or administrative authority supporting the procedural requirements; and (c) the existence of credible monitoring and enforcement mechanisms.

3. There have been modest changes in sentencing outcomes, particularly some increases in prison use, in jurisdictions that have adopted sentencing reforms. These increases in sentence severity were typically found in previously marginal prison cases—cases that might or might not have resulted in short prison terms in the past. Less ambiguous cases, including both more serious cases for which prison terms were fairly certain outcomes and less serious cases for which prison terms were relatively rare, have experienced little change in sentencing outcomes.

4. The substantial increases in prison populations in jurisdictions that have adopted sentencing reforms continue pre-existing trends in sentencing and do not appear to be substantially caused by these sentencing reforms. (Blumstein et al. 1983, 28–31)

Another reform issue concerns possible reform impacts on prison populations. Evaluation research on this policy issue has frequently asked whether the sentencing reforms have overcrowded state prisons. A typical answer to this research question is that while there is a strong tendency toward prison overcrowding, no hard evidence attributes rising prison population and accompanying overcrowding problems to sentencing reforms.

The fact that insufficient prison capacity to house convicted defendants may serve as an independent variable inhibiting the implementation process has received little attention. A few states have taken steps to develop prison population control mechanisms in response to the new sentencing schemes. With the absence of some "safety-valve" control mechanisms or prison expansion projects to accommodate inmates serving longer definite sentences, the overcrowding issue turns into a reform backlash exerting pressures on the judicial process. The panel highlights the prison population issue as part of sentencing policies:

1. Prison populations increased steadily in the 1970s, and further increases are projected throughout the 1980s. This growth in prison populations appears to continue preexisting trends and is only marginally related to recent sentencing reforms.

2. Prison populations have increased more rapidly than has available prison capacity. Many institutions are crowded, and little immediate relief from population pressures is in sight.

3. Responsible formulation of sentencing policy requires baseline projections of the size and composition of prison populations with no policy changes, as well as estimates of the impact of various policy options. Analytical techniques for this purpose, although still crude, can be applied to estimate the effects of proposed policy changes, thereby making the value choices explicit.

4. A continuation of the current rate of prison admissions, in the absence of some new prison population "safety-valve" mechanisms, is likely to result in a dramatic rise in prison populations.

5. Evidence from evaluations of these programs suggests that these alternatives have been used more frequently as a supplement to existing nonincarcerative sanctions for use with offenders who would have remained in the community rather than as an alternative sanction for offenders who

would otherwise have been incarcerated. (Blumstein et al. 1983, 32–36)

The sentencing reforms empirically evaluated here and elsewhere suggest that key criminal justice actors charged with the responsibility of carrying out intended reform goals have been less than enthusiastic in realizing these goals. At times, a set of organizational goals such as caseload reduction and maintaining high levels of certainty toward conviction tend to be in conflict with reform goals (Eisenstein and Jacob 1977). For instance, when the officials disapprove of reform elements as unnecessarily inconvenient, and when monitoring and sanctioning mechanisms for enforcement are weak, organizational resistance hampers attainment of reform goals.

The post-reform effects of policy innovations, under these and other unfavorable circumstances, have been to the benefit of affected offenders. Criminal sanctions, not necessarily harsher after reform policies have been instituted, tend to become less frequently imposed and served to the entire terms specified.

While this type of implementation problem is consistent with plausible explanations grounded in organization and implementation theory (Mazmanian and Sabatier 1983), prior research findings reported in the literature remain inconclusive (Cohen and Tonry 1983; Tonry 1987).

The typical design used in most evaluation studies of sentencing reform is weak. The typical study bases its evaluation analysis on short observation periods, six months to one year, before and after the reform became effective. The typical interpretation is that the observed post-reform changes between the two periods compared are attributable to the reform effects. Methodological flaws are inherent in a research design that precludes an effort to examine trends present in the pre-reform period. A short post-reform period does not allow for exploration of evolutionary or delayed types of reform effects.[1]

According to the Panel on Sentencing Research, there are several key methodological concerns about the validity of reform impact evaluations:

---

1. See Campbell and Stanley (1966, 7–12), Cook and Campbell (1979, 99–103), and Bingham and Felbinger (1989, 175–90) for methodological discussion on this one-group pretest-posttest design with respect to statistical regression, maturation, and other threats to internal validity.

1. While changes in system operations and sentence outcomes have been observed, almost all the impact studies suffer from methodological problems that limit our ability to attribute these changes to the sentencing reforms. Inadequate observation periods mar many of the impact studies.

2. The validity of impact studies is seriously jeopardized if they fail to investigate the considerable opportunities for differential filtering of cases before and after the implementation of new rules or precedures. To date, impact studies have been too narrowly focused, examining changes only in those parts of the process directly affected by a sentencing reform.

3. The validity of the conclusions of many impact studies is limited because of their failure to control adequately for changes in the mix of cases before and after the change takes effect. (Blumstein et al. 1983, 31–32)

It is crucial to include multiple observations over extended periods so that reform effects can be assessed in the presence of the preestablished trends. The California evaluation studies make a good case in point.[2] The time series observed for both early guilty plea and prison use rates at this research site provides no defensible evidence that a shift from the pre-reform normal level has taken place after the reform.

Another concern addressed by the panel is the need for outcome measures at all levels of case processing. Thus, official circumvention of procedural requirements with an even chance of taking place at any stage of criminal procedures can be investigated. There is also need for adequate controls for changes in case attributes and for qualitative analysis of system functioning (Blumstein et al. 1983, 221–24).

CONCLUSION

Mandatory minimum sentencing laws have been widely accepted in the United States. The rhetoric of these laws emphasizes the

---

2. Several major studies that take into account historical patterns of criminal justice behavior in California include research evaluations done by Brewer et al. (1980), Casper et al. (1982), and Lipson and Peterson (1980). See Cohen and Tonry (1983, 375–83), particularly figures 7–1 and 7–2 for presentation of California' Guilty Pleas at Initial Appearance and Prison Use time series.

mandatory minimum element of procedural reform requirements intended to increase certainty and severity of punishment as a means for promoting crime reduction.

The use of mandatory minimum sentences has been widely directed toward certain violent offenses committed with the unlawful use of a firearm. Some states treat illegal firearm use as a separate punishable offense that requires mandatory minimum sentence in addition to the primary offense punishment. Firearm sentencing enhancements have been established in many other states.

Within the mandatory minimum structure, ranges within which judges may set incarcerative terms without giving reasons remain wide. While incarcerative sentences must be imposed on conviction of certain offenses specified in the statute, judicial discretion to determine sentence lengths varies from state to state, but in most cases it remains large. For states with great concern over sentence disparities, the ranges between statutory minimum and maximum terms specified are narrower.

Determinate sentencing laws emphasize determination of sentence lengths at the time of sentencing. The pure form of flat sentence suggests elimination of parole release discretion. A few states have abolished parole boards, but they tend to shift some discretionary power to the Department of Corrections charged with mandatory supervised release as in Illinois. Where the authority of parole boards has been curtailed, there is a tendency toward widened judicial discretion to determine the length of supervised release.

The sentencing guidelines model emphasizes more consistent sentencing practices across judges. The penalty structure of presumptive guidelines reflects several theoretical principles of proportionality and just deserts. Elaborate procedural requirements must be followed to rank offense severity and criminal history scores. Both in/out decisions and incarcerative terms are usually presented in a matrix. Departure from specified ranges requires compelling written reasons. Appellate review of sentences outside permitted ranges serves as an effective monitoring mechanism to promote judicial compliance.

In the National Institute of Justice Issues and Practices in Criminal Justice publication series, Tonry summarizes seven key points of empirical findings drawn from the sentencing reform impact literature as follows:

1. Mandatory sentencing laws increase the proportion of offenders imprisoned among persons convicted of the pertinent offense but tend to elicit widespread efforts by judges and lawyers to circumvent their application.

2. Voluntary sentencing guidelines, where evaluated, have generally not resulted in significantly altered sentencing patterns.

3. Presumptive sentencing guidelines, like those in Minnesota and Washington, can, under favorable circumstances, achieve substantial changes in sentencing patterns, compared with past practices, and can increase consistency in sentencing.

4. Statutory determinate sentencing laws, like those in California and North Carolina, under certain circumstances, can produce demonstrable changes in sentencing outcomes, including increased consistency.

5. Parole guidelines can achieve relatively high levels of accuracy, consistency, and accountability in decision making and can offset disparities in the lengths of prison sentences imposed by judges.

6. Neither jury trial rates, trial rates, nor average case disposition times necessarily increase under statutory determinate sentencing laws, presumptive sentencing guidelines, or plea bargaining bans (increases in trial rates and case processing times have often been hypothesized as a likely result of such systems, because defendants could expect little incremental increase in sanctions after trial convictions, compared with sanctions following plea bargains).

7. Appellate review of sentences need not generate a caseload that overwhelms the appellate courts, as has been hypothesized by those concerned with judicial caseloads and apprehensive about the litigious proclivities of prisoners. (1987, 2–3)

All in all, certain patterns of sentencing reform impacts exist in some systematic fashion associated with reform types adopted. The mandatory minimum sentencing schemes such as those in Massachusetts, Michigan, and New York tend to be the most vulnerable to the systems' efforts to circumvent procedural requirements. This type of vulnerability may apply to the mandatory determinate sentencing schemes as implemented in Illinois. The presumptive determinate sentencing schemes with narrow prison sentence ranges have higher potential to achieve consistency in sentence lengths as opposed to the mandatory minimum scheme. With sentencing commission and appellate sentence review provisions as in Minnesota and Washington, presumptive guidelines are more likely to obtain judicial compliance than are voluntary guidelines.

While prior evaluations of sentencing reform impacts have demonstrated a strong tendency toward internal resistance to change in the sentencing process, methodological limitations of most impact studies make their interpretations ambiguous. Weaknesses of these impact studies are inherent in the research designs they employ. This study recognizes these inherent research problems. An attempt will be made to strengthen the research methodology of this study. For those who are interested in the methodological details (that distinguish the multiple interrupted time-series quasi-experiment design from the pooled time-series quasi-experiment design) and statistical procedures (including both interrupted time-series analysis and pooled time-series analysis) employed in this study, please refer to appendixes A and B. In chapter 6, the respective evaluation models specified in appendix A will be applied to evaluate the impacts of sentencing reform policies on courts, prisons, and crime in the United States.

Before reporting our research findings, chapter 5 calls attention to what we call the counterintuitive nature of court community systems. The system dynamics of the court community drive people who work at courthouses, especially those key actors who belong to the courtroom work groups, to behave in ways that run against the whole thrust of the policy maker's intentions and also much of what the general public believe they should do to reduce crime, and in ways that eventually produce contrary and unforeseen results.

CHAPTER 5

The Court Community's Response to Sentencing Reforms

Criminal courts perform critical roles in the criminal justice system. From the crime control perspective, the proper role of the courts is to suppress crime and, thus, protect the rights of law-abiding citizens (Packer 1968). In the fight against crime, courts decide whether the defendant brought before them is guilty or innocent and, if the defendant is found guilty, they impose appropriate penalties.

The role of the courts in the fight against crime has long been at the center of the public's attention. In 1970 the National Commission on the Causes and Prevention of Violence recommended that, in fighting against crime, "we should give concrete expression to our concern about crime by a solemn national commitment to double our investment in the administration of justice and the prevention of crime, as rapidly as such an investment can be wisely planned and utilized" (1970, 233). The National Conference on the Judiciary, held in Williamsburg in March 1971, reached the unanimous conclusion that "the courts are appropriately the subject of close scrutiny in the fight against crime." In 1973 the National Advisory Commission on Criminal Justice Standards and Goals recommended speed and efficiency in determining a defendant's guilt or innocence as a top priority. Faster and more efficient criminal processing, the commission believed, would not only increase the deterrent impact of the law but also ease the task of rehabilitating offenders, and thus reduce crime (1973c, 7).

Under due process of law provisions, courts apply and interpret the law in specific cases through an adversary system, which is viewed as the best way to determine guilt while protecting the rights of the accused. That is, the role of the courts in the fight against crime must be accomplished within the framework of law

(Neubauer 1979, 9–14). The criminal courts are charged not only with convicting the guilty but also with protecting the innocent, and they must maintain a proper balance between effectiveness and fairness (President's Commission on Law Enforcement and Administration of Justice 1967b, 1). Ideally, the court should perform the following functions: (1) swiftly determine the guilt or innocence of those persons who come before it; (2) sentence guilty offenders in such a way that their rehabilitation is possible, and that others are deterred from committing crimes; and (3) protect the rights of society and the offender (National Advisory Commission on Criminal Justice Standards and Goals 1973a, 93).

The courts apply the criminal law through a complicated process known as criminal procedure. Criminal procedure varies from state to state. In this chapter, the flow of criminal cases will be employed to describe the sequence of events that happens to accused persons as they move through the criminal justice system. Decisions are made at various stages in case processing and these decisions determine how criminal cases are disposed. These are the everyday realities of courthouse dynamics and the way in which courthouse regulars respond to sentencing reforms.

THE FLOW OF CRIMINAL CASES

The criminal justice system operates as the "case processing machinery" that produces an orderly flow of managerial decisions in handling criminal cases (Gibbons 1968, 75). Despite the fact that criminal cases may be handled differently in individual jurisdictions, there are some similarities. The sequence of events that happens to arrested offenders as they move through the criminal justice system can be generalized. The President's Commission on Law Enforcement and Administration of Justice (1967a, 8–9) offers a simplified view of caseflow through the criminal justice system that finds wide acceptance. The criminal case begins with the arrest of a suspect (an entry into the system) and ends on the completion of correctional treatment (an exit out of the system). At any phase of the criminal justice process, a number of the accused or suspects are released, dismissed, acquitted, discharged, or otherwise returned to the general population. The remaining offenders are prosecuted, tried, convicted, and incarcerated or placed on probation.

Criminal cases are handled through a complicated process that consists of numerous and sometimes redundant procedures. The purpose is to ensure that individual rights are protected (Neubauer 1979, 31). What is the sequence of events in the criminal process? The flow of the criminal case can be broken down into five major phases of case processing: entry into the system, prosecution and pretrial services, adjudication, sentencing and sanctions, and corrections (U.S. Dept. of Justice Bureau of Justice Statistics 1988, 56–60).

Much crime has gone unreported. Only a small fraction of offenses known to police have been cleared by arrest. Suspects are sometimes apprehended at the scene; others are identified and apprehended after an extensive investigation. An arrest made by police is "simply the action of taking a person into custody for the purpose of charging with a crime." Most arrests are made in the field without an arrest warrant. A police officer can make an arrest without a warrant only when it is reasonably certain that "the person being arrested is indeed the offender" (Inciardi 1987, 143).

A suspect accused of a crime must be brought before a judge or magistrate without unnecessary delay. At the initial appearance, the defendant is given formal notice of the charges and also notified of his or her fundamental rights. Bail is usually set as a guarantee that the defendant will later appear for trial. At the preliminary hearing, the presiding magistrate seeks to determine whether there is probable cause to believe that the defendant committed a crime. The defendant may be released and the charges dismissed for lack of probable cause (National Advisory Commission on Criminal Justice Standards and Goals 1973c, 12; Neubauer 1979, 35; Inciardi 1987, 145).

The formal determination of charges is available through an indictment or information. Where a grand jury is not applicable, the prosecutor files a charging document called the information and presents the case in open court, usually at the preliminary hearing. If the hearing is waived, the information document is not tested before a magistrate. Where a grand jury is required, a formal charging document based on a grand jury's determination that probable cause exists is called the indictment. At this phase of case processing, the defense may examine whether the indictment or information of formal charges issued is valid or certain evidence is admissible. Any procedural error will lead to release of the defendant. This step provides another check on unwarranted prosecution (Inciardi 1987, 145).

The actual trial process begins with the arraignment, at which the defendant is asked to enter a plea. The defendant can plead not guilty, guilty, or nolo contendere (no contest but do not admit), or stand mute. Usually the guilty plea is entered; in some jurisdictions the defendant can elect to have a bench trial or a jury trial. Before the case is actually tried to determine the guilt or innocence of the defendant, either the prosecution or the defense may file pretrial motions—formal, written requests for the judge to make a legal ruling. Most motions are filed by the defense, for instance, to suppress evidence obtained from illegal search or to suppress a confession by contending that the confession was coerced.

The trial process involves the adversary determination of guilt or innocence, a system under which the prosecutor has the burden to prove the defendant guilty beyond a reasonable doubt. The formal trial proceedings usually begin with opening statements by prosecution and the defense introducing witnesses and evidence to be used later in the case. Presenting the state's case, the prosecutor calls and examines the witnesses and evidence, followed by their cross-examination by the defense. The defense argues for dismissal on the grounds that the prosecution failed to establish guilt beyond a reasonable doubt. Closing arguments by the defense, followed by those of the prosecutor, are made after all of the evidence and testimony is in. The jury then retires to consider the facts of the case and deliberate a verdict. Next, they return to the courtroom with a verdict to be announced by the court: guilty or not guilty.

If a guilty verdict is returned, it proceeds with a conviction. If the prosecution failed to establish guilt beyond a reasonable doubt, a verdict of not guilty is returned, leading to acquittal of the defendant. However, the case of a bench trial disregards those steps involving the jury, leaving to the judge the determination of innocence or guilt. The complete formal trial process represents the premise of the adversary system: a battle between the two parties, the prosecution and the defense, viewed as the best way to determine guilt while protecting the fundamental rights of the accused (Inciardi 1987, 146–47).

Most criminal prosecutions do not involve this adversarial determination of guilt or innocence through trial. Only a small proportion of defendants actually go to trial; most of them plead guilty. A guilty plea must be entered voluntarily and with an understanding of its full consequences. "Most findings of guilts," as Neubauer explains, "result not from a trial verdict but by a voluntary plea by the defendant" (1979, 37).

Sentencing follows the trial process that results in conviction or the entry of a guilty plea. Convicted offenders may receive a sentence for a certain period of time or be placed on probation. The judge usually has discretion to determine the type of sentence to be imposed. Sentences can also take the form of fines, community based corrections, imprisonment, and even death. An appeal to a higher court by the defendant may take place after conviction. A defendant may appeal on the basis of claims that due process was violated, that new evidence has emerged, or that cruel and unusual penalty was imposed, in violation of constitutional rights (Inciardi 1987, 148).

The offender who has served the time specified in the sentence will be released. Parole is a conditional release after some portion of the sentence has been served. Release from prison through pardon, a forgiveness for the crime committed, is another type of release. A reprieve delays the execution of a sentence; commutation reduces the severity of a sentence (Inciardi 1987, 148).

In sum, the flow of criminal cases resembles "a streamlined process with defendants entering at the arrest stage and steadily moving through the various stages until conviction and eventual sentencing." Not all cases handled are automatically advanced to the next step. There are numerous detours during early stages. The steps of the criminal process, acting as a series of screens, sort defendants into various categories. As a result, many cases are sometimes rerouted or terminated (Neubauer 1979, 32–33). However, the probability that an arrested person will be routed along alternative paths varies with the type of crime, characteristics of the accused (such as age and prior criminal record), and characteristics of the processing stage (President's Commission on Law Enforcement and Administration of Justice 1967c, 57). These multiple checkpoints of the criminal process can cause inefficiency and complexity. The flow of the criminal case can be viewed as discretionary, assembly line, and more administrative than judicial (President's Commission on Law Enforcement and Administration of Justice 1967a, 130; Neubauer 1979, 29–31).

THE DYNAMICS OF THE COURT COMMUNITY SYSTEMS

Mastering the basic legal concepts underlying the criminal court process is necessary, but by no means adequate, to understanding how American courts actually dispense justice. While it is the right of the accused to be presumed innocent until proven guilty of alleged crimes beyond a reasonable doubt, most defendants not screened out by rejection or dismissal are most likely to plead guilty. Although the premise of the adversary system suggests that the best way to apply the law is through a formalized conflict— the fact finding process with the accused's right to cross-examination—only a few cases go to trial. Today court operations are less likely to be hard-fought contests aimed at determining guilt, but rather directed more toward setting the appropriate penalty. These important features highlight how legal theory (law on the books) is actually applied on a daily basis (law in action). Moreover it is essential to understand why the law as practiced deviates from the seeming intent of the formal rules. The day-to-day realities of the courthouse that describe such deviations need further consideration (Neubauer 1979, 29).

The court is the pivot on which the wheel of criminal justice turns. Any formal action concerned with defendants must be funneled through the courts. Although the three major components of the criminal justice system are theoretically independent of each other, they are bound together in a variety of ways. Not only is it necessary that these three components work together daily, but the decisions one agency makes become raw materials for another agency. Thus, the criminal justice system can be viewed as an integrated whole (President's Commission on Law Enforcement and Administration of Justice 1967b). It is a system of interrelationships often marked by conflict and even hostility. Such tension stems from each of the three components viewing the common task of case processing from different perspectives (National Advisory Commission on Criminal Justice Standards and Goals 1973c, 5).

For others, the overall process has become "so fragmented, splintered, divided, and decentralized that there is no overall coordination in the American justice process." Tensions and conflicts among police, courts, and corrections that arise from their competing goals can provide effective checks on each other and are, therefore, desirable. All these checks and balances make the three components a "living system" of criminal justice, "where the work of each component is evaluated by others: the police make arrests, yet the decision to charge is made by the prosecutor; the judge and jury rate the prosecutor's ability" (Neubauer 1979, 5).

Because the application of law is a dynamic process of applying abstract rules to concrete situations, at various stages of processing criminal cases, prosecutors, defense attorneys, and judges exercise discretion where the formal rules do not provide precise guidelines. These actors believe it is the best way to make the system fair. This line of argument concludes that discretion lies at the heart of the criminal justice process.

Empirical evidence suggests that exogenous factors, such as caseload, may have little impact on case dispositions. A study of two Connecticut courts, one with a heavy caseload and the other with a light one, found no substantial differences in how cases were processed and disposed. Both courts relied heavily on guilty pleas and imposed roughly similar penalties. The same amount of time was spent per case (Feeley 1979). These results suggest that "trying to understand the criminal courts on the basis of excessive caseloads omits too much of importance" (Neubauer 1979, 105).

The concept of courts as communities explains how courts handle cases the way they do. Judges, prosecutors, defense attorneys, and clerks who are courthouse regulars depend on each other for getting their respective jobs done at courthouses. Working together on a daily basis, they learn how to cooperate and maintain good relationships. What happens at courthouses, particularly within the courtroom work groups, determines the outcomes of cases (Eisenstein et al. 1988).

The Courtroom Work Group

It is essential to understand the dynamics of courthouse justice by employing the "courtroom work group" concept proposed by James Eisenstein and Herbert Jacob (1977). This concept stresses the complex network of ongoing relationships among judges, prosecutors, and defense attorneys, who work together daily on cases as work groups. Some level of cooperation exists among these principal actors who, at times, engage in casual conversations. They are also likely to compromise and maintain good relationships within work groups in settling their cases.

The courtroom work group functions like a case processor. The same group of courthouse regulars assembles in the same courtroom performing the same tasks. None of these work group members can get their work done alone. Neither can they decide about cases independently. For instance, the defense attorney must consider what type of plea agreement the prosecutor will offer, what kind of sentence the judge is likely to impose, the possibility that a jury will return a guilty verdict, and whether the probation officer will recommend probation. In addition, members of the work group cooperate to produce mutual benefits in disposing of cases. Their shared goals of handling cases expeditiously, reducing uncertainty in the outcomes of cases, maintaining group cohesion, and doing justice influence how a particular case is handled and resolved (Eisenstein and Jacob 1977).

Within courtroom work groups, decisions are usually made on a joint basis. Judges who set bail, adjudicate guilt, and impose sentences often rely on others for information. For instance, they may routinely follow the prosecutor's bail recommendations, accept plea agreements previously reached between the prosecutor and the defense attorney, or grant probation according to the pre-sentence report prepared by the probation officer. However, these recommendations are mainly based on judges' previous decisions.

The courthouse regulars possess a set of shared norms. They seek to reduce uncertainty caused by external factors. A second set of shared norms concerns standards of personal and professional conduct. Sanctions will be imposed if such rules are violated. Policy standards or going rates emerge from a group sense of justice as a solution to the problems the work groups encounter. Cases are categorized according to type of crime and type of offender before being disposed of on the basis of a set pattern.

The socialization process at courthouses teaches newcomers not only the formal requirements of the job but the informal rules of behavior. Both sanctions (sticks) and rewards (carrots) are employed to reinforce the work group norms. For example, cooperative defense attorneys are likely to receive more case information from prosecutors. In return, they are also expected not to file unnecessary motions. By contrast, prosecutors are less likely to offer good deals to uncooperative defense attorneys.

Among members of the courtroom work group, the prosecutor is the most influential actor, possessing more information about the case than anyone else. Police reports, records of previous arrests and convictions, physical evidence, and laboratory tests are the prosecutor's major source of case information. Others involved in a case must react to the decisions made by the prosecutor. A prosecutor's actions are, in turn, shaped by other members of the courtroom work group (Neubauer 1979, 138–39).

Judges are the most prestigious members of the courtroom work group. Some are active leaders of the courtroom work group, while others are not. Variation exists among judges in how they run their courtroom and how they think cases should be handled. Judges depend heavily on other members of the work group and often share their legal powers with prosecutors and probation officers by following their recommendations (Neubauer 1979, 158–59).

Defense attorneys are the least powerful members of courtroom work groups. Defense attorneys tend to maintain good relationships with judges, prosecutors, and clerks in exchange for cooperation. While cooperative defense attorneys are rewarded, those who violate the work group's norms will be sanctioned. Inexperienced attorneys are sometimes too unpredictable and can cause administrative problems. Some attorneys are "gamblers" who take an aggressive, fighting, and hostile posture. However, those presenting the majority of defendants work within the system; they tend to cooperate, discern a good deal offer, and are willing to encourage their clients to accept such an offer (Neubauer 1979, 183–84).

Whether the defendant's best interests are eroded by the defense attorneys' ties to the court community remains a debatable topic. It is often taken for granted that the defendants are guilty and they are treated as such. Frequently, it is the defense attorney who first suggests that defendants plead guilty. Thus, the defendants' best interests to be presumed innocent until proven guilty beyond a reasonable doubt are not represented. Working within the system will prevent the client from being penalized by the court community's sanctions, such as those of the prosecutor by not reducing charges or recommending a higher than normal prison sentence, for the hostility of the defense attorney. Cooperation with the court community can make the defense attorney a better counselor to the defendant. From this viewpoint, the defendant's best interests are not eroded by the defense attorney's ties to the court community (Neubauer 1979, 185).

Plea Bargaining

A steady flow of guilty pleas is the result of the courtroom work group's cooperative effort to administer justice. But if most defendants go to trial, the whole system would collapse or otherwise would undoubtedly lower the quality of justice. Yet would providing every defendant with a full trial make a just system (President's Commission on Law Enforcement and Administration of Justice 1967b, 10)? There is no way every defendant could have a trial unless there were enough judges, prosecutors, defense attorneys or public defenders, clerks, and courtrooms. "We've got to have plea bargaining—it's a matter of necessity," said Judge Williams. Plea bargaining was once called "a necessary evil that society would be hard put to do without." Former Supreme Court Chief Justice Warren Burger has called plea bargaining "an essential component of the administration of justice. Properly administered, it is to be encouraged" (Neubauer 1979, 103).

Plea bargaining can be defined as "a process through which a defendant pleads to a criminal charge with the expectation of receiving some consideration from the state" (Neubauer 1979, 308). Typically plea negotiations take one of three forms. Through charge bargaining a prosecutor offers a reduction of charges in return for a plea of guilty. For instance, a defendant may be allowed to plead guilty to robbery rather than the original charge of armed robbery. This type of plea bargaining is frequently found in jurisdictions where the state's criminal code carries severe penalties. Sometimes prosecutors routinely overcharge to begin with. In count bargaining, the defendant agrees to plead guilty to one or more criminal charges in return for dismissal of all other pending charges. For instance, a prosecutor accepts a defendant's pleading guilty to only one burglary charge and agrees to dismiss the other remaining accusations. A plea of guilty entered in exchange for a promise of leniency in sentencing is called sentence bargaining. In sentence bargaining, there may be a promise that the defendant will be placed on probation or that the prison term will be no more than going rates (Neubauer 1979, 309–10).

The bargaining process by which a plea agreement is reached varies from courtroom to courtroom within a particular courthouse. Agreement from an active participating judge is typically that if the defendant enters a plea of guilty, a specific sentence will be imposed. Where judges refuse to participate in bargaining at all, prosecutors dominate the bargaining process. A slow plea is sometimes employed by the defendant, who at trial "does not contest the issue of guilt but rather presents favorable evidence in hopes that the judge will impose a light sentence" (Neubauer 1979, 311).

As a case reaches trial stage, the courtroom work group presumes that the defendant is probably guilty or would otherwise have been dismissed earlier in the process. Given this presumption of guilt, the courtroom work group discusses and analyzes how the crime was committed, the nature of the victims and witnesses, and the background of the defendants. Costs and risks of trial are something all participants seek to avoid through bargaining. Not only is establishing the defendant's guilt through trial costly and time-consuming, but winning a case at trial is also unpredictable. There is no way that all trials can be avoided, "But through plea bargaining the scarce resources of trial can be applied to the types of cases that should be tried" (Neubauer 1979, 313).

In determining what to do with the guilty, the courtroom work group adjusts the penalties to the specifics of the crime and the defendant. The state's criminal code and penalty structure have a close relationship with plea bargaining practices. Members of the courtroom work group participate in plea negotiation because they perceive the penalties to be inappropriately harsh. In Michigan, a defendant charged with nighttime burglary might plead to daytime burglary. In Kansas, a prosecutor may allow a defendant to plead guilty to a lesser offense of third-degree burglary in a case initially charged first-degree burglary. A widespread use of charge reduction in both states resulted from new sentencing provisions that were deemed too inflexible (Neubauer 1979, 314–15).

Plea negotiation involves a contest in which each side endeavors to secure the best arrangement possible. Where there is sufficient evidence for conviction, the prosecutor proceeds with plea bargains to reward cooperative defendants. While the defendant benefits from the possibility of a lenient sentence, the prosecutor can obtain a conviction from the defendant's pleading guilty. Where the case is weak, the prosecutor tends to increase the certainty of conviction by offering such a good deal the defendant cannot refuse it. Judges tend to accept a plea agreement. If judges are reluctant to participate directly in plea negotiation, the prosecutors and the defense attorneys are more likely to engage in charge or count bargaining in order to mitigate penalties the judge might impose. Some judges are active participants, letting the defense attorney know what penalty will be imposed. When judges are playing an active role, prosecutors are more likely to initiate sentence bargaining (Eisenstein and Jacob 1977).

A plea of guilty involves "a defendant's waiver of the most vital rights of the court process: presumption of innocence, jury trial, and confrontation of witnesses" (Neubauer 1979, 324). Thus, a guilty plea is acceptable only when entered intelligently and voluntarily. A judge may reject a guilty plea unless the defendant fully admits guilt. Some courts require that a plea agreement be placed on the record.

The Sentencing Process

Understanding the sentencing process from the standpoint of formal rules of law is by no means adequate. It is essential to know how the informal rules and practices of the courtroom work groups operate to shape outcomes of the sentencing process. Sentencing is not merely the judge's legal authority to pass a sentence, but rather "involves a collective decision-making process" within which the courtroom regulars play an influential role (Neubauer 1979, 392). In the vast majority of jurisdictions, a pre-sentence investigation is conducted prior to passing a sentence. The pre-sentence reports, usually prepared by the court's probation agency or pre-sentence office, summarize the defendant's present offense, previous criminal record, sociological background, employment history, and psychological evaluation. In jurisdictions where sentence bargaining predominates, judges tend to follow the prosecutor's sentence recommendations. Thus sentencing can be best described as "a collective decision-making process that involves recommendations of the prosecutor, the defense attorney, the judge, and sometimes the pre-sentence investigator" (Inciardi 1987, 457).

Sentencing is not an easy task; it is indeed the most difficult part of the job for most judges. Although judges are empowered to pass sentence within the statutory framework that establishes the range of sentencing alternatives, determination of an appropriate sentence "requires weighing the possibility of rehabilitation, the need for protecting the public, popular demands for retribution, and any potential deterrent value in the sentence" (Neubauer 1979, 396). The President's Commission on Law Enforcement and Administration of Justice (1967b, 18) recognized the necessity of systematic procedures that provide relevant information about the offense and the offender to the sentencing judge. Several procedures that meet the information needs for sentencing include the pre-sentence investigation and report, the sentencing hearing, and the diagnostic commitment.

Certain forms of pre-sentence reports are prepared in most felony convictions to aid the court in arriving at a fair and just sentence. It is the defense counsel's primary duty to verify and challenge both the completeness and the accuracy of such information contained in the report. A sentence based on incomplete and inaccurate information may be either too lenient for the protection of society or unduly harsh for the offender to be reintegrated into the community. Another way to improve the accuracy of pre-sentence reports is to conduct the sentencing hearing. Diagnostic commitments may be requested for a psychiatric evaluation of the defendant, a valuable aid to the sentencing judge (President's Commission on Law Enforcement and Administration of Justice 1967b, 18–21).

The National Advisory Commission on Criminal Justice Standards and Goals (1973d, 184) has recommended that "a pre-sentence report should be presented to the court in every case where there is a potential sentencing disposition involving incarceration and in all cases involving felonies or minors." The pre-sentence report should be made available to both defense counsel and the prosecution within a reasonable time prior to the date set for the sentencing hearing. All sentencing decisions should rely on an official record of such sentencing hearing. The reasons for selecting the particular sentence imposed should be provided and made available to the defendant or defense counsel for purposes of appeal (National Advisory Commission on Criminal Justice Standards and Goals 1973d, 195).

Sentencing is a human process. A study on judicial attitudes and practices in sentencing revealed that wide variation exists among judges in their commitment to various goals when imposing sentences (Hogarth 1971). Some reject stiff prison sentences as the answer to the crime problem, while others see little deterrent effect of the law. In a typical felony case, the judge must choose between probation or imprisonment on the basis of available information presented to the court. A study of sentencing decisions in California found that judges were more likely to follow the pre-sentence report prepared by probation officers when probation was recommended than when incarceration was recommended (Carter and Wilkins 1967, 507). Probation officers work closely with judges and in some cases the probation department is part of the judiciary.

There are several important ways prosecutors can influence sentencing decisions. By agreeing to either count or charge reduction bargains, prosecutors can anticipate the maximum penalties a judge may impose. In sentence bargains, they may make a specific sentence recommendation based on the penalty that has already been agreed on. The judge almost invariably imposes the sentence as recommended. During the pre-sentence investigation some prosecutors let the probation officer know about the sentence agreement the defense attorney has already accepted. Other prosecutors can also bring to the court's attention during the sentencing hearing factors that would increase the penalty (aggravating circumstances) or factors that would lessen the penalty (mitigating circumstances).

In seeking to obtain the best sentence possible, the defense attorney must advise the client to choose between going to trial or pleading guilty. The defense attorney must also try to convince other members of the courtroom work group during plea negotiation and pre-sentence investigation why the defendant deserves a lenient sentence. Judges must exercise their formal legal authority to impose sentences by working within the limits established by the consensus of the courtroom work groups (Neubauer 1979, 392–96). When they deviate "too far from expectations by imposing a sentence either substantially more lenient or more severe than the one agreed on by defendant, defense lawyer and prosecutor, it becomes more difficult for the prosecutor and defense counsel to negotiate future agreements" (Rosett and Cressey 1976, 81).

There are at least four important factors that courtroom work groups employ to consider appropriate sentences: the seriousness of the offense, prior criminal record, aggravating or mitigating circumstances, and social stability. These factors are used to develop a classification of "normal crimes" as a mechanism that facilitates plea negotiation. Based on the shared concept of normal crimes and normal penalties, both the prosecutor and the defense attorney employ plea bargains wherever possible as the way to avoid a trial (Sudnow 1965, 255–76; Gibbons 1968, 83). Upward and downward adjustments are made around these normal penalties. The initial step after conviction is to decide whether to incarcerate the defendant or grant probation. The second step is to determine how long the sentence should be (Neubauer 1979, 396).

Courtroom work groups vary in their view of the seriousness of the offense and the severity of the penalties to be applied. The more serious the offense, the less likely the decision to grant probation and the longer the prison sentence to be imposed. In setting normal penalties on the basis of the seriousness of offense, the courtroom regulars agree to the "The punishment should fit the crime" principle. The second factor, the defendant's prior record, is also taken into consideration in order to "let the punishment fit the criminal." Moreover, another factor considered is how the crime was committed. Aggravating circumstances such as the use of firearms and personal injury to the victim lead to higher penalty. By contrast, mitigating factors, such as the defendant's lack of mental capacity, lower penalty. In granting probation, judges tend to consider the defendant's social stability (marital status, family relationship, length of employment, and alcohol and drug abuse record). In addition to these four basic factors in sentencing, the method of disposition (plea or trial) and public opinion toward the court's role in reducing crime are also considered by courtroom work groups in arriving at a fair and appropriate sentence (Neubauer 1979, 392–400).

THE DISPOSITION OF FELONY CASES

What is the outcome of the process described above? In 1987 it was officially estimated that 2,266,467 adults were arrested for the eight index offenses but only 241,887 offenders were committed to state and federal institutions (Jamieson and Flanagan 1989, 482, 614). Based on these data, a rough estimate of those arrested for felonies being incarcerated is 10.7 percent. By this simple computation, the rate of incarceration can be measured at the state level in a particular year and the result is fairly accurate. Between 1979 and 1986 the rate of incarceration based on the simple computation ranges from 10 percent to 11 percent. Using the Prosecutor's Management Information System (PROMIS) database from the participating jurisdictions, Boland et al. (1988, 1989) found that only about 12 percent to 13 percent of all those arrested for felonies brought by the police for prosecution were sentenced to incarceration for more than one year. Clearly, the overall effect is that most persons arrested go free or receive minimal punishment, even in felony cases.

Case Attrition

Case attrition occurs at the early stages of the criminal court process by rejection and dismissal. Rejection at initial screening and the decision to charge by the prosecutor rely mainly on a review of the facts of the crime or evidence, witnesses, victim(s), and information about the defendant such as criminal history and alcohol or drug use. Based on available evidence mainly obtained by the police, the prosecutor then decides whether to charge the accused with the felony charge brought by the police, to charge the accused with a lesser offense, or to reject the entire case.

In a general sense, screening refers to "the discretionary decision to stop, prior to trial or plea, all formal proceedings against a person who has become involved in the criminal justice system" (National Advisory Commission on Criminal Justice Standards and Goals 1973a, 17). Cases may be rejected at initial screening on the basis of insufficient evidence to convict a suspect or suspects. If there is insufficient evidence to prove the elements of the offense, cases should be dropped or reduced to a lesser charge. However, a prosecutable case does not necessarily satisfy probable cause to meet the standards of proof beyond a reasonable doubt necessary to convict the defendant (Neubauer 1979, 230–34).

Legal scholars have drawn attention to the prosecutorial control of the charging decision. The prosecutor who is allowed to exercise discretion whether to charge or not to charge becomes the gatekeeper who regulates the flow of cases to the courts (Neubauer 1979, 227). Abuse of such discretionary power can cause irreparable damage to an innocent person when charges are brought against him or her unduly and later dismissed. In Justice Jackson's famous statement, "the prosecutor has more control over life, liberty, and reputation than any other person in America" (Boland et al. 1983, 5). On the contrary, the decision not to charge, as Davis points out, is almost always final and immune from review (1969, 188–98).

The decision to nolle or dismiss a case after filing can also lead to case attrition. A "nolle prosequi" is an action on the sole authority of the prosecutor to drop a case. At the post-filing stages, the prosecutor's reluctance to nolle weak cases filed can also lead to a dismissal. A proportion of 1979 filed cases that were nolled or dismissed varied across jurisdictions, ranging from 14 percent in Kalamazoo County, Michigan, Louisville, Kentucky (Jefferson County), and New Orleans, Louisiana (Orleans Parish), to 45 percent in Cobb County, Georgia, and Golden, Colorado (First Judicial District). Considering all fourteen jurisdictions, it was estimated that about 28 percent of cases filed were nolled and dismissed. The average proportion of cases dismissed after a grand jury or preliminary hearing in seven jurisdictions including Los Angeles County, California, Kalamazoo County, Michigan, Louisville, Kentucky (Jefferson County), Manhattan, New York, Rhode Island (entire state), Cobb County, Georgia, and St. Louis, Missouri, was 15 percent. Two basic reasons for case attrition are witness problems and evidence-related deficiencies (Boland et al. 1983, 7–9).

Guilty Plea and Trial

Most cases not rejected or dismissed are commonly disposed of by a guilty plea. According to the Task Force Report on Science and Technology's 1965 estimate, there were about 168,000 felony cases carried forward. A total of 160,000 felony defendants were convicted. While 130,000 defendants pleaded guilty, only 38,000 went to trial and 8,000 were acquitted (President's Commission on Law Enforcement and Administration of Justice 1967c, 60–61). Based on these figures, guilty pleas accounted for 77.4 percent of cases carried forward to the courts or as high as 81.25 percent of total convictions obtained.

Boland et al. (1983, 12) found consistent results in their study of the fourteen jurisdictions participating in the PROMIS project. This study revealed that in 1979 all these jurisdictions experienced no less than 80 percent of total convictions resulting from a guilty plea. Nine out of fourteen jurisdictions studied, namely, Salt Lake County, Utah, Los Angeles County, California, Kalamazoo County, Michigan, Geneva, Illinois (Kane County), Golden, Colorado (First Judicial District), St. Louis, Missouri, Manhattan, New York, Cobb County, Georgia, and Rhode Island (entire state) have shown more than 90 percent of total convictions through a guilty plea. On the average, guilty pleas accounted for 92 percent of all convictions in these fourteen jurisdictions.

It becomes obvious that the criminal court process relies most heavily on a guilty plea in obtaining felony conviction. In 1982, based on the data from thirty-seven jurisdictions, guilty pleas accounted for 94 percent of total convictions (Boland et al. 1988, 2). Later, in 1986, felony cases disposed of through a guilty plea rose to 96 percent of total convictions (Boland et al. 1989, 2). These findings confirm the conventional view that the vast majority of convictions result from a guilty plea rather than a guilty verdict.

Not all guilty pleas are negotiated. The negotiated plea, as defined by the President's Commission on Law Enforcement and Administration of Justice, involves "discussions looking toward an agreement under which the accused will enter a plea of guilty in exchange for a reduced charge or a favorable sentence recommendation by the prosecutor" (1967b, 9). In a study of guilty dispositions in New Haven, Connecticut, the evidence showed that most guilty pleas were not in fact bargains. Plea discussions did not focus solely on concessions in return for a guilty plea but actually on the facts and circumstances surrounding the crime (Feeley 1979).

The percentage of guilty pleas that result from negotiations varies across jurisdictions. The University of Pennsylvania Law Review study of plea bargaining in 1964 found that more than half of the prosecutors' offices reported more than 70 percent of the defendants pleaded guilty, and at least 30 percent to 40 percent of these guilty pleas resulted from negotiations. It was also found that in about 11 percent of the offices, more than 70 percent of all guilty pleas were negotiated (President's Commission on Law Enforcement and Administration of Justice 1967b, 9).

Cases go to trial when the risks of trial are low, that is, when there is a chance of acquittal. But if a prison sentence is likely to be imposed, a slim chance of an acquittal may be worth taking the risks of the trial penalty. In Los Angeles, as Neubauer (1979, 322–23) points out, serious crimes such as murder, rape, and robbery were more likely to go to trial than property offenses. In those serious cases, a defendant, if convicted, is likely to receive a sentence that is already severe. Thus, going to trial still has a chance of a not guilty verdict. As of 1979 similar patterns of the defendant's going to trial were found associated with crime type in seven jurisdictions: Indianapolis, Indiana (Marion County), Los Angeles

County, California, Louisville, Kentucky (Jefferson County), Milwaukee County, Wisconsin, New Orleans, Louisiana (Orleans Parish), St. Louis, Missouri, and Washington, D.C. The proportion of violent crimes going to trial was substantially higher than that for property crimes. In all jurisdictions, homicide was the most likely crime to go to trial. A trial is not recommended if the evidence is strong unless the case is very serious. Boland et al. (1983, 17) explain this point: "In a very serious case, the defendant is likely to go to prison regardless of whether he pleads guilty or goes to trial and therefore has little to lose by going to trial and a small chance of a considerable gain—acquittal."

Incarceration and Probation

In setting the penalty, a sentencing judge determines whether the defendant convicted of criminal offenses will be granted probation and, if not, how many years in prison should be imposed. Choosing between prison and probation reflects our "ambivalent expectations over the causes of crime, the nature of criminals, and the role of the courts in reducing crime" (Neubauer 1979, 374). Sentencing has at least four competing and often contradictory goals: retribution, incapacitation, deterrence, and rehabilitation. None standing alone seems adequate. However, these sentencing philosophies have been the most widely held justification for imposition of prison sentences or probation.

Judges hold differing views on imprisonment. Judge Roy W. Seagraves of Redwood City, California, for example, opposes the use of stiff prison sentences as the answer to the crime problem. "If we jailed everyone we could, we would bankrupt the country to pay for their imprisonment," he said. "But the popular concept that punishment is a deterrent in crime is a fallacy. A criminal doesn't consider the punishment at all because he doesn't think he is going to get caught." Judge Harry J. Pearce of Bismarck Municipal Court believes sentencing should be viewed "as a punishment rather than as a rehabilitative measure," and also "as setting an example while protecting society" (Neubauer 1979, 384).

The sentencing process requires information about the defendant's situation necessary to determine an appropriate sentence. Prior to actual sentencing, a pre-sentence investigation may be conducted in order to prepare pre-sentence reports. Even though pre-sentence investigations are not compulsory, the National

Advisory Commission has recommended that they be conducted in all felony cases. Furthermore, in every case where incarceration for more than five years is a possible disposition, a full pre-sentence report should be prepared with a complete file on the offender regarding background, prospects of reform, and details of the crime for which he or she has been convicted (1973b, 184).

A sentencing hearing is held afterward and the presiding judge then imposes the sentence. If the defendant receives multiple sentences for various crimes committed, prison sentences may be imposed either concurrently or consecutively (Inciardi 1987, 468–69).

In his analysis of the sentencing process, Neubauer (1979, 392) called attention to the informal rules and practices of the courtroom work groups. As he explains, judges do not work alone in imposing sentences. They almost invariably impose the sentence already agreed upon by the prosecutor and the defense attorney. It is also likely that the prosecutor talks to the probation officer about the sentencing agreement already obtained.

The National Advisory Commission on Criminal Justice Standards and Goals (1973d, 150–56) admitted the fact that "there are some offenders whose aggressive, repetitive, violent or predatory behavior poses a serious threat to the community." They are considered unresponsive to correctional programs. Lengthy prison sentences should be imposed for the "dangerous" offender. There are at least three reasons that justify confinement of the dangerous offender. First, there is undue risk that the offender will commit another crime if not confined. Second, the offender is in need of correctional services that can be provided effectively only in an institutional setting, and such services are reasonably available. Third, any other alternative will depreciate the seriousness of the offense.

In examining the imposition of prison sentences in eight jurisdictions, Boland et al. (1983, 18–19; 1988, 2; 1989, 2) found that in 1979 more than 75 percent of defendants arrested for felonies and convicted of felonies or misdemeanors were incarcerated in jail or prison in Los Angeles County, California, and New Orleans, Louisiana (Orleans Parish). In Golden, Colorado (First Judicial District), Indianapolis, Indiana (Marion County), Louisville, Kentucky (Jefferson County), and St. Louis, Missouri, the rates of convictees sentenced to incarceration were no less than 60 percent. On the average, about three out of five defendants convicted of felonies were incarcerated in 1979. In 1982, based on the data from the thirty-seven prosecutors' offices studied, of those convicted 52 percent received incarceration sentences to be served in local jails or state prisons. In 1986 it was estimated that about 22 percent of convictions were sentenced to incarceration of more than one year, compared with one-third sentenced to incarceration of one year or less.

A sentence of probation is imposed with conditions that are necessary to benefit the offender and provide protection to the public. While this is "an act of leniency moderating the harshness of confinement," the court retains authority "to modify or enlarge the conditions of probation at any time prior to expiration or termination of sentence" (National Advisory Commission on Criminal Justice Standards and Goals 1973d, 158–59).

Viewed as an alternative to incarceration, probation possesses a set of advantages in that it reintegrates the offender into the community, avoids the isolating and labeling effects of imprisonment, and mitigates the financial burden on the state. In 1965 about 53 percent of the offenders sentenced to correctional treatment were placed on probation nationwide (President's Commission on Law Enforcement and Administration of Justice 1967c, 27–28). More recently it was estimated that more than 40 percent but less than half of felony cases convicted were sentenced to probation or other conditions during 1979 and 1986 (Boland et al. 1983, 1988, 1989).

Typical Outcomes of Felony Arrests

In the Prosecution of Felony Arrests series, Boland et al. attempted to describe statistically what happens to felony cases processed in prosecutors' offices across the country. The outcome of the criminal court process was analyzed from data on felony cases that reached a final disposition during a particular year. The studies focused on the following four critical decision points: (1) screening or intake of those cases eligible for prosecution; (2) post-filing dismissals either by prosecutor or court to terminate a case accepted for prosecution; (3) choosing between going to trial or pleading guilty; and (4) imposition of sentences to incarceration or probation.

In 1979 the overall case attrition was as high as 50 percent of total cases that were brought by police for prosecution. At the initial screening, about 20 percent of all cases were rejected on the basis of insufficient evidence or other reasons; another 30 percent were subsequently nolled or dismissed at the post-filing stages. While 45 percent of typical felony arrestees entered a guilty plea, only 5 percent went to trial. Four out of five defendants were found guilty at trial and one was acquitted. Of the forty-nine defendants convicted of a felony or misdemeanor, twenty-nine were sentenced to incarceration either in jail or prison (Boland et al. 1983, 2).

In 1982 and 1986 cases were less likely to be screened out. The proportion of case attrition both by rejection and dismissal dropped slightly from 50 percent in 1979 to 49 percent in 1982 and continued to drop to 45 percent in 1986. Taking dismissal alone, there was a substantial reduction in attrition by dismissal from 21 percent to 18 percent between 1982 and 1986. As more cases were carried forward, there was also a substantial increase in guilty pleas associated with lenient sentences imposed.

In recent years, prosecutors' offices have experienced a steady increase in the proportion of felony arrests resulting in guilty pleas from 45 percent in 1979 to 47 percent in 1982 and as high as 52 percent in 1986. Sentencing patterns were found associated with such steady increase in guilty pleas for the same period. The defendants who received sentences to probation or other conditions rose from 20 percent in 1979 to 24 percent in 1982. Those who were sentenced to incarceration for one year or less rose substantially from 13 percent in 1982 to 18 percent in 1986. At the same time, the number of persons sentenced to incarceration for more than one year dropped slightly from 13 percent to 12 percent. The association between guilty plea dispositions and lenient sentences imposed, as discussed above, implies the existence of guilty plea negotiations.

ADAPTIVE RESPONSES TO SENTENCING REFORMS

There are many reasons to believe that the effects of sentencing reforms are nullified or subverted. Despite popular dissatisfaction with the role of the courts in reducing crime, the court system has proven relatively resistant to change (National Advisory Commission on Criminal Justice Standards and Goals 1973c, 2). Based on the empirical findings of major impact evaluations, the Panel on Sentencing Research has concluded that compliance with procedural requirements of sentencing innovations has been found only in form rather than in substance (Blumstein et al. 1983, 28). Sentencing reforms, particularly mandatory sentencing laws, tend to elicit widespread efforts by courthouse regulars to avoid their application (Tonry 1987, 4).

There are good reasons to observe the court community's adaptive responses or accommodative reactions to sentencing reforms through changes in the rate of incarceration. Unlike previous studies that relied on the samples of cases that have already reached the felony courts, the solution to this sample selection problem is straightforward. The rate of felony arrests that are finally committed to state institutions—a fairly accurate measure used earlier in this chapter—allows us to follow cases from arrest through the system to the final disposition. Measuring the rate of incarceration in this manner yields the overall probability that persons charged with a felony will be imprisoned. This measure reflects the actual certainty that an incarcerative sentence is imposed for a given number of felony arrests. Any changes that occur in case attrition prior to conviction can be detected and accounted for.

As far as the implementation process is concerned, compliance with the intent of sentencing reforms by members of the court community can be observed in the shift in the rate of incarceration associated with the adoption of sentencing innovations. This study evaluates the court community's response to sentencing reforms as reflected by the certainty of imprisonment for felony arrestees. The interrupted time-series procedure is applied to data on each jurisdiction's incarceration rate measured annually from 1967 to 1984. The use of eighteen annual observations on the rate of incarceration is to rule out the plausibility of the maturation argument, a methodological problem that is present in the simple "before-after" research design employed in most of the impact evaluations reviewed in chapter 4. By use of this statistical procedure, any preexisting trend in the severity of sentencing will be taken into account prior to the estimation of the true effect on the rate of incarceration. The results obtained are further analyzed to derive any generalizable pattern of sentencing reform impacts. An attempt will be made to compare the way in which court communities respond to sentencing reforms from state to state. If there is an increase in the use of incarcerative sentences, this evaluation will conclude that widespread compliance among implementing officials has been achieved. By contrast, a substantial reduction in the rate of incarceration would suggest that court communities' accommodative reactions have occurred.

Mandatory Minimum Sentencing Laws

In general, mandatory minimum sentencing laws are too inflexible. Members of court communities take steps to avoid what they consider unduly harsh or unjust for the defendants. Prosecutors in Michigan, for example, avoided application of the mandated prison sentences simply by filing charges for offenses that are similar but not eligible to mandatory sentences. Such charge reduction makes the law inoperative, as does the use of waiver trial. In Detroit, Michigan, judges sidestepped the 1977 Felony Firearms Statute by use of sentence adjustments to offset the mandatory two-year term they would otherwise impose (Heumann and Loftin 1979; Cohen and Tonry 1983, 344).

Based on evidence from recent studies conducted in New York, Massachusetts, and Michigan, the operation of mandatory minimum sentencing laws has brought about changes in the case processing pattern: (1) courthouse regulars, especially defense attorneys and judges, will attempt to avoid application of the laws they consider inappropriate; (2) the implementation of mandatory minimum sentencing laws will elevate dismissal rates at early stages of the criminal process; (3) defendants who are carried forward tend to make all-out efforts to avoid conviction; (4) defendants who are convicted of the eligible offense tend to receive more severe penalties; (5) a decline in conviction rates is likely to be offset by an increase in imprisonment rates on conviction and thus the rates of incarceration among felony arrestees remain relatively stable in these jurisdictions (Tonry 1987, 26–27).

As of 1983 the majority of American states have adopted the mandatory minimum sentencing laws. Thirty-three out of thirty-six states (Georgia, Montana, and Vermont are excluded due to missing data) are included in this analysis. The interrupted time-series procedure is applied to their respective rates of incarceration from 1967 to 1984, except in Alaska, Arkansas, and Delaware, where data are available only from 1971 to 1984. The results based on application of this statistical procedure are reported in table 5.1. There is little evidence to demonstrate that court communities are committed to the intent of mandatory minimum sentencing laws. Only a few states have shown a statistically significant increase in their rates of incarceration, which indicates their substantive compliance with the new laws.

In the states of Alabama, Alaska, Arizona, Delaware, Missouri, and New York, the overall probability that felony arrestees are sentenced to incarceration in state institutions went up substantially after the mandatory minimum sentencing laws became effective. This implies that the court communities in these six jurisdictions respond favorably to sentencing innovations. In Alabama and Delaware, application of the mandatory minimum sentencing laws increased the likelihood that a person arrested for a felony offense would receive an incarcerative sentence. The effects of such new laws take the form of an abrupt permanent increase— termed a step function of policy impact—in the rates of incarceration in both jurisdictions.

Another pattern of reform effects is found in Alaska, Arizona, Missouri, and New York, where the rates of incarceration are found to rise gradually and persistently. A gradual permanent increase—termed a ramp function of policy impact—in the use of incarcerative sentences reflects substantive compliance by court communities in these four states in making imprisonment more predictable. In Alaska, where it was found recently that plea bargaining bans apparently achieved high levels of compliance (Tonry 1987, 19–20), court communities responded to the mandatory minimum sentencing statute with a relatively high level of compliance. In New York, application of the mandatory prison sentence for drug offenders, effective on September 1, 1973, resulted in a substantial drop in the rate of incarceration. Members of the court communities consider the mandatory incarcerative sentence prescribed for a drug felony too severe (Tonry 1987, 28). When prison terms become mandatory for other violent and firearm felonies, court communities tend to agree that severity of punishment should be increased. Court communities are convinced that, under certain circumstances, mandatory minimum sentencing laws can lead to an increase in the incarceration rate that reflects an increase in the certainty of imprisonment.

In the majority of mandatory minimum sentencing states, however, court communities' noncompliance or accommodative reactions result in no significant change in the rates of incarceration. That is, the levels of certainty in the use of incarcerative sentences remain unaltered and stable. Massachusetts' and Michi-

Table 5.1
Estimated Change in the Rate of Incarceration
(New Court Commitments per Ten Thousand Felony Arrests)
Associated with Mandatory Minimum Sentencing Laws, 1967–84

State	Effective Date	Change in the Incarceration Rate[b]	Intervention Pattern
Alabama	1980	870.4*	Step
Alaska[a]	1980	328.0*	Ramp
Arizona	1978	72.9*	Ramp
Arkansas[a]	1981	-44.8	Step
Delaware[a]	1982	269.1*	Step
Florida	1976	-137.2*	Step
Hawaii	1976	-132.8	Pulse
Idaho	1979	-142.1	Step
Iowa	1978	-390.1*	Step
Kansas	1976	-93.7	Step
Kentucky	1975	-370.8	Step
Louisiana	1978	-34.1	Step
Maryland[a]	1976	-354.0*	Step
Massachusetts	1974	-57.5	Step
Michigan	1977	-58.2	Step
Mississippi	1977	-1033.8*	Step
Missouri	1979	34.7*	Ramp
Nebraska	1977	-278.6*	Step
Nevada	1973	-11.9	Step
New Hampshire	1981	43.6	Step
New Jersey	1979	-49.7	Step
New York	1978	38.7*	Ramp
North Dakota	1975	-232.4*	Step
Ohio	1974	174.1	Step
Oklahoma	1976	-316.7*	Step
Oregon	1977	-157.1	Step

State	Effective Date	Change in the Incarceration Rate[b]	Intervention Pattern
South Carolina	1975	1211.9	Step
South Dakota	1978	-810.3*	Step
Tennessee	1982	180.6	Step
Texas	1977	52.1	Step
Virginia	1975	-158.8	Step
West Virginia	1981	115.7	Step
Wyoming	1979	20.2	Step

*The t statistic is significant at $p < .05$.
[a]1971–84.
[b]The time-serial correlation structure is reduced to a random "white noise" process.

gan's mandatory minimum sentencing laws are good case studies that explain how court communities operate to nullify application of mandatory sentences. Thus, the probability that a person arrested in a felony case will go to prison did not change substantially. The same pattern of noncompliance observed in nineteen jurisdictions can be explained by the nullification of mandatory sentences court communities consider inappropriate and, thus, circumvent them. Therefore, it seems more accurate to conclude that, under most circumstances, imprisonment did not become more certain under mandatory minimum sentencing laws.

There are at least two reasons that seem plausible in explaining the lack of the effects mandatory minimum sentencing laws were initially intended to produce. First, a reduction in the conviction rate following the enactment of the laws, as shown in prior studies in Massachusetts and Michigan (Beha 1977; Carlson 1982; Cohen and Tonry 1983; Heumann and Loftin 1979; Loftin and McDowall 1981; Tonry 1987), can reduce the number of convictees eligible for mandatory minimum sentences. Changes in case screening at the prosecutor's office and the rates of dismissals at preliminary hearings or at trials and acquittals at trials influence the rate of convictions.

Second, the effects of the laws on the plea process influence disposition outcomes. In the plea process, either charges, sentences, or evidentiary facts on cases are negotiated, generally by prosecutors and defense counsel, with or without participation by judges. Under certain circumstances, prosecutors' concessions can lead to conviction on reduced or substituted charges. When charges under mandatory minimum sentence provisions are reduced or substituted in exchange for guilty pleas, convicted offenders may no longer be eligible for mandatory minimum sentences.

Inconsistent with the intent of the new mandatory sentencing laws to increase the certainty of minimum prison sentences, the rates of incarceration have been in substantial decline in eight states: Florida, Iowa, Maryland, Mississippi, Nebraska, North Dakota, Oklahoma, and South Dakota. The empirical evidence that felony arrestees are less likely to be incarcerated leads to the implication that court communities exercise discretion to offset the severity of mandatory minimum prison sentences. As Neubauer explains, harsher sentencing laws are associated with the exercise of increased discretion: "The more severe the penalty, the less likely it will be imposed because the severity of the penalty exceeds the limits of punishment viewed as appropriate. The final result is that more produces less. Increasing the severity of the punishment does not increase the threat of punishment; it reduces it" (1979, 415).

Mandatory Determinate Sentencing Laws

In Connecticut, Illinois, and Maine, both mandatory sentencing and determinate sentencing schemes are combined in a single system. While the determinate sentencing scheme eliminates discretionary parole release, discretion can be exercised by courts in setting a prison term within a broad minimum and maximum range. Prison terms set by judges under mandatory determinate sentencing laws are subject to no further adjustments by the parole board (Galvin 1983). The determinacy of a prison sentence, a system in which parole release has been abolished, lets members of the courtroom work group know at the time of sentencing or shortly thereafter the duration of a prison sentence to be served. There is no doubt that mandatory determinate sentencing laws have substantial impacts on the plea bargaining process. Court communities vary in their level of compliance from state to state. The fact that judges can exercise discretion within broad statutory ranges may encourage sentencing bargaining. Prosecutors can also strengthen their position by use of charging discretion in plea negotiations. In general, court communities have easily accommodated mandatory determinate sentencing laws (Tonry 1987, 77–79).

The rates of incarceration in Connecticut, Illinois, and Maine are analyzed by application of the interrupted time-series procedure to determine whether court communities comply with sentencing reforms. The results, as displayed in table 5.2, are mixed. An increase in the rate of incarceration in Illinois is statistically significant in its gradual steady rise throughout the implementation period. This is not the case in Maine. The analysis shows a statistically significant reduction in the rate of incarceration associated with the new law in Maine. For every ten thousand felony arrests, Maine's state prisons received an estimated 146 fewer new inmates to serve their determinate sentences since the new law

Table 5.2
Estimated Change in the Rate of Incarceration
(New Court Commitments per Ten Thousand Felony Arrests)
Associated with Determinate Sentencing Laws, 1967–84

State	Effective Date	Change in the Incarceration Rate[b]	Intervention Pattern
a) Mandatory Determinate Sentencing Laws			
Connecticut[a]	1981	-339.8*	Pulse
Illinois	1978	133.3*	Ramp
Maine	1977	-146.3*	Ramp
b) Presumptive Determinate Sentencing Laws			
California	1977	56.9*	Ramp
Colorado	1976	-150.2	Step
Indiana	1977	497.0	Step
New Mexico	1979	31.3	Step
North Carolina[a]	1977	-339.4	Pulse

*The t statistic is significant at $p < .05$.
[a]1971–84.
[b]The time serial correlation structure is reduced to a random "white noise" process.

took effect. In Connecticut, the effect of the new law on the rate of incarceration is only temporary.

Even though the Illinois data reveal a significant increase in the rate of court commitments per ten thousand arrests, to what degree one can attribute such increase to the law is ambiguous. This finding contradicts research results reported elsewhere. Two studies based on disposition data yield different findings. Among defendants whose cases were disposed of on felony charges, the risk of imprisonment has been in decline since the enactment of the new law. The data on felony dispositions in Illinois indicate that many offenders charged with Class X felonies (the charges that carry the most severe sanctions) were convicted on reduced or substituted non-Class X offenses to avoid mandatory prison sentences (Schuwerk 1984; Witayapanyanon 1992).

In both Maine and Illinois, the effects of their similar statutes are both statistically significant but in opposite directions. Drawing a general conclusion from these results is difficult. Court communities appear to have adopted some form of accommodative reactions in Connecticut. While compliance with the new rules seems to have taken place in Illinois, there appears to be general noncompliance in Maine. It is reasonable to conclude that mandatory determinate sentencing laws have failed to increase incarceration rates in a consistent and systematic manner across jurisdictions.

Presumptive Determinate Sentencing Laws

The five presumptive determinate sentencing states (California, Colorado, Indiana, New Mexico, and North Carolina) are analyzed and tested by comparing their rates of incarceration with the advent of their new laws. The interrupted time-series analysis is applied to evaluate both magnitude and type of changes in the rate of incarceration for every state. The results of these evaluations are presented in table 5.2.

California is the only state that shows a statistically significant increase in the incarceration rate during the post-reform period. Prior studies show that the shift toward increased punitiveness in California was caused by an increase in the proportion of offenders committed to prison for less serious crimes, who had prior conviction records (Ku 1980; Sparks 1981; Utz 1981). Unlike Connecticut and Illinois statutes, presumptive sentences prescribed by the California code are relatively short for all classes of felonies. If the use of incarcerative sentences for serious crimes continues its previous trend, the overall use rate of incarceration is likely to increase. This is particularly the case where imprisonment of short duration becomes more acceptable and thus replaces probation and jail sentences among marginal cases (Brewer et al. 1980; Casper et al. 1982). Past studies of reform impacts in California included only a few post-reform observations and their interpretation relied solely on graphical presentations of time series without application of statistical significance tests (Blumstein et al. 1983, 209). Unlike these evaluation studies, extended post-reform observations are included in the present evaluation. Thus, in California, the evidence suggests that the rate of incarceration has risen substantially beyond its normal preexisting trend and continued to escalate from year to year in a cumulative manner since the law took effect.

What happened at California's courthouses determines the outcomes of felony cases. Judges largely complied with the sentencing reform requirements. However, prosecutors still retained their considerable discretion in initial charging and post-filing dismissal practices. Thus determinate sentencing provisions become important bargaining chips. Plea agreements for defendants to accept prison terms would result in dropping these allegations to avoid application of determinate sentences (Tonry 1987, 80). An increase in the rate of incarceration is attributable to imprisonment of less serious or marginal offenders. Such increases in prison use, as some would believe, are viewed as continuations of preexisting trends toward increased severity of sentencing in California—and not due to the effects of the determinate sentencing law. Since the interrupted time-series procedure employed here can take such upward trends into account, this rival argument is no longer plausible.

The data from Colorado, Indiana, New Mexico, and North Carolina tell a different story. Presumptive determinate sentencing laws have no consistent, statistically significant impact on the use of incarceration in these four states. Although Indiana's impact is larger in magnitude than California's, it is not statistically significant. The unique experience with presumptive determinate sentencing in California cannot be generalized for all five states evaluated here. Comparison of interrupted time-series analysis among these five states indicates no consistent and systematic pattern of changes in the incarceration rate as a result of their laws. With the exception of California, other presumptive determinate sentencing states have witnessed the court community's accommodative reactions to nullify application of the new laws. The nullification by court communities' discretion describes the operation of courtroom work groups in these jurisdictions.

Presumptive Sentencing Guidelines

Unlike other reformed sentencing procedures, presumptive guidelines introduce the dispositional criteria that presume an in/out decision has already been made. The Minnesota guidelines prescribe prison sentences for serious offenses (crimes against persons) and repeaters of serious offenses while reducing the use of imprisonment for first conviction of less serious offenses (property crimes without bodily injury or use of dangerous weapons). Early evaluation studies of the Minnesota guidelines implementation show Minnesota's success in shifting prison sentences from property to person offenses (Blumstein et al. 1983, 215). Despite a steady increase in the rate of dispositional departures during the first three years under the guidelines, the in/out departure rate of this period remains less than half that of the preguidelines rate. Because this rate is calculated from total convictions, charging and bargaining adjustment prior to conviction cannot be detected.

Research shows that the plea process has been shifted from sentence to charge negotiation because the Minnesota guidelines rely solely on the charge of conviction (Rathke 1982, 278–84; Tonry 1987, 72). Such deliberate charge adjustment in plea negotiation can reduce the severity level of the convicted offense so the case is no longer eligible for a presumptive prison sentence. This pattern of charge negotiation leading to conviction on reduced severity levels has occurred in more than 25 percent of all cases in Minnesota (Knapp 1984, 78; Tonry 1987, 72).

It is important to note that an increase in the rate of imprisonment among convictees does not neccessarily reflect an increase in the overall rate of imprisonment among arrestees. If the combined proportion of dismissals and acquittals increases, as found in Massachusetts (Rossman et al. 1979) and Michigan (Heumann and Loftin 1979), the conviction rate among all dispositions would decrease. A decline in the conviction rate can offset an increase in the rate of imprisonment among convicted defendants.

Table 5.3
Estimated Change in the Rate of Incarceration (New Court
Commitments per Ten Thousand Felony Arrests) Associated with
Sentencing Guidelines, 1967–84

State	Effective Date	Change in the Incarceration Rate[b]	Intervention Pattern
a) Presumptive Sentencing Guidelines			
Minnesota[a]	1980	-124.5*	Pulse
b) Voluntary Sentencing Guidelines			
Pennsylvania	1982	22.0	Step
Rhode Island[a]	1982	124.0*	Step
Utah	1978	-9.7	Step
Wisconsin	1982	-93.5	Step

*The t statistic is significant at $p < .05$.
[a]1971–84.
[b]The time serial correlation structure is reduced to a random "white noise" process.

A decline in the conviction rate also involves prosecutorial discretion and strategy in handling criminal cases and reducing uncertainty of case outcome (Albonetti 1986). There is a tendency for the prosecutor to screen out more "no win" cases in order to keep the "win" record high. It is clear that the decision to "nolle prosequi" charges will reduce the overall conviction rate.

Table 5.3 shows that there was a significant drop in the rate of new court commitments, controlling for the total number of arrests in Minnesota. This measure of incarceration reflects several concerns mentioned above. The analysis indicates that the incarceration rate dropped temporarily, only for the period of initial implementation phase and returned to the pre-reform normal level once the sentencing process has been fully adjusted to the guidelines. Washington is excluded from the analysis due to insufficient data to measure policy impact on the rate of incarceration.

Voluntary Sentencing Guidelines

Voluntary sentencing guidelines were implemented in Pennsylvania, Rhode Island, Utah, and Wisconsin. Pennsylvania, not surprisingly, has experienced much higher levels of dispositional and durational departures from the guidelines recommendations than Minnesota. Even though the data on plea bargaining adjustment presented in the 1984 and 1985 studies by the Pennsylvania Commission on Sentencing were not directly evaluated, some indirect evidence exists. The Pennsylvania evidence suggests that the plea process adapted to the guidelines. In sentence bargaining, conviction on the offense charged can be negotiated for a substantial reduction in sentence length or from a prison to nonprison sentence. In charge bargaining, the parties may negotiate for conviction of a reduced or substituted charge leading to the anticipated dispositional outcome the guidelines recommend. Either pattern of adaptation in the plea process can undermine the guidelines in Pennsylvania as well as other guidelines states (Tonry 1987, 62–67).

Alternative explanations that plea bargaining can undermine the success of the guidelines are consistent with the data from Pennsylvania, Utah, and Wisconsin presented in table 5.3. The traditional patterns of incarceration continue with relatively stable incarceration rates under the guidelines implemented in these three states. Rhode Island is an exception in this regard. The incarceration rate increased significantly under the Rhode Island guidelines, effective since 1982. How much one can attribute the increase in the incarceration rate to the guidelines is not clear.

Policy Implications and Research Agendas

There is no systematic and consistent evidence that the five types of sentencing reforms have succeeded in achieving the declared goal of increasing the certainty of severe punishment in most implementing states nationwide. While only a few implementing jurisdictions, or nine out of forty-six states (Georgia, Montana, Vermont, and Washington are excluded due to the data problem), have achieved their stated goal of increasing the certainty of incarcerative sentences, there appear to have been reasons other than sentencing reform that explain these behavioral changes. Even if one can attribute some of these changes to the reform, the weight of the overall evidence indicates reform failure in the majority of the forty-six states evaluated.

The overall findings conform to the conclusion that the court communities comply with sentencing reforms after certain adjustments have been arranged to nullify their application. These adaptive responses are not conducive to any generalizable pattern of sentencing reform impacts across the nation and within certain types of sentencing reforms. The generalizable conclusion is that sentencing reforms as practiced in respective states have not achieved their intended goal of getting tough with criminal offenders. There are only a few states, namely, Alabama, Alaska, Arizona, California, Delaware, Illinois, Missouri, New York, and Rhode Island, which have demonstrated potential successes. Among these nine implementing states, there is no systematic or consistent pattern of sentencing outcomes that enables us to decide what kind of sentencing reform has worked. By contrast, the vast majority of implementing states have failed to achieve higher levels of sentencing severity. None of the sentencing reforms have proven to be an effective choice in general.

Such generalization is defensible but limited to the research design. This case-by-case approach offers no significance test that compares changes in the incarceration rate across jurisdictions. In order to strengthen the evaluation quality, this study adopts a pooled time-series approach to examine reform impacts. This technique provides an evaluation design that compares post-reform sentencing practices to pre-reform norms within the same state relative to the national trends during the pre-reform period, controlling for other variables that can influence the incarceration rate. The discussion will turn to the pooled time-series analysis of the incarceration rate under the five sentencing reform types in the next chapter.

It is quite difficult to find consistent patterns of sentencing behavior. The context and dynamics of court communities vary from jurisdiction to jurisdiction. These variations explain why courtroom work groups behave the way they do in response to sentencing reforms. The pooled time-series procedure provides a solution to this inherent problem. Nationwide variations in court communities' response to the five types of sentencing reforms will be statistically examined using this analytical procedure in the following chapter.

CONCLUSION

In response to sentencing reforms, the courtroom work group performs its critical role in determining guilt and setting appropriate sentences for guilty offenders. A proper balance between convicting the guilty and protecting the innocent must be maintained in the fight against crime. This is not an easy task. The dynamic of courthouse justice is the key to understanding why the law as practiced and applied on a daily basis deviates from the legal codes. There are numerous factors that jointly determine the final dispositional outcomes of the sentencing process. We have demonstrated how administrative, rather than judicial, discretion has been exercised in advancing criminal cases from checkpoint to the next.

The court community's adaptive response to the five competing types of sentencing innovation has been empirically tested in forty-six implementing states nationwide. There is little chance that court communities would achieve the higher levels of sentencing severity intended. Only nine states actually did. The probability of being successful is thus less than 0.2 chances in one. The most plausible explanation is that application of the sentencing reforms has been nullified or even resisted by members of the court community in the majority of the implementing states nationwide.

CHAPTER 6

Consequences of Sentencing Reforms

Sentencing reforms have both intended and unintended consequences. They are aimed at a common set of declared goals such as consistency and predictability in sentencing outcomes, leading to reduction of sentencing disparities. No doubt policy makers often have other goals in mind. Sometimes these goals are explicit, such as reducing the discretion of criminal justice officials, increasing the certainty and severity of punishment, incapacitating dangerous criminals, and deterring violent crime. Sentencing reforms are most attractive to people who believe it is the answer to the crime problem, especially government officials who can appear to be fighting crime without having to increase state budgets. They can offer symbolic support for "tough on crime" legislation even though many of them realize severe penalties are not likely to be enforced.

To evaluate policy successes or failures, one requires a set of criteria to be measured against a set of policy goals. Reflection suggests that sentencing reforms are likely to produce unintended consequences, which are termed "side effects" or "hidden costs." This study addresses both intended and unintended consequences of sentencing reforms on courts, prisons, and crime. Have the court communities achieved the goal of increasing the certainty of imprisonment? Or have sentencing reforms caused prison populations to increase substantially beyond normal trends? Have they reduced violent crime rates? To answer these basic questions this study relies on empirical analyses of both the multiple interrupted and pooled time-series evaluations applied to annual rates of incarceration, prison population size, and violent crime in forty-seven states (all except Georgia, Montana, and Vermont due to missing data) from 1959 to 1987.

THE LIMITS OF SEVERE PENALTIES

Evaluations of the court community's response to sentencing reforms within particular states in the previous chapter reveal what policy analysts term "unintended consequences" of policy implementation. These separate state-by-state evaluations indicate that court communities have resisted the intent of sentencing innovations to increase the certainty of a prison sentence. The outcome has been that courts have failed to increase the risks of imprisonment for those arrested for a felony in substantially more than half the jurisdictions evaluated in this study. It is discouraging to see that imprisonment is even less predictable and becomes less risky for arrested felons in about one of every four implementing states nationwide. The research findings based on multiple interrupted time-series evaluations analyzed in the previous chapter imply that harsher sentencing laws, particularly those that require mandatory and determinate prison sentences, have been substantially undermined by the way in which court communities handle cases. Until now, there has been no claim for convincing empirical evidence that the system works where it has been adopted and implemented. Moreover, there is no single kind of sentencing innovation that has proven its potential success by assuring increased use of a prison sentence. Most of the implementing states have failed to carry out the intent of sentencing reforms in getting tough on crime. There are at least eleven implementing states—mainly the mandatory minimum sentencing states—which show substantial reduction in their rate of incarceration.

Based on evaluation results from the previous chapter, we have arrived at a generalization that none of the sentencing innovations have made severe penalties truly nondiscretionary. This finding is not new. It is consistent with a widely accepted assertion that "No one should assume that any judicial outcome can be made truly 'mandatory'—discretion removed from one place in the criminal justice system tends to reappear elsewhere in it" (Wilson 1975, 187). Neubauer agrees with this line of argument: "In particular harsher sentencing laws are associated with the exercise of increased discretion and negative side effects" (1979, 414).

Although the strength of the separate interrupted time-series designs allows us to compare court communities' response patterns within the same type of sentencing reforms, no statistical tests can be conducted that lead to generalizations concerning these response patterns. However, in most circumstances, accommodative reactions by court communities have been devised to absorb the effect of severe penalties mandated by the sentencing innovations. There is no doubt that court communities respond variably to the five competing models of sentencing reforms. The pooled time-series evaluation model will be employed to test this research hypothesis.

Type of Sentencing Reforms

The adoption of sentencing innovations intended to increase the certainty and severity of punishment in the fight against crime is easier in theory than in practice. The law that in theory aims to increase the certainty of severe penalties for target offenses tends to reduce their certainty in practice. As Currie observes, "The tougher mandatory penalty apparently spurred defendants to go to trial to seek acquittal (rather than accepting a lighter penalty in exchange for a guilty plea). Accordingly, there were more verdicts of not guilty, more dismissals, more appeals, and more new trials" (1985, 63). Why is the law not really enforced? To answer this question, Wilson explains that "the more severe the penalty, the more unlikely that it will be imposed. To ensure a conviction, avoid an expensive trial, reduce the chances of reversal on appeal, and give expression to their own views of benevolence, prosecutors and judges will try to get a guilty plea, and all they can offer in return is a lesser sentence" (1975, 179).

What in fact has taken place in the implementing states nationwide can only be investigated through a pooled time-series evaluation (see appendixes A and B for details on research methodology and statistical procedure). Also included in the evaluation model as a control variable is the violent crime rate of the previous year. For a deterrent advocate, the courtroom work groups are expected to play a critical role in fighting crime. The work groups should tend to increase their prison use in response to a rise in violent crime. Recent research findings do not suggest this pattern of response, but rather its rival argument, the system overload thesis, which is more likely to be operating.

The explanation of the courthouse dynamics based on excessive caseloads focuses on pressures to move cases quickly. At busier courthouses, not much time can be spent on any typical case from start to finish. A large number of felony cases have been settled on the basis of plea negotiation in order to avoid the time and expense of a trial. A reduced charge or a lighter sentence is offered in exchange for a guilty plea. As Wilson describes the rela-

tionship between excessive caseloads and the leniency in sentencing, "Though congested dockets are not the only reason for this
practice, an increase in congestion increases the incentives for such
bargaining and thus may increase the proportion of lighter sentences" (1975, 67). Taking the rate of violent crime in the previous year to represent the degree of caseloads, we would expect a
rise in violent crime to be followed by a reduction in the certainty
and severity of sanctions imposed.

Variations in court communities' response to sentencing
reforms are empirically evaluated on the basis of the national incarceration data during 1971–84 in all forty-seven states. In a carefully
designed pooled time-series evaluation, five dummy variables that
represent the presence or absence of the five sentencing innovations
and the rates of total violent crime per one hundred thousand population during 1970–83 are simultaneously regressed on the rates
of incarceration per ten thousand felony arrests during 1971–84.
The four-step least squares regression is applied to the pooled time-
series data set. The results of this evaluation reported in table 6.1
will be discussed with specific attention paid to their interpretations
and policy implications concerning how the court communities
have responded to the five competing models of sentencing reform.

The pooled time-series evaluation results offer no solid empirical evidence to draw a generalizable conclusion that the adoption
of sentencing reforms has brought about a statistically significant
increase in the likelihood that felony arrestees would be imprisoned. We are more convinced that, in response to the sentencing
innovations, court communities have devised procedural adaptations to sidestep the new rules. It is estimated that, of ten thousand
typical felony arrests, there have been, on the average, approximately ninety-eight fewer persons being sentenced and committed
to state prisons in a particular year in a given state of the thirty-
three mandatory minimum sentencing states. The estimation
implies that about one percent of those arrested for a felony, who
would have gone to prison, received lighter sentences (such as less
than a year term in jail), were placed on probation, or even went
unpunished. The actual certainty of imprisonment for those
arrested felons was reduced by one percent from what it used to
be without mandatory minimum sentences. To estimate roughly,
there were more than 22,200 arrested felons who "got away with
crime" and were put back on the streets throughout the United
States in 1987.[1]

Table 6.1
Pooled Time-Series Analysis of Sentencing Reform Impacts on the
Rate of Incarceration (New Court Commitments per Ten Thousand
Felony Arrests) Applying the Four-Step Least Squares Procedure in
Forty-Seven States, 1971–84

Independent Variables	*Regression Estimates*	*Standard Error*	*t-test*
Constant	17.091	10.918	1.565
Mandatory Minimum	-98.219	19.213	-5.112***
Mandatory Determinate	-282.268	143.208	-1.971*
Presumptive Determinate	-116.756	41.355	-2.823**
Presumptive Guidelines	7.645	35.082	0.218
Voluntary Guidelines	66.220	29.735	2.227*
Violent Crime Rate[a]	-18.735	9.977	-1.878*

$R^2 = 0.90$

$\lambda = 2386$

Unit-Based RSTD Ratio Range = 0.72–1.14

Time-Based RSTD Ratio Range = 0.78–1.45

*p < .05.
**p < .01.
***p < .001.
[a]This variable is measured at time *t-1*, 1970–83.

There is a clear pattern that mandatory determinate sentencing has the greatest level of policy impact on sentencing behavior
and ways in which the court community operates. Key actors of
the court community in general and all the parties of the courtroom work group in particular adapted their ways of handling
cases in the individualized manner that they think is the most efficient and just possible. These adaptations by the members of the
court community have resulted in more felony cases being

1. In 1987 it was reported that 2,266,467 adults were arrested for the eight FBI-
UCR index offenses throughout the United States. Thus, 0.98 percent reduction of these total arrests is 22,211 arrested persons who would have been
imprisoned.

screened out, more lenient sentences being imposed, and, thus, less incarcerative sentences being applied. If this analysis is true, then the rates of incarceration would fall in the jurisdictions that adopted this sentencing scheme. The data support the adaptive-response hypothesis.[2]

In the mandatory determinate sentencing states (Connecticut, Illinois, and Maine), the rates of incarceration have been in decline by 282 persons for every ten thousand felony arrests. On the average, the risk of getting mandatory determinate sentences for serious crimes has been reduced by 2.82 percent from what it was for the same offenses prior to the new laws. This 2.82 percent average reduction in the annual rates of incarceration is almost three times greater than that in the mandatory minimum sentencing states and about two and a half times greater than that of the presumptive determinate sentencing states. That is, 2.82 percent of those arrested felons, who would otherwise have gone to prison, were given lighter sentences, granted probation, or even released without conviction.

Likewise, the presumptive determinate sentencing states that include California, Colorado, Indiana, New Mexico, and North Carolina have experienced an average reduction in the rate of incarceration by about 117 persons for every ten thousand typical felony arrests in a given year since the new laws went into effect. This finding suggests that the chance of imprisonment for those arrested for a felony has been reduced from what it was prior to the new laws by approximately 1.17 percent in a particular year for a particular state adopting the presumptive determinate sentencing law.

Both presumptive and voluntary sentencing guidelines are quite different in their effects on the incarceration rate. The estimate of impact coefficient that is not statistically significant indicates that the rates of incarceration in Minnesota, relative to Washington's, under the presumptive sentencing guidelines continues at their pre-reform normal level. The voluntary sentencing guidelines states (Pennsylvania, Rhode Island, Utah, and Wisconsin) have experienced some increase in incarceration, with an estimate of sixty-six

---

2. In table 6.1, the estimate for the mandatory determinate sentencing laws specified in the regression equation has a negative sign that passes statistical tests.

more new court commitments per ten thousand felony arrests in a particular year under the voluntary guidelines system as a whole. While the certainty of imprisonment remains unaltered under presumptive sentencing guidelines, the court communities are more willing to use incarcerative sentences for those arrested for felony charges under voluntary sentencing guidelines.

It is reasonable to raise a rather methodological question: Does this increase in the incarceration rate reflect the significant shift in Rhode Island alone? In considering the results of interrupted time-series analysis applied to each of the four voluntary sentencing states case by case, there appears to be no systematic pattern of change in sentencing outcomes across all four implementing states. But, in comparison with sentencing norms elsewhere during the same period nationwide through the pooled time-series analysis, the four states implementing voluntary guidelines seem to achieve greater certainty in sentencing. This case is a good example of how we can improve the generalizability of research findings through the pooled time-series evaluation design. Between the two evaluation designs, the results based on the pooled time-series analysis are more defensible in their external validity. Its methodological strength allows for statistical tests of policy impacts to be generalized across time and space within the same group of states adopting voluntary sentencing guidelines.

The overall pattern of reform impact in terms of its magnitude and direction can be explained by variation in the rigidity of legislative control over judicial sentencing discretion. Both presumptive and voluntary guidelines share a similarity in the positive sign of their impact estimates. Apparently, the guidelines system is the most flexible reform type. All types of rigid control—mandatory minimum, mandatory determinate, and presumptive determinate sentencing—have a negative impact on judicial sentencing behavior. The mandatory reform that prescribes lengthier sentences and also removes parole release discretionary power in the form of mandatory determinate sentencing laws is the most rigid legislative control. This rigid reform type appears to have experienced a net negative impact of the largest magnitude either in absolute terms or in percent of its pre-reform averaged level. On the rigidity scale of legislative control imposed on both judicial and administrative discretionary powers, the list of sentencing reform ranges from the most to the least rigid type: mandatory determinate, presumptive determinate, mandatory minimum, presumptive guidelines, and voluntary guidelines. A corresponding pattern of policy impact exists from the greatest negative to the greatest positive impact as follows: -2.82, -1.17, -0.98, 0.08, and 0.66 percent of total felony arrests in mandatory determinate, presumptive determinate, mandatory minimum, presumptive guidelines, and voluntary guidelines states, respectively.

Taking the states that adopted voluntary sentencing guidelines as a group, it is the only system of sentencing reform that appears to have the most impact in the right direction. It is also the system that allows for the most discretion on a voluntary basis. Meanwhile it seems to be the effort to reduce discretion, the mandatory determinate sentencing law, which appears to be the most resisted. It is almost as though the less discretion, the more the system operates in the wrong direction.

In response to rising crime, the courts are expected to play their punitive role in sentencing by increasing the certainty of imprisonment. But this is not usually the case. The pooled time-series evaluation provides no findings to support such an outcome. The empirical evidence is that court communities do not respond punitively to the rise in violent crime. As the rate of violent crime increases by one incident per one hundred thousand population, there is a statistically significant reduction in the rate of incarceration of approximately nineteen persons who are incarcerated in state prisons for every ten thousand felony arrests. This association between a rise in the rate of violent crime and a decline in the certainty of severe punishment supports the heavy caseloads explanation.

To explore further the apparent resistance of court communities to reforms, one should consider pre-reform sentencing norms, which can be measured by the average rates of incarceration in the implementing states during the pre-reform period. It is estimated that about 1,477 of every ten thousand felony arrestees went to prison in the mandatory minimum sentencing states before the new system went into effect (see table 6.2). That is, about 14.77 percent of total felony arrestees were imprisoned. In the mandatory determinate sentencing states, about 1,271 of every ten thousand felony arrestees or 12.71 percent ended up going to prison during the pre-reform period and so did about 10.93 percent of total felony arrestees in the presumptive determinate sentencing states. But only 5.46 percent of total felony arrestees in the presumptive sentencing guidelines states, compared with 5.14 percent in the voluntary sentencing guidelines states, were imprisoned. Between 1979 and 1986 the national rates of incarceration ranged from 10 percent to 11 percent of total felony arrests (Boland et al. 1988, 1989). We have found that the average rate of incarceration in the mandatory minimum sentencing states, which are the majority of the implementing states, is well above the national average. Also higher than the national norms are the mandatory determinate sentencing states. The presumptive determinate sentencing states' average rate of incarceration is close to the national average, while those of both the presumptive and voluntary sentencing guidelines states are well below the national average.

There is evidence that states with higher levels of punitiveness in sentencing are more likely to adopt harsher and more rigid sentencing reforms. Since the average rates of incarceration in more punitive states were already at their high levels, it would be more difficult to achieve the greater certainty of imprisonment. The higher the average rates of incarceration, the greater the degree of court communities' internal resistance to reforms. If this argument holds, one would find a corresponding pattern in the estimates of net impact obtained from the pooled time-series evaluation. It is fair to say that such a pattern exists. The post-reform averaged rates of incarceration can be roughly estimated by simple calculation. For example, the estimate of the averaged rate of incarceration for the post-reform period is 1379.05 per ten thousand felony arrests or about 13.79 percent in the mandatory minimum sentencing states. The same calculation yields the post-reform aver-

Table 6.2

Substantive Significance of Net Impact of Sentencing Reform on the Rate of Incarceration (New Court Commitments per Ten Thousand Felony Arrests) Relative to Pre-Reform Average Levels by Reform Type

Sentencing Reform Type	Pre-Reform Average	Net Impact	Relative Impact
Mandatory Minimum	1477.27	-98.219	-6.65%
Mandatory Determinate	1271.09	-282.268	-22.21%
Presumptive Determinate	1092.65	-116.756	-10.69%
Presumptive Guidelines	545.50	7.645	1.40%
Voluntary Guidelines	513.95	66.220	12.88%

aged rates of incarceration that are equal to 9.89 percent for the mandatory determinate sentencing states, 9.76 percent for the presumptive determinate sentencing states, 5.53 percent for the presumptive sentencing guidelines states, and 5.80 percent for the voluntary sentencing guidelines states, respectively.

The risks of imprisonment for felony arrestees remain higher than the national average in the mandatory minimum sentencing states. Under the mandatory and presumptive determinate sentencing systems, the likelihood that felony arrestees will be imprisoned is slightly below 10 percent, which is the nation's norms. Despite a substantial increase in the certainty of a prison sentence, the risks of imprisonment remain below 6 percent of total felony arrests under both presumptive and voluntary sentencing guidelines systems.

Table 6.2 demonstrates that the net impact of mandatory determinate sentencing laws amounts to a 22.2 percent decrease from the pre-reform average. Determinate sentences tend to be shorter in presumptive sentencing states, particularly California and Colorado, with 10.7 percent decrease from the average level prior to the reform. Where parole release discretion is not entirely removed, the net decrease in the mandatory minimum sentencing states is only 6.7 percent below the already most punitive norms. An increase in the incarceration rate under voluntary guidelines (12.9 percent) reflects sentencing adjustment toward more punitive norms in states where the incarceration rate was extremely low. And this is probably a reason these states adopted a voluntary approach to reform.

In sum, a systematic and consistent decline in the certainty of imprisonment among arrestees charged with violent crimes is opposite the original legislative intent of the sentencing reforms. A tendency toward fewer prisoners committed to state institutions reflects a shift toward reservation of limited prison resources for those most serious offenders to serve their lengthier prison terms. There is also a consistent tendency toward deliberate evasion or adaptive responses to the sentencing reform laws and guidelines nationwide.

The Prison Crowding Issue

Table 6.3 presents the proportion of rated prison capacity occupied by the total prison population in state institutions at the year-end of 1977, 1979, and 1983. The average occupancy rate above or below rated capacity is then calculated for the post-reform period. Those state prisons operating beyond their rated full capacity are considered as crowded facilities. By this definition, about two-thirds of the forty-seven states under study have been operating their state prisons beyond their rated capacity after the states' sentencing reforms. In 1983 Hawaii, Oregon, and Indiana ranked highest on the list of states with crowded state prisons. The higher the occupancy rate over 100 percent, the higher the degree of prison crowding. If the prison crowding variable has a role in determining the incarceration rate, the higher the degree of crowding, the lower the incarceration rate should be.

In the second pooled time-series evaluation model, we treat all five competing types of sentencing innovation alike, while retaining the violent crime rate as a control variable and adding the prison crowding index into the equation. Both the sentencing innovations and the violent crime rate have shown their relationship to the rate of incarceration. The inclusion of the prison crowding index in the equation is intended to test the argument that predicts a reduction in the rate of incarceration as a response to prison crowding. We recognize the limitations of the prison crowding measure, which does not represent an annual variation, but rather reflects cross-sectional variation of the post-reform period.

The results of the pooled time-series evaluations are summarized in table 6.4. It is estimated that of ten thousand typical felony arrests, there would be, on the average, about ninety-seven persons who can avoid a prison sentence under the new rules. Regardless of variation in the type of sentencing reform, for an increase in one violent crime incident per one hundred thousand population, the rate of incarceration reduces by twenty-seven persons from those who are otherwise imprisoned for every ten thousand felony arrests. We also found a positive relationship between prison crowding and the incarceration rate that is not in the postulated direction. This does not mean that court communities in the implementing states with more crowded prisons would increase their use of imprisonment. A better argument would be that court communities do not respond to actual prison crowding situations directly by deciding not to imprison but, rather, they react to altered patterns of plea bargaining practices that threaten the certainty of conviction.

Table 6.3
Percent of Rated Prison Capacity Occupied for Selected Years and the
Degree of Prison Crowding During the Post-Reform Period

State	Survey Periods[a]			Post-Reform Average Prison Crowding Index
	1977	1979	1983	
a) Mandatory Minimum Sentencing States				
Alabama	95.2	90.1	114.0	14.00
Alaska	72.9	92.5	130.0	30.00
Arizona	144.9	99.3	114.0	6.65
Arkansas	99.3	99.0	100.0	0.00
Delaware	98.8	109.2	107.0	7.00
Florida	131.6	89.1	110.0	10.23
Hawaii	119.0	115.4	155.0	29.80
Idaho	115.7	111.7	134.0	34.00
Iowa	97.5	91.0	105.0	-2.00
Kansas	101.6	88.2	119.0	2.93
Kentucky	129.6	124.4	95.0	16.33
Louisiana	110.7	89.9	100.0	0.00
Maryland	140.7	119.4	123.0	27.70
Massachusetts	89.3	97.2	141.0	9.17
Michigan	125.9	104.0	110.0	7.00
Mississippi	95.2	92.6	101.0	-3.20
Missouri	128.6	112.0	91.0	-9.00
Nebraska	79.2	81.0	122.0	-5.93
Nevada	110.7	91.8	113.0	5.17
New Hampshire	75.9	86.7	107.0	7.00
New Jersey	138.1	92.0	111.0	11.00
New York	95.3	89.4	107.0	-1.80
North Dakota	64.9	60.3	87.0	-29.26
Ohio	88.0	92.2	108.0	-3.93
Oklahoma	151.0	101.7	123.0	25.23
Oregon	123.4	113.2	150.0	31.60
South Carolina	149.5	128.3	129.0	35.60

State	Survey Periods[a]			Post-Reform Average Prison Crowding Index
	1977	1979	1983	
South Dakota	88.5	96.9	107.0	1.95
Tennessee	148.9	121.9	122.0	22.00
Texas	93.0	110.2	91.0	-1.93
Virginia	88.2	94.3	105.0	-4.16
West Virginia	64.1	83.8	105.0	5.00
Wyoming	84.5	124.5	115.0	19.75
b) Mandatory Determinate Sentencing States				
Connecticut	97.7	104.8	112.0	12.00
Illinois	100.7	97.3	115.0	6.15
Maine	99.9	91.3	114.0	1.73
c) Presumptive Determinate Sentencing States				
California	88.3	94.9	124.0	2.40
Colorado	91.3	89.0	106.0	-4.56
Indiana	123.1	91.0	146.0	20.03
New Mexico	143.2	115.5	103.0	9.25
North Carolina	104.2	106.7	95.0	1.97
d) Presumptive Sentencing Guidelines States				
Minnesota	85.2	97.7	90.0	-10.00
Washington	113.3	104.9	129.0	29.00
e) Voluntary Sentencing Guidelines States				
Pennsylvania	94.0	90.2	124.0	24.00
Rhode Island	81.0	88.4	98.0	-2.00
Utah	103.9	82.7	105.0	-6.15
Wisconsin	107.8	107.3	123.0	23.00

[a]The data on rated capacity in 1977, 1979, and 1983 are based on *Sourcebook of Criminal Justice Statistics —1978,* table 6.41 (Parisi et al. 1979); *Sourcebook of Criminal Justice Statistics —1979,* table 6.21 (Flanagan et al. 1980). The occupancy rate, percent of rated capacity occupied, is measured in percent of prison population at year-end to rated capacity of that year. The post-reform averaged prison crowding measure is computed by subtracting 100 from the post-reform average of the occupancy rates.

Table 6.4
Pooled Time-Series Analysis of Sentencing Reform and Prison Crowding
Impacts on the Rate of Incarceration (New Court Commitments per Ten
Thousand Felony Arrests) Applying the Four-Step Least Squares
Procedure in Forty-Seven States, 1971–84

Independent Variables	Regression Estimates	Standard Error	t-test
Constant	22.137	10.787	2.052*
Reform Interventions	-97.463	17.854	-5.459***
Prison Crowding	2.267	1.029	2.204**
Violent Crime Rate[a]	-27.604	10.272	-2.687**

$R^2 = 0.90$

$\lambda = 2359$

Unit-Based RSTD Ratio Range = 0.74–1.28

Time-Based RSTD Ratio Range = 0.72–1.47

*p < .05.
**p < .01.
***p < .001.
[a]This variable is measured at time t-1, 1970–83.

THE GROWTH OF PRISON POPULATIONS

The prison population in state institutions, either in absolute terms or relative to the size of the state, rose sharply over the past fifteen years by more than 130 percent. By 1986 nearly half the states had a rate of over two hundred prison inmates per one hundred thousand population. Some twelve states, mainly the southern states, have rates over two hundred fifty. The top five states, with scores as high as three hundred, include Alaska, Delaware, Louisiana, Nevada, and South Carolina (Flanagan and Jamieson 1988, 486–87). A cursory analysis of these figures leads many observers to conclude that sentencing reforms account for most of this huge increase of prison inmates in state institutions.

Studies show that even though the overall imprisonment rate declined (Beha 1977; Heumann and Loftin 1979; Loftin and McDowall 1981; Schuwerk 1984), the average length of sentence and actual stay increased somewhat after the reform went into effect (Brewer et al. 1980). In a sense, due to limited prison space, imprisonment has been reserved for use only by those relatively serious offenders, who received longer sentences. For example, after the reform in California, Brewer et al. (1980) found that an increase in sentence length was applied to offenders convicted of robbery and assault with a deadly weapon.

Casper (1984) hypothesized that prison population growth is affected by legislative control over parole release criteria. In the mandatory minimum sentencing states, the laws require the service of certain minimum prison terms, minus good-time, before inmates become eligible for parole. In both mandatory and presumptive determinate sentencing states, prison terms are subject to further modification only by good-time credits. Experiencing prison crowding problems, many states (for example, Georgia, Illinois, and Michigan) began to reduce prison terms by moving forward parole eligibility dates in order to acquire more available space (Galvin 1983). Others are considering adoption of a similar policy. At the same time, California and some other states are experimenting with intensive surveillance programs and house arrest as alternatives to imprisonment (Petersilia et al. 1985).

Despite an overall reduction in the incarceration rate (see tables 6.1 and 6.2), it appears that reform provisions in other areas—sentence length and parole eligibility reforms, and reduction of prison terms with good-time credit—have an impact on the increase of inmates in state institutions. Another relevant factor is the violent crime rate. The rising crime rate and a corresponding rise in arrested offenders tend to increase the number of convicted and incarcerated defendants, thereby increasing total admissions.

The conventional argument that sentencing reforms account for the growth in the prison population size is evaluated in table 6.5. The pooled time-series evaluation model is employed to estimate effects on the rate of prisoners per one hundred thousand population during the 1972–85 period for the five types of sentencing reforms. To estimate the effects of these sentencing reforms more accurately, the incarceration and violent crime rates are included in this evaluation. This pooled time-series evaluation allows at least one year for both the sentencing innovations and the control variables to produce their effects on the size of the prison population.

Even though a rise in prison populations occurred throughout the 1980s, there has been thus far no strong evidence from prior evaluations that attributes the growth of prison populations and accompanying prison crowding problems to implementation of sentencing reforms. Consider how the Panel on Sentencing Research addresses this policy issue: "Prison populations increased steadily in the 1970s, and further increases are projected throughout the 1980s. This growth in prison populations appears to continue preexisting trends and is only marginally related to recent sentencing reforms" (Blumstein et al. 1983, 32). This pooled time-series evaluation will attempt to assess the plausibility of this argument by use of the specification above. If the rise in prison populations is simply the continuation of pre-reform normal trends, there would be no demonstrable shifts in the size of prison populations in the implementing states. A substantial shift in the rates of inmates per one hundred thousand population beyond their nor-

Table 6.5

Pooled Time-Series Analysis of Sentencing Reform Impacts on the Size of Prison Population (Prisoners per One Hundred Thousand Population) Applying the Four-Step Least Squares Procedure in Forty-Seven States, 1972–85

Independent Variables[a]	Regression Estimates	Standard Error	t-test
Constant	2.125	0.536	3.965***
Mandatory Minimum	17.887	1.807	9.897***
Mandatory Determinate	28.326	4.034	7.021***
Presumptive Determinate	9.077	3.641	2.493**
Presumptive Guidelines	6.389	2.560	2.458**
Voluntary Guidelines	18.536	2.884	6.427***
Violent Crime Rate	14.905	1.082	13.771***
Incarceration Rate	0.00334	0.00163	2.054*

$R^2 = 0.96$

$\lambda = 1249$

Unit-Based RSTD Ratio Range = 0.73–1.07

Time-Based RSTD Ratio Range = 0.75–1.34

*p < .05.
**p < .01.
***p < .001.
[a]All independent variables are measured at time $t-1$, 1971–84.

mal trends during the post-reform period will be a good reason for us to reconsider what we have learned in the past. If this is the case, the assertion that "The substantial increases in prison populations in jurisdictions that have adopted sentencing reforms continue pre-existing trends in sentencing and do not appear to be substantially caused by these sentencing reforms" (Blumstein et al. 1983, 31) would become less plausible.

The national data on the rate of inmates per one hundred thousand population between 1972 and 1985, as displayed in table 6.5, provide strong and verifiable empirical evidence that there have been statistically significant shifts in the size of prison populations one year after the reforms became effective in all five groups of the implementing states nationwide. We have both substantive and empirical reasons to believe that these shifts in the size of prison populations are affected by application of the sentencing reforms. In the mandatory determinate sentencing states, the rate of sentenced inmates serving terms in state prisons rose by twenty-eight inmates per one hundred thousand population. Even though it was found that court communities reduced their use of incarcerative sentences from about 12.71 percent to 9.89 percent of total felony arrests under the mandatory determinate sentencing system, this type of sentencing innovation has proved to have the greatest magnitude of the impact estimate on the size of prison populations due to the absence of the so-called safety-valve control mechanisms.

Likewise, the estimate of the mandatory minimum sentencing laws' impact on the size of prison populations is an increase of eighteen inmates per one hundred thousand population beyond its normal trends. Although there has been a substantial drop in the rate of incarceration from 14.77 percent to 13.79 percent of total felony arrests after the new law, rising prison populations in the mandatory minimum sentencing states would result in part from longer prison terms for those violent and persistent offenders. Since parole eligibility after the completion of mandatory minimum prison terms served as in Massachusetts, Michigan, Ohio, and Kansas can be devised to control the size of prison populations, a rise in prison populations is not as drastic as that of the mandatory determinate sentencing laws.

The presumptive determinate sentencing states have a modest increase in prison population size, which amounts to nine inmates per one hundred thousand population, although it was found that the rate of incarceration dropped from 10.93 percent to 9.76 percent of total felony arrests during the same period. Other states also experienced an increase in prison population under both presumptive and voluntary sentencing guidelines. A significant shift in the incarceration rate from 5.14 percent to 5.80 percent of total felony arrests during the evaluation period can be taken to explain a corresponding increase in the size of prison population in the voluntary guidelines states. Finally, a slight increase (only six inmates per one hundred thousand population) in prison population in the presumptive guidelines states (Minnesota and Washington) is attributable to their relatively short but determinate sentences.

The net effects on prison population size are expressed in percent of the pre-reform average level (in table 6.6) to compare with changes in the incarceration rate (in table 6.7). Both presumptive determinate and presumptive guidelines states experienced the smallest increases (less than 10%) in prison populations. The prison population control mechanisms differ between the two types. Sentencing guidelines are more flexible than sentencing laws to shorten the length of presumptive sentences without revisions of the codes. With that flexibility, the presumptive guidelines states can keep their incarceration rates stable. Despite adjustment to reduce prison sentences, the prison population still increased by 8.6 percent in the presumptive determinate sentencing states and by 19.6 percent in the mandatory minimum sentencing states. Although the incarceration rate decreased by 22 percent in the mandatory determinate sentencing states, their relatively longer determinate sentences led to the 47 percent increase in prison populations.

In addition to the crime rate and the incarceration rate included in the regression model, several policy variables influence the growth in prison populations. Mandatory minimum prison sentences, determinate sentences, penalty schedules, and judicial adjustment in making incarceration decisions—all have an important role in determining the number of admissions, sentence length to serve in prisons, actual time served, and parole release or supervised release decisions.

THE RISE IN VIOLENT CRIME

One of the most important policy issues raised during the formulation of sentencing reform policies is violent crime. This issue

Table 6.6
Substantive Significance of Net Impact of Sentencing Reform on the Size
of Prison Population (Prisoners per One Hundred Thousand Population)
Relative to Pre-Reform Average Levels by Reform Type

Sentencing Reform Type	Pre-Reform Average	Net Impact	Relative Impact
Mandatory Minimum	91.4	17.9	19.57%
Mandatory Determinate	60.1	28.3	47.12%
Presumptive Determinate	105.2	9.1	8.63%
Presumptive Guidelines	76.3	6.4	8.37%
Voluntary Guidelines	59.1	18.5	31.39%

Table 6.7
Substantive Significance of Net Impact of Sentencing Reform on
the Rate of Incarceration (New Court Commitments per
Ten Thousand Felony Arrests) and the Size of Prison Population
(Prisoners per One Hundred Thousand Population) Relative to
Pre-Reform Average Levels by Reform Type

Sentencing Reform Type	Change in the Rate of Incarceration	Change in the Size of Prison Population
Mandatory Minimum	-6.65%	19.57%
Mandatory Determinate	-22.21%	47.12%
Presumptive Determinate	-10.69%	8.63%
Presumptive Guidelines	1.40%	8.37%
Voluntary Guidelines	12.88%	31.39%

involves the crime control effects of mandatory minimum and determinate sentence laws, a major concern raised by the conservative advocates of sentencing reforms. Both types of sentencing schemes emphasize the certainty of punishing violent offenders as a deterrent measure in reducing criminal offenses committed with the use of dangerous weapons, particularly firearms. It should be noted that presumptive determinate sentencing and other sentencing guidelines aim at other policy issues, namely more consistent and equitable sentencing practices. Therefore, these latter types of sentencing reforms are not expected to reduce violent crimes. The goal of increasing consistency and equity in sentencing practices is, however, beyond the scope of this evaluation.

Interrupted Time-Series Evaluations: Murder, Rape, Robbery, and Aggravated Assault

This multiple interrupted time-series evaluation design is employed to analyze individual states' annual rates of murder, rape, robbery, and aggravated assault per one hundred thousand population between 1959 and 1987. The purpose of applying this interrupted time-series procedure to each of the four serious criminal offenses on a state-by-state basis is to test empirically whether particular sentencing reforms as practiced in particular jurisdictions caused a reduction in any of their violent crime rates. Evaluation results as reported in tables 6.8–6.10 provide empirical grounds for comparisons from which a systematic and consistent pattern of crime reduction can be generalized from state to state and from one type of sentencing innovation to another.

In the mandatory minimum sentencing states, the rates of murder, rape, robbery, and aggravated assault per 100,000 population in 31 states are analyzed. Evaluation results, as reported in table 6.8, demonstrate merely a few cases of crime reduction, mixed with nearly twice as many cases of rising violent crime rates, and the majority of cases appear unaffected by the new laws. The rates of murder per 100,000 population fell by a proportion of 2.34 in Maryland, 2.16 in Michigan, 1.97 in Oklahoma, and 1.58 in South Carolina. On the contrary, murder incidents per 100,000 population rose by .97 in New Jersey, 1.57 in

Table 6.8
Estimated Change in Four Violent Crime Rates per One Hundred Thousand Population Associated with Mandatory Minimum Sentencing Laws, 1959–87[a]

State	Murder	Rape	Robbery	Assault
Alabama	-.17	2.92	24.27*	3.16
Alaska	-2.30	14.77*	-20.88	-16.13
Arizona	.50	8.96*	17.47	-8.48
Arkansas	-.26	-3.30*	-5.76	-29.80

Table 6.8 (continued)

State	Murder	Rape	Robbery	Assault
Delaware	-1.77	.35	-10.86	69.17
Hawaii	-.36	1.86	5.93	8.40
Idaho	-.45	2.02	3.49	43.40*
Iowa	.19	-.57	5.77	8.00
Kansas	.29	4.04*	-6.03	9.31
Louisiana	.73	2.74	29.77	9.41
Maryland	-2.34*	.70	-38.60	-36.07
Massachusetts	.14	-1.75	32.12	-19.83*
Michigan	-2.16*	4.30	-81.73*	-4.09
Mississippi	.81	2.46	1.68	-12.55
Missouri	.69	5.53	22.94	16.00
Nebraska	.47	-3.07	9.34	-17.71
Nevada	.56	11.57	62.82*	48.02*
New Hampshire	.01	-1.72	-6.16	-30.38*
New Jersey	.97*	3.33*	32.35	6.34
New York	-1.05	-1.23	26.20	-5.38
North Dakota	.18	-1.81	1.49	8.63*
Ohio	1.57*	1.05	47.68*	14.35
Oklahoma	-1.97*	-1.05	-23.20	19.06
Oregon	-.15	2.68	-16.00	-10.33
South Carolina	-1.58*	1.42	-20.82*	57.03*
South Dakota	-.17	.72	-.61	-19.54
Tennessee	-.04	-3.48	15.50*	-1.02
Texas	1.33*	5.88	6.98	25.32
Virginia	.54	.66	20.08*	38.66*
West Virginia	-.68	-1.60	.67	-12.26*
Wyoming	.08	4.22	-.45	72.14*

*The t statistic is significant at p < .05.
aThe results of the interrupted time-series procedure applied yield a random "white noise" process in its residuals.

Ohio, and 1.33 in Texas. In most of the mandatory minimum sentencing states, the rates of murder did not deviate significantly from their normal fluctuations.

This evaluation reveals a similar pattern for rape, robbery, and aggravated assault. Rape fell by 3.3 incidents per 100,000 population in Arkansas but rose by about the same amount (3.3) in New Jersey and (4.04) in Kansas, almost three times as much (8.96) in Arizona, and more than four times as much (14.77) in Alaska. A drop in the robbery rate per 100,000 population is estimated to be 20.82 in South Carolina and about four times as much (81.73) in Michigan. Under the mandatory minimum laws, the rates of robbery per 100,000 population increased by 15.50 in Tennessee, 20.08 in Virginia, 24.27 in Alabama, 47.68 in Ohio, and 62.82 in Nevada. While the rates of aggravated assault fell in Massachusetts, New Hampshire, and West Virginia, they rose in Idaho, Nevada, North Dakota, South Carolina, Virginia, and Wyoming.

Of thirty-one states empirically tested by use of the interrupted time-series procedure, only eight have succeeded in reducing their violent crime rates: Arkansas, Maryland, Massachusetts, Michigan, New Hampshire, Oklahoma, South Carolina, and West Virginia. Since none of these states have achieved their declared goals of increasing the rates of incarceration, the declining crime rates they experienced cannot be fully attributable to perceived threats of punishment based on the actual certainty of imprisonment in these jurisdictions.

Many of us are inclined to accept the deterrence notion that "effective application of penalties, even rather modest ones, will deter certain forms of behavior" (Wilson 1975, 176). If this argument holds, the violent crime rates in Alabama, Alaska, Arizona, Delaware, Missouri, and New York, where those arrested felons faced the greater risks of imprisonment caused by the mandatory minimum sentencing laws, would have been reduced. Not only did their violent crime rates not go down, but they rose for robbery in Alabama and for rape in Alaska and Arizona. As frequently found elsewhere, less certain imprisonment produces more crime. If this relationship exists, then the rates of violent crime in Florida, Iowa, Maryland, Mississippi, Nebraska, North Dakota, Oklahoma, and South Dakota, where the chance of going to prison is lowered, should have risen. The data indicate, however, that their violent crime rates, except the rate of aggravated assault in North Dakota, did not increase.

There are fourteen out of thirty-one mandatory minimum sentencing states that faced a rise in at least one or more offenses of violent crime: Alabama, Alaska, Arizona, Idaho, Kansas, Nevada, New Jersey, North Dakota, Ohio, South Carolina, Tennessee, Texas, Virginia, and Wyoming. We cannot simply blame it on the courts coddling criminals. Alabama, Alaska, and Arizona have succeeded in increasing the risks of imprisonment for those arrested for a felony but not in reducing violent crime rates.

The deterrent effect of increasing the certainty of imprisonment is not supported by research findings discussed above. The greater risks of a prison sentence for felony offenders did not deter violent crime in the mandatory minimum sentencing states. The reasons for a reduction in violent crime in some jurisdictions have no association with their rates of incarceration at all. This pattern of crime rates and the certainty of imprisonment suggests a generalizable conclusion that the mandatory minimum sentencing laws are unlikely to deter violent crime.

Table 6.9 summarizes the results of multiple interrupted time-series evaluations of violent crime in the mandatory and presumptive determinate sentencing states. In Connecticut, Illinois, and Maine, where the mandatory determinate sentencing laws were adopted, there is no substantial decline in the rates of murder, rape, and robbery. By contrast, robbery rose in Connecticut and so did rape in Illinois. The aggravated assault rates have been indifferent to both mandatory and presumptive determinate sentencing laws, except in Connecticut. Since the presumptive determinate sentencing laws went into effect, the rates of murder went up substantially in California and New Mexico and so did North Carolina's rape rate. In Colorado, the rates of rape and robbery per 100,000 population decreased by 12.79 and 33.53, respectively.

Evaluation results for the six jurisdictions implementing the sentencing guidelines systems are reported in table 6.10. Four states whose violent crime rates fell include Washington, Pennsylvania, Rhode Island, and Wisconsin. These systems do not deter murderers in all implementing states. There are less rape incidents in Pennsylvania, and less aggravated assault incidents in Rhode Island. There are more murder incidents in Washington and Utah,

Table 6.9
Estimated Change in Four Violent Crime Rates per One Hundred
Thousand Population Associated with Determinate Sentencing Laws,
1959–87[a]

State	Murder	Rape	Robbery	Assault
a) Mandatory Determinate Sentencing Laws				
Connecticut	.68	-1.84	36.87*	-19.38*
Illinois	.17	5.69*	-14.46	4.59
Maine	.19	1.59	.76	.64
b) Presumptive Determinate Sentencing Laws				
California	1.12*	2.99	7.13	2.32
Colorado	-.33	-12.79*	-33.53*	-1.10
Indiana	.43	2.51	.56	-9.44
New Mexico	1.82*	2.39	3.45	21.85
North Carolina	-.65	1.66*	-6.68	10.66

*The t statistic is significant at $p < .05$.
[a]The results of the interrupted time-series procedure applied yield a random
"white noise" process in its residuals.

Table 6.10
Estimated Change in Four Violent Crime Rates per One Hundred
Thousand Population Associated with Sentencing Guidelines, 1959–87[a]

State	Murder	Rape	Robbery	Assault
a) Presumptive Sentencing Guidelines				
Minnesota	.26	.49	6.06	-7.70
Washington	.80*	1.41	1.17	-22.82*
b) Voluntary Sentencing Guidelines				
Pennsylvania	-.43	-2.50*	-16.81*	7.40
Rhode Island	.07	.90	20.57*	-28.72*
Utah	.52*	2.26	-2.82	28.74*
Wisconsin	.02	-2.07*	4.91	-3.25

*The t statistic is significant at $p < .05$.
[a]The results of the interrupted time-series procedure applied yield a random
"white noise" process in its residuals.

more robbery incidents in Rhode Island, and more aggravated assault incidents in Utah.

Pooled Time-Series Evaluations:
Murder, Rape, Robbery, and Aggravated Assault

While the multiple interrupted time-series evaluations yield empirical evidence with specific details for each state, it allows no statistical tests to generalize research findings across individual states. It is thus essential to conduct the pooled time-series procedure with an attempt to draw a generalizable conclusion about the relationship between the sentencing reforms and violent crime rates.

To begin with, the rates of total violent crimes per one hundred thousand population in forty-seven states between 1972 and 1985 are analyzed in a regression equation that includes the five policy intervention variables and the incarceration rate during the 1971–84 period (see appendix A for further explanation on this model specification). If there is a negative relationship between the rates of crime and imprisonment, crime declines when imprisonment goes up, and rises when imprisonment falls. Since it appears that the rate of incarceration fell in the mandatory minimum, mandatory determinate, and presumptive determinate sentencing states, one would anticipate that the rate of total violent crime would rise. A decline in the total violent crime rate is anticipated in the states that adopted the voluntary sentencing guidelines system, where their incarceration rate went up. The evaluation results in table 6.11 support some of these anticipated patterns.

In the mandatory minimum sentencing states, the rate of total violent crime rose by 0.42 incidents per 100,000 population. This crime rate also rose by 0.38 in the presumptive determinate sentencing states and by 0.24 in the voluntary sentencing guidelines states. Other variables are not statistically significant. A reduction in the risk of imprisonment explains a rise in the total violent crime rate in the mandatory minimum and presumptive determinate sentencing states, but not in the mandatory sentencing states.

One would argue further that potential perpetrators of different violent crimes might respond to sentencing reforms quite differently. This argument relies on the notion that different types of violent crime tend to constitute different patterns of criminal violence between the offender and the victim. A study of criminal vio-

Table 6.11
Pooled Time-Series Analysis of Sentencing Reform Impacts on the
Aggregate Violent Crime Rate per One Hundred Thousand Population
Applying the Four-Step Least Squares Procedure
in Forty-Seven States, 1972–85

Independent Variables[a]	Regression Estimates	Standard Error	t-test
Constant	0.3178	0.0161	19.717***
Mandatory Minimum	0.4199	0.0554	7.585***
Mandatory Determinate	-0.1820	0.1657	-1.098
Presumptive Determinate	0.3806	0.1472	2.585**
Presumptive Guidelines	0.0712	0.1749	0.407
Voluntary Guidelines	0.2372	0.0975	2.431**
Commitment Rate (1,000s)	-0.0157	0.0441	-0.357

$R^2 = 0.96$

$\lambda = 3262$

Unit-Based RSTD Ratio Range = 0.71–1.31

Time-Based RSTD Ratio Range = 0.59–1.28

*$p < .05$.
**$p < .01$.
***$p < .001$.
[a]All independent variables are measured at time $t\text{-}1$, 1971–84

lence suggests that the patterns of interactions in violent coercion differ between murder and robbery and between coercion with the use of a gun and coercion without the use of a gun (Luckenbill 1984). Thus, studies of sentencing reforms distinguish between offenses with the use of firearms and those with the use of other weapons in evaluating the impact of mandatory prison sentences on firearm-related crimes (Deutsch and Alt 1977; Pierce and Bowers 1981; Loftin et al. 1983; Loftin and McDowall 1984; McPhethers et al. 1984). Due to data limitations, gun robbery cannot be distinguished from nongun robbery in this study. Thus, violent crime rates must be disaggregated simply into murder, rape, robbery, and aggravated assault.

The same evaluation model is applied to each crime type. The rates of murder, rape, robbery, and aggravated assault per one hundred thousand population are evaluated for the same period (1959–87) for all forty-seven states under study. Because the incarceration rate does not have an impact on the aggregate violent crime rate, it is dropped from this model. The results of pooled time-series analysis on these four types of violent crimes are reported in tables 6.12–6.15.

For murder, the rate per one hundred thousand population increased by 0.34, 0.48, and 0.84 for mandatory minimum, mandatory determinate, and presumptive determinate sentencing states, respectively. No matter what types of sentencing reforms were adopted, rape continued to rise by about 6 or more incidents per one hundred thousand population in the mandatory and determinate sentencing states, and from 3 to 7 incidents per 100,000 population in the sentencing guidelines states.

Table 6.12

Pooled Time-Series Analysis of Sentencing Reform Impacts on the Murder Rate per One Hundred Thousand Population Applying the Four-Step Least Squares Procedure in Forty-Seven States, 1959–87

Independent Variables	Regression Estimates	Standard Error	t-test
Constant	0.0330	0.0296	1.116
Mandatory Minimum	0.3409	0.0967	3.525***
Mandatory Determinate	0.4861	0.2508	1.938*
Presumptive Determinate	0.8423	0.3587	2.348**
Presumptive Guidelines	0.2528	0.2781	0.909
Voluntary Guidelines	0.3137	0.2308	1.359

$R^2 = 0.92$

$\lambda = 10119$

Unit-Based RSTD Ratio Range = 0.99–1.00

Time-Based RSTD Ratio Range = 0.64–1.48

*p < .05.
** p < .01.
*** p < .001.

Table 6.13

Pooled Time-Series Analysis of Sentencing Reform Impacts on the Rape
Rate per One Hundred Thousand Population Applying the Four-Step
Least Squares Procedure in Forty-Seven States, 1959–87

Independent Variables	Regression Estimates	Standard Error	t-test
Constant	0.4489	0.0927	4.844***
Mandatory Minimum	6.6212	0.4557	14.531***
Mandatory Determinate	5.9948	0.9923	6.041***
Presumptive Determinate	6.2800	1.1012	5.703***
Presumptive Guidelines	6.9443	1.9883	3.493***
Voluntary Guidelines	3.1890	1.0316	3.091***

$R^2 = 0.94$

$\lambda = 4779$

Unit-Based RSTD Ratio Range = 0.90-1.03

Time-Based RSTD Ratio Range = 0.53-2.19

*p < .05.
**p < .01.
***p < .001.

Robbery per 100,000 population also went up about 10.80 in
the mandatory minimum sentencing states, 12.52 in the presumptive determinate sentencing states, and 15.29 in the presumptive
sentencing guidelines states. The rates of robbery in the states that
adopted both mandatory determinate sentencing laws and voluntary sentencing guidelines did not change. Finally, it is clear that
there are more aggravated assault rates in all five reform categories. Aggravated assault per 100,000 population is estimated to
increase by 22.6 in the presumptive guidelines states, 26.7 in the
mandatory determinate sentencing states, 30.2 in the voluntary
guidelines states, 42.5 in the mandatory minimum sentencing
states, and 47.8 in the presumptive determinate sentencing states.

In short, the data reveal no crime reduction effects of the
reform on any crime type nationwide. Both murder and robbery
rates remain unaffected in some states, but increased significantly
in the remaining part of the country. Similarly, both rape and
aggravated assault rates increased significantly throughout the

Table 6.14
Pooled Time-Series Analysis of Sentencing Reform Impacts on the
Robbery Rate per One Hundred Thousand Population Applying the
Four-Step Least Squares Procedure in Forty-Seven States, 1959–87

Independent Variables	Regression Estimates	Standard Error	t-test
Constant	1.6705	0.4993	3.346***
Mandatory Minimum	10.7968	1.7198	6.278***
Mandatory Determinate	6.5984	4.5096	1.463
Presumptive Determinate	12.5154	5.2006	2.407**
Presumptive Guidelines	15.2904	8.0000	1.911*
Voluntary Guidelines	1.4716	4.4512	0.331

$R^2 = 0.96$

$\lambda = 7523$

Unit-Based RSTD Ratio Range = 0.65–1.10

Time-Based RSTD Ratio Range = 0.51–2.16

*p < .05.
**p < .01.
***p < .001.

United States. The evidence of no deterrent effects is consistent across all crime types.

POLICY IMPLICATIONS AND CONCLUSION

This chapter has explored the negative side effects of sentencing reforms in terms of the limitations of severe penalties, the growth of prison population, and the rise in violent crime. The five types of sentencing reform have different impacts on the incarceration rate and the size of prison population. Although policy modifications during the reform implementation process made prison sentences less frequently imposed, a growth in prison population ensued. The types of sentencing reforms adopted explain variation in their impacts on the incarceration rate and the growth in prison populations. Sentencing reform standards that rely largely on rigid control and prescribe lengthy sentences tend to experience a

Table 6.15

Pooled Time-Series Analysis of Sentencing Reform Impacts on the
Aggravated Assault Rate per One Hundred Thousand Population
Applying the Four-Step Least Squares Procedure in Forty-Seven States,
1959–87

Independent Variables	Regression Estimates	Standard Error	t-test
Constant	3.9857	0.7054	5.651***
Mandatory Minimum	42.5331	3.5381	11.965***
Mandatory Determinate	26.7273	11.5027	2.324***
Presumptive Determinate	47.8364	10.5115	4.551***
Presumptive Guidelines	22.6245	10.2138	2.215*
Voluntary Guidelines	30.1567	6.9995	4.308***

$R^2 = 0.95$

$\lambda = 5531$

Unit-Based RSTD Ratio Range = 0.84–1.04

Time-Based RSTD Ratio Range = 0.53–2.40

*p < .05.
**p < .01.
***p < .001.

greater reduction in the incarceration rate. Less rigid sentencing standards with shorter sentences received less internal resistance and adaptive responses to the reform. Under the reform, state prisons have experienced severe prison crowding problems. Finally, there is no evidence that the reforms deterred violent crime such as murder, rape, robbery, and aggravated assault.

Nullification by the Court Community

This study found no empirical support for the sentencing reform hypothesis that restriction of judicial discretion can increase the predictability of sentencing decisions, thereby increasing the certainty of incarceration. The data analyzed in this evaluation are consistent with the Panel on Sentencing Research's assertion that judges, prosecutors, and defense counsel can adapt their case-handling routines in an effort to circumvent new rules and procedures. As the panel states, "Increased case screening or other early disposition of cases effectively avoids application of sentencing laws" (Blumstein et al. 1983, 220). If this avoidance or nullification hypothesis holds true, the use of incarcerative sentences among adult arrestees would decline or at least remain stable during the post-reform period.

The research findings pertinent to this nullification hypothesis are: (1) the most rigid control under mandatory determinate sentencing laws appears to have elicited the greatest level of internal resistance and deliberate evasion of the new sentencing standards; (2) mandatory sentence reforms tend to have greater impact than presumptive sentencing; and (3) both lengthier prison sentences and elimination of parole release discretion can influence sentencing decisions and the growth in the prison population. However, the degree of prison crowding has no effect on the incarceration rate, beyond the overall sentencing reform impact. Despite a significant pattern of adjusted implementation to nullify the effects of reform, only the growth in the size of prison populations can be attributed to determinacy in sentencing.

Policy Constraints on State Prison Facilities

There is little doubt that the reforms have significant impact on the size of prison populations. One important implication for state policy makers is that carrying out the intent of sentencing reforms requires corresponding prison policies. There are three general strategies available to cope with the crowding problem: (1) expansion of capacity through changes in existing facilities and the construction of new prisons, (2) limitation on admissions through use of alternatives to imprisonment, and (3) direct regulation of prison populations through controls on intake and release (Blumstein et al. 1983, 246). The first alternative requires financial capital and long-term planning on projected prison population growth. At the same time, the second alternative requires a compromise between sentencing policies and prison policies. The third alternative, prison population control mechanisms through the use of good-time for sentence reduction, conflicts with the legislative intention of increasing the certainty of punishment.

If judges send all eligible offenders to serve mandatory determinate sentences in prisons, what consequences can one anticipate in the long term? Is the criminal justice system ready to carry out legislative intent to achieve the greater certainty of imprisonment? The public demands punitive policy in handling criminals. Carrying out such a policy requires the construction of new prisons. But taxpayers are reluctant to pay for them. Several alternatives to imprisonment have been explored. Experimental intensive surveillance programs (ISPs) in several states may extend their coverage to grant convicted felons more probationary sentences under electronic monitoring devices. Specific program designs and their effectiveness require more research and experimentation.

Crime Control Reconsidered

The goal of crime control rests on the idea that new sentencing policies to increase the certainty and severity of legal sanctions, particularly mandatory imprisonment and determinate sentences, should produce the deterrent and incapacitative effects advanced by deterrence theory. This idea of reducing crime by getting tough with criminals relies on the assumption that potential criminals are rational individuals who calculate the cost of being punished against the benefit of breaking laws. The state-level data on both aggregate and disaggregate violent crime rates indicate that the new laws lack deterrent and incapacitative effects in reducing crime.

The findings of no significant increases in the incarceration rates in the majority of the forty-seven states evaluated may explain why the violent crime rates were not affected by the new sentencing laws. Changes in the laws do not seem to have been put into practice as orginally intended. Consequently, the level of certainty and severity of legal sanctions remain more or less unchanged. Under certain conditions, such as lack of cooperative efforts from judges and prosecutors, circumvention of new rules and procedures, and limited resources, the rate of incarcerative sentences among adult arrestees has been in decline in most states. With an increase in use of nonincarcerative alternatives, legal sanctions would appear to be less certain and more lenient for offenders. Moreover, the low rate of police arrests per crime being committed represents a major gap in the logic of the certainty and severity argument.

As Tappan has said about the criminal law, the "law in books" is not equivalent to "law in action" (1960, 25). The complexity of the criminal justice system with a series of decision stages in the process of carrying out sentencing reforms creates numerous sources of uncertainty in the process of handling offenders. There are also numerous factors that affect crime beyond the reach of the criminal justice system.

Since deterrence relies mainly on perceptions of legal sanctions that are certain and severe, one would expect no crime reduction effects because the fundamental assumptions of deterrence have not been met. This study has shown that rates of murder, rape, robbery, and aggravated assault continued to rise in the United States. The findings of no deterrent effects of the sentencing reforms add another important piece of evidence to the existing literature on deterrence reviewed elsewhere (Blumstein et al. 1978).

CHAPTER 7

Sentencing Reform:
Simple Theory, Hard Reality

The nominal goal of sentencing reform legislation in the United States was to deter crime by increasing the rates of incarceration for a variety of high-priority crimes. The evidence, detailed in the preceding chapter, is that sentencing reform laws did not have anticipated impacts on either criminal courts' sentencing behavior or crime rates. Why did these sentencing reforms fail? In part, there appear to be several logical gaps or outright fallacies in the policy theories underlying mandatory and determinate sentencing laws (Mazmanian and Sabatier 1983). Primarily, legislators may not have anticipated the extent to which criminal court communities could adapt in ways contrary to the intent of new sentencing reform laws.

A SUMMARY OF EVALUATION RESULTS

Both interrupted time-series and pooled time-series quasi-experiments evaluate the impacts of sentencing reforms in terms of behavioral changes in the target population across forty-seven states. These two approaches to a comparative study of public policy complement each other. The former deals with the impacts of sentencing reform policies within particular jurisdictions that were, in turn, generalized across jurisdictions. The latter compares the impacts of sentencing reform policies across jurisdictions using statistical significance tests on the pooled cross-sectional and time-serial data. The pooled cross-sectional time-serial analysis provides an estimate of the net effect of each sentencing reform across all states that implemented the reform. However, the state-by-state comparison, though complicated by the specificity of within-state policy impacts, is equally if not more important. If a reform is to be judged effective, it should show a consistent pattern of policy impact in the expected direction across all states that implemented the reform. Within multiple comparison groups and policy intervention staggered across different years, this pooled quasi-experiment is a very powerful evaluation design.

Empirical evidence from interrupted time-series quasi-experiments is immune to the threats to the internal validity of an evaluation for several reasons. Unlike prior evaluations of the reform using only pretest-posttest data, these interrupted time-series quasi-experiments cover eighteen years of annual observations on the incarceration rate. The interrupted time-series technique employed can account for both short- and long-term patterns of behavioral changes in the sentencing process over the period under study. This technique provides a general time-series procedure to identify and describe any systematic variation in the incarceration rate that reflects a changing pattern of sentencing behavior. A rise in the incarceration rate series, for instance, exemplifies a tendency toward increased punitiveness in sentencing. In addition, statistical tests can be used to determine the significance of such a shift in the incarceration rate.

This evaluation design addresses several methodological concerns of previous studies on the same subject. The strengths of the interrupted time-series design lie in its comparative analysis of evaluation results across forty-six states. The comparative strategy prevents researchers from drawing erroneous conclusions based on an unrepresentative sample of jurisdictions. In fact, with a national study in which almost all of the American states are analyzed, concerns about the study's external validity are minimal.

Empirical Evidence
from Interrupted Time-Series Quasi-Experiments

Sentencing reform impacts on the incarceration rate per ten thousand felony arrests in forty-six states are summarized in table 7.1. Conclusions from interrupted time-series analyses are divided into four categories: significant increase, nonsignificant increase, significant decline, and nonsignificant decline. Nine states in column (a) have succeeded in increasing their incarceration rates, as the reforms purport to dictate. The number of success cases is only

Table 7.1
A Summary of Interrupted Time-Series Evaluations of Sentencing Reform Impacts on the Rates of Incarceration in Forty-Six States, 1967–84

Change in the Expected Direction			
(a) Significant Increase (9)		*(b)* Nonsignificant Increase (10)	
Alabama	MMSL[a]	Indiana	PDSL
Alaska	MMSL	New Hamshire	MMSL
Arizona	MMSL	New Mexico	PDSL
California	PDSL	Ohio	MMSL
Delaware	MMSL	Pennsylvania	VSGS
Illinois	MDSL	South Carolina	MMSL
Missouri	MMSL	Tennessee	MMSL
New York	MMSL	Texas	MMSL
Rhode Island	VSGS	West Virginia	MMSL
		Wyoming	MMSL

Change in the Opposite Direction			
(c) Significant Decline (11)		*(d)* Nonsignificant Decline (16)	
Connecticut	MDSL	Arkansas	MMSL
Florida	MMSL	Colorado	PDSL
Iowa	MMSL	Hawaii	MMSL
Maine	MDSL	Idaho	MMSL
Maryland	MMSL	Kansas	MMSL
Minnesota	PSGS	Kentucky	MMSL
Mississippi	MMSL	Louisiana	MMSL
Nebraska	MMSL	Massachusetts	MMSL
North Dakota	MMSL	Michigan	MMSL
Oklahoma	MMSL	Nevada	MMSL
South Dakota	MMSL	New Jersey	MMSL
		North Carolina	PDSL
		Oregon	MMSL
		Utah	VSGS
		Virginia	MMSL
		Wisconsin	VSGS

[a]MMSL—mandatory minimum sentencing laws; MDSL—mandatory determinate sentencing laws; PDSL—presumptive determinate sentencing laws; PSGS—presumptive sentencing guidelines systems; VSGS—voluntary sentencing guidelines systems.

about a fifth of the total cases evaluated. In ten states listed in column (b), there were some, but minimal, increases in incarceration rates. Unforeseen by the proponents of the reforms have been substantial declines in the incarceration rates in eleven states in column (c). Sixteen states in column (d) experienced some but minimal declines in their incarceration rates. In short, the lack of sentencing reform impacts on courts is evident in the majority of the implementing states under study.

The comparative analysis of interrupted time-series evaluation results yields several primary findings:

1. Felony arrestees have faced higher risks of imprisonment after the advent of sentencing reforms in nineteen jurisdictions.

2. There are only nine states with substantial increases in the rate of incarceration: Alabama, Alaska, Arizona, California, Delaware, Illinois, Missouri, New York, and Rhode Island.

3. Sentencing reforms tended to elicit adaptive responses by the court community actors with efforts to circumvent application of the new rules in at least twenty-seven states, where the certainty of a prison sentence imposed for a felony has been in decline after the reforms.

4. Presumed behavioral adjustments in implementing the reforms and the evasion of the new sentencing standards have been observed in eleven jurisdictions: Connecticut, Florida, Iowa, Maine, Maryland, Minnesota, Mississippi, Nebraska, North Dakota, Oklahoma, and South Dakota, where the incarceration rate has dropped substantially relative to prior practices.

5. Mandatory minimum sentencing laws have been effectively implemented to increase the proportion of incarcerated offenders among those arrestees charged and convicted of violent offenses in six jurisdictions: Alabama, Alaska, Arizona, Delaware, Missouri, and New York; whereas their side effects characterized as internal resistance and deliberate evasion of the new provisions have been substantial as found in the following eight states: Florida, Iowa, Mary-

land, Mississippi, Nebraska, North Dakota, Oklahoma, and South Dakota.

6. Mandatory determinate sentencing laws as adopted in Connecticut and Maine have been most likely to encounter similar efforts to nullify the reform impacts.

7. Presumptive determinate sentencing laws have received modest compliance with procedural requirements in Indiana and New Mexico and substantial compliance in California, but have been resisted in Colorado and North Carolina.

8. Voluntary sentencing guidelines have failed to bring about significant changes in sentencing outcomes, compared with previous practices, except in Rhode Island, whereas presumptive sentencing guidelines, as adopted in Minnosota, have experienced a substantial reduction in the incarceration rate.

These primary research findings undermine the "get tough on crime" premise of sentencing reforms intended to make prison sentences more certain as well as more consistent. In most implementing jurisdictions, changes in sentencing behavior to comply with procedural requirements have largely been compliance in form rather than compliance in substance. However, there is sufficient empirical evidence to assert that internal resistance and deliberate evasion of the new pertinent rules have been prevalent in the United States. No specific type of sentencing reforms has demonstrated the ability to achieve a substantial level of internal support for the reform; to establish the most effective form of statutory or administrative authority to promote compliance and commitment to the desired goals; and to develop and utilize credible monitoring and enforcement mechanisms.

A summary of evaluation results in table 7.2 illustrates a similarly mixed pattern of sentencing reform impacts on the rates of the four violent crime types. Only a few states experienced a significant reduction in the violent crime rates of murder, rape, robbery, and aggravated assault. These violent crime rates remain unaffected by sentencing reforms in most of the remaining states. Obviously, sentencing reforms have not yet proven to be efficacious anticrime measures.

Table 7.2
A Summary of Interrupted Time-Series Evaluations of Sentencing Reform
Impacts on Four Violent Crime Rates in Forty-Five States, 1959–87

Crime Type	Change in the Expected Direction	
	Significant Decline (Number of States)	Nonsignificant Decline (Number of States)
Murder	4	14
Rape	4	10
Robbery	4	13
Assault	6	15
Crime Type	Change in the Opposite Direction	
	Significant Increase (Number of States)	Nonsignificant Increase (Number of States)
Murder	7	20
Rape	6	25
Robbery	7	21
Assault	7	17

Empirical Evidence from Pooled Time-Series Quasi-Experiments

The pooled time-series quasi-experimental design was employed to evaluate the impacts of sentencing reforms on courts, prisons, and violent criminals. With this cross-sectional and time-serial quasi-experiment, one can estimate the net effects of these five major reform types while accounting for control variables. The estimates of their net effects were derived from the pooled time-series data across the forty-seven states.

The results of the pooled time-series quasi-experiments about sentencing reform impacts on incarceration rates, prison populations, and violent crime rates are summarized in table 7.3. First, associated with the advent of sentencing reforms have been significant declines in the incarceration rates per ten thousand felony arrests in jurisdictions that adopted mandatory minimum sentencing laws, mandatory determinate sentencing laws, and presumptive determinate sentencing laws. While both presumptive and voluntary sentencing guidelines appear to increase the incarceration rate, only jurisdictions implementing voluntary sentencing

Table 7.3
A Summary of Pooled Time-Series Evaluations of Sentencing Reform
Impacts on the Rate of Incarceration, the Size of Prison Population, and
the Aggregate Violent Crime Rate by Reform Type

Reform Type	Incarceration Rate		Prison Population Size		Aggregate Violent Crime Rates	
Mandatory Minimum	-	*	+	*	+	*
Mandatory Determinate	-	*	+	*	-	
Presumptive Determinate	-	*	+	*	+	*
Presumptive Guidelines	+		+	*	+	
Voluntary Guidelines	+	*	+	*	+	*

Legend: + indicates an increase in the post-reform time-series level; - indicates a reduction in the post-reform time-series level; * denotes that *t* is statistically significant at p < .05.

Note: The five types of sentencing reform were intended to reduce violent crime rates by increasing the rate of incarceration per felony arrests (the certainty of imprisonment), which will result in the growth of prison populations.

guidelines have potential successes in achieving higher levels of certainty in imprisonment. The evidence leads to a general conclusion that imprisonment is unlikely to become more certain under sentencing reforms.

Second, the pooled time-series analysis of sentencing reform effects on prison population sizes during the 1972–85 period revealed evidence of a significant growth in the population of prisoners in state institutions. If every imprisoned offender receives a one-year sentence, prison populations grow at least 25 percent (Petersilia and Greenwood 1978). A significant increase in the size of prison populations has been an inescapable outcome that has burdened state prisons since sentencing reforms went into effect throughout this country. Legislative responses to the greater demands for prison space require a larger slice of the state government budget pie to finance the operation of prisons and their expansions. More likely than not, state prisons under financial difficulty have been operating well beyond their rated capacity. By legal definition, the majority of state prisons have been severely crowded.

Finally, the evidence shows that sentencing reforms did not deter violent crimes in this country. The pooled time-series analyses of the aggregate violent crime rate (murder, rape, robbery, and aggravated assault combined) as well as the rates of disaggregated violent crimes during the 1959–87 period revealed no evidence of a reduction in violent crimes in response to sentencing reforms in the United States.

The findings of no increase in the incarceration rate suggest that mandatory sentences and other sentencing reforms have not been carried out as they were initially intended. However, this does not necessarily mean that fully enforced mandatory sentences would have reduced violent crimes (general deterrence) and recidivism among released offenders (specific deterrence). Deterrence is a complex psychological process. The focus on certain punishment by changing the penalty structure and sentencing behavior represents only one aspect of the deterrence process.

Overall, both interrupted time-series and pooled time-series quasi-experiments revealed that: (1) legislative control over judicial sentencing discretion has failed to increase the certainty of imprisonment; (2) despite some adjustment in reducing the rate of incarceration, the prison population sizes rose sharply; and (3) violent crime rates were not deterred by the new sentencing policies.

SENTENCING REFORM ON TRIAL: A SIMPLE POLICY THAT FAILS

The failure of sentencing reform at least in the major areas evaluated here requires some explanation. One explanation may involve the theories incorporated into the design of sentencing reforms. Another set of hypotheses generated by the court community model will be considered in light of the empirical evidence suggested by this evaluation.

A Fallacy of Sentencing Reform Models

Many conceptual problems contribute to difficulties confronting sentencing reforms. These conceptual difficulties lie in at least five interrelated assumptions and factors inherent in most of the reforms implemented.

First, the assumption that a statute can turn judges into mindless robots, who can be programmed in advance to do what legislators tell them to do with strict obedience, is naive. This implicit assumption about automatic application of equal sanctions for diverse cases vaguely classified and labeled the same crime is seriously flawed. This fallacy of sentencing reform reflects a wide range of conceptual problems deeply rooted in the mechanistic view of the criminal justice process.

Cressey has argued that all criminal laws cannot and should not be merely enforced as written without any adjustment that fits the specific circumstances of the offense (1980, 59). There is little doubt that any reform that mandates automatic application of the law is impractical and will be resisted. Thus, one should not expect judges to perform as computerized robots because they must be given room to exercise their own common sense (Cressey 1980, 62).

Second, another misleading assumption of sentencing reform is that impeccable sentencing standards are written into reform laws or rules. A major problem with any reform is that sentencing standards do not cover all the nuances of situation, intent, and social harm that condition the gravity of particular criminal acts (Cullen and Gilbert 1982, 162). It is difficult, if not impossible, to standardize sentencing decisions through explicitly stated rules that are both specific in substance and general in meaning at the same time. The problem with standardization is that equal treatments are prescribed for unequal, diverse criminal acts legally and conveniently defined under the same vague labels (Cressey 1980, 61). Many who appeal to equal justice do not acknowledge that "offense labels can mask significant variations in actual seriousness" of crimes (Feeley 1983, 194).

The precept of "treating like cases alike and different cases differently" (Hart 1961, 155) is difficult to translate into specific and articulated sentencing standards. The real issue extends beyond equality; equal punishment is not necessarily *equitable* punishment (Zimring 1983, 116).

Third, it is politically attractive to increase rather than decrease sentence lengths. This trend toward increased prison sentences is particularly true in Colorado, Indiana, Illinois, and Ohio (Greenberg and Humphries 1980, 221). In response to the public demand for longer prison sentences due to increasing fear of crime, it is hard to imagine that politicians will vote for a reduction in sentence lengths. As a result, prison terms become unrealistically longer. In most of mandatory minimum sentencing states, long prison terms will be substantially reduced by good-time and parole release discretion. Politicians in general prefer a system that barks louder (lengthy prison sentences listed on the books and imposed in court) than it actually bites (substantially reduced actual time served due to good-time and parole release discretion). A system that does not bark (fewer short prison sentences prescribed and imposed), but bites more severely—that is, no further modifications of prison terms under statutory determinate sentencing laws—is less politically appealing (Cullen and Gilbert 1982, 155).

Fourth, it is inaccurate to assume that "little or no human element is necessary to justice" (Rosett and Cressey 1976, 163). The lack of clarity and specificity in laws necessitates discretionary adjustment by experienced professionals. They must mediate between the "law on the books" and the "law on the streets" (Cressey 1980, 59). It is such adjustment that can prevent gross injustices caused by equal treatments for diverse cases of unequal seriousness even under the same legal labels. Such adjustment may moderate, or it may augment sanctions prescribed by "the book." Criminal justice officials cannot just enforce the law. When they adjust punishment to fit the crime by modifying unduly harsh statutory penalties, in light of the nuances of individual cases, they "do justice" (Rosett and Cressey 1976, 164). For this reason many reformers were reluctant to recommend abandonment of plea negotiation.

Finally, sentencing reform in the United States seems to be guided by the maxim "Half a loaf is better than none" (Zimring 1983, 113). Partial reform seeks to restrict or eliminate discretionary power at certain decision points in the criminal justice process. Ironically, however, restrictions over judicial sentencing discretion lead to an increase in prosecutorial discretion that remains unregulated (Cullen and Gilbert 1982, 162; Feeley 1983). Uncertainty exists at various stages of the sentencing process. Thus, reduction in uncertainty at a particular decision point cannot lead to an overall increase in the certainty of punishment. That is, an increase in the certainty of judicial sentencing decisions may be offset by changes in the opposite direction.

Some Concluding Thoughts

New policies have been implemented to reform the criminal sentencing process in the United States. These new policies usually did not have the intended effect on the output of criminal courts or outcomes regarding crime control, and did have unintended consequences on the size of state prison populations. The failure of these sentencing reform policies is manifested by the courts' inability to increase the certainty of imprisonment. With respect to the efficacy of anticrime measures, violent crime rates were not generally affected by these "get tough with crime" policies. Finally, these policies enlarged the size of prison populations, a major factor leading to prison crowding.

Explaining exactly why sentencing reform policies have failed in the United States requires additional empirical data to test alternative hypotheses about the everyday functioning of criminal courts. These hypotheses must be formulated in light of how courts appear to respond to new sentencing policies. An organizational perspective helps explore the courts' responses to these new policies. The court community model is a strong candidate because it explains what happens in courthouses during the processing of criminal cases. From this organizational perspective, one expects that courtroom work groups tend to develop ways of resisting, evading, circumventing, or adjusting to changes in their environment, such as new sentencing standards. Testing this adaptive response hypothesis requires further exploration that is beyond the scope of this study. In order to explore the adaptive response hypothesis more fully, one would need to examine changes in the process of screening, charging, plea bargaining, and convicting. However, given the results of this evaluation, it appears that the data are at least consistent with adaptive-response behavior on the part of court community work groups.

Sentencing reform policies encountered many obstacles in implementing changes imposed by state legislatures. Like most other reform policies, sentencing reforms were formulated with high expectations in achieving their policy goals, that is, crime control and fairness in sentencing. Ambitious policies are likely to be disappointing merely because their goals are unattainable. Criminal sentencing is and always will be a human process (Hogarth 1971). Removal of human elements in decision making—that is, official discretion in sentencing—requires remarkable effort and a body of knowledge that theorists have not yet discovered. Beautifully simple theory can find a way of turning into ugly practice. The complexity of criminal court operations, suggested by the court community model, makes efforts to change criminal justice extremely difficult. Courts as communities, like most human organizations, can find ways to resist changes in their everyday operations. Policy innovations tend to generate a typical response by members of complex organizations, including court communities, "What's wrong with the way we have been doing things for years?" (Eisenstein et al. 1988, 297).

SIMPLE THEORY, HARD REALITY

We have now completed our task in evaluating the consequences of sentencing reforms as practiced in the United States in the past two decades on courts, prisons, and crime. Readers, including those who support "punitive" crime policies in various forms of "get tough on crime" legislation, who have read this far may be disappointed with the empirical results of this evaluation study. Some blame it on courts for coddling criminals by evading mandatory prison sentences. Others consider all those who belong to the court community responsible for their resistance to change and failure to comply with policy makers' intentions. Many blame legislators for the failure to make substantial investment in the criminal justice system required for its effective implementation. The arguments go on from different perspectives. Adherents of deterrence would argue that the court community's response to crime must be correspondingly bitter and more aggressive by adopting the tough attitudes of the embattled public. Opponents of deterrence would raise some theoretical questions and call for new crime policies. We are not prepared to propose any resolution to these theoretical and ideological issues. But the theory of criminal sentencing reform can provide the overall and clear picture of how key factors are interrelated and how policy consequences revealed in this study should be interpreted.

In formulating crime policy, policy makers adhere to deterrence theory and develop a simple theory that predicts that if the penalties prescribed by the revised statutes become more severe, then violent crime rates will be reduced. By reducing more complex systems of human behavior to such a relatively simplistic form of cause and effect, the legislators make certain assumptions: that judges and others in the court community will strictly adhere to the new laws, making a prison sentence more certain and lengthier, and that criminals are rational persons deterred by swift, certain, and severe punishment actually applied.

Application of the theory of sentencing reform reveals that legislators who make these assumptions have seriously mistaken how the court community would respond to the sentencing reform. This theoretical framework helps explain the rise in violent crime rates due to declines in the certainty and severity of imprisonment actually imposed in jurisdictions that adopted mandatory minimum and presumptive determinate sentencing laws. Accompanied with the advent of determinacy in sentencing has been the uncontrollable explosion of prison populations in state institutions throughout the United States. Sentencing reforms have produced undesirable but inevitable side effects that require immediate and innovative remedies.

What the theory of sentencing reform explains is the reverse of the policy maker's intentions. The theory of sentencing reform reveals widespread resistance to change (noncompliance) associated strongly with the elimination of discretionary control. The court community model explains why the courtroom work group actors behave the way they do on a daily basis. What the theory of sentencing reform actually explains is the basic theme of the present study: a "simple theory" that drives policy makers and laypersons alike to make policy choices based on simple-minded notions of human behavior confronting "hard reality."

The simple theory is what Jay W. Forrester calls the "mental model." The mental model is "fuzzy," "incomplete," and "imprecisely stated." Policy makers tend to use this mental model to communicate in political campaigns. To persuade their policy advocates, certain fundamental assumptions are made but never brought into the open. Moreover, practical consensus often leads to laws and policies that fail in their declared goals or produce unforeseen ensuing difficulties greater than those that have been relieved (Forrester 1971, 54).

This is true for sentencing reform policy. All the arguments based on deterrence and incapacitation reduce to unambiguous and straightforward policy expectations that the revised codes that prescribe harsher penalties will reduce crime rates. Several theoretical assumptions are made regarding the nature of human behavior: criminals are rational people who seek to maximize pleasure and minimize pain, are threatened by infliction of pain, and thus are deterred by legal threats (refraining from crime that causes sanctions). The main thrust of legislative control over judicial decisions in sentencing emerges from the Beccarian assertion that "It is the 'Legislators' that determine the penalties, and it is the duty of magistrates to inflict such penalties exactly as they have been prescribed" (Mannheim 1973, 41). Most observers deny that America has such a "rational, consistent, and even-handed" system of sanctioning that deterrence requires to be effective (Neubauer 1979, 372). Something must be wrong with our intuitive thinking and these theoretical assumptions. Policy actions taken in the form of sentencing reform to alleviate the crime problem can actually make matters worse. Crime rates continue to rise sharply. While the simple theory suggests that the rigidity of the discretionary control promotes uniformity in sentencing, what happens in reality is the opposite. We have demonstrated with strong evidence that the greater the rigidity of legislative control, as in mandatory and determinate sentencing, the higher the degree of internal resistance to change. It should be emphasized that the system of least control of discretion, as in voluntary sentencing guidelines, is most likely to produce desired outcomes. There are chances that policy options guided by intuition can alter the system in the wrong direction.

To recapitulate, we tend to reduce complex reality to simple cause and effect relationships that are proximate in time and space. We are often caught in situations that are much more complicated than we can conceptualize and driven by simple theory to adopt policy options based on simple-minded notions of human behavior. In reality, incentives, such as what motivates a judge's behavior, are enmeshed in complex systems that promote very different responses from those anticipated. The hard reality results in the frustration of intentions by the more complex systems of human interactions described by the court community model. While the simple theory is essentially the operation of "conventional wisdom" in directing policy choices, the "hard reality" is the dynamics of the court community systems.

This study teaches us at least two lessons. One lesson is that severe punishment, lengthier prison sentences prescribed by the revised statutes, is unlikely to be enforced. In light of the counterintuitive nature of the court community systems, one can expect to see more appropriate prison sentences being more predictably imposed. The second lesson is that the dynamics of the court community systems, like that of any other social system, can drive those who belong to the court community to behave in a counter-intuitive manner running against most of what they would normally do in grappling with the crime problem. If compulsory actions have been widely resisted, consider voluntary actions that further compliance.

No further erroneous assumptions should be made about the nature of human behavior or the dynamic behavior of social systems of which we have become a part. What we have learned from this study is not only that the dynamics of court community systems can produce policy outcomes that are sometimes inefficacious, unanticipated, or detrimental, but also that we have so little knowledge about the way in which court community systems behave in response to policy innovations. Before any further policy actions can be taken toward sentencing reform, we must be aware of the possibility that taking these actions will make the problems worse. Research that pertains to the dynamics of court community systems is urgently needed. Then we can expect a far sounder basis for policy actions. But if we still follow our "simple theory" or conventional wisdom in making policy choices, the trends of our past experiences will continue into the "hard reality" of deepening difficulty that frustrates policy intentions.

APPENDIX A

Research Methodology

As the survey of previous evaluations of sentencing reform reviewed in chapter 4 suggests, better research designs are needed to improve the quality of future evaluation. It is crucial to include time-series observations for comparison between pre- and post-reform periods in order to distinguish reform impacts from any preexisting trends in sentencing practices and outcomes. More cases are also needed for comparison if evaluation results are to be generalized for policy considerations. The Panel on Sentencing Research views time-series analysis as one of many possible options (Blumstein et al. 1983, 278). This study endorses this view, and uses pooled cross-sectional time-series data in a quasi-experimental evaluation of sentencing reform impacts in the United States.

Drawing on Donald T. Campbell and his associates (Campbell and Stanley 1966; Cook and Campbell 1979), this study employs an interrupted time-series (ITS), comparison-group quasi-experiment in order to identify patterns of reform impacts across jurisdictions. This goal can be achieved by increasing the number of jurisdictions included. If all or most jurisdictions show the same post-reform impact pattern, the evaluation can draw clear conclusions. However, if different patterns of impacts are found, the conclusion will be ambiguous. This problem calls for a more robust research design. Pooled time-series (PTS) quasi-experiments can address research questions regarding broad policy concerns about reform impacts, and allow crucial policy-relevant variables to be introduced into the analysis as control factors.

This appendix describes measures of the concepts under study and their sources, a conceptual framework for evaluation of sentencing reform impacts in the United States, and research design issues. The discussion then turns to interrupted time-series analyses and specification of impact types. The first evaluation model specification will be applied to the incarceration rate time series in order to illustrate how to identify and overcome statistical problems inherent in pooled time-series data.

173

DATA SOURCES

This evaluation is conducted at the time when criminal sentencing reform policies have been in place in the United States for several years. It is difficult to gather original data for the years before the reforms without financial support for data collection and cooperation from criminal justice officials. Collection of original data for this evaluation demands both time and supporting staff.

A major problem encountered in previous research is that the data on court dispositions are too difficult to acquire, at least in most jurisdictions where evaluations have been completed. The data published by the National Center for State Courts contain only a few annual observations for some jurisdictions and none for many others. Without the data for the pre-reform period, this published data source cannot be used.

To solve this data limitation, this study turns to another source. The National Prisoners Statistics (NPS) of the U.S. Department of Justice's Bureau of Justice Statistics published the data on movement of sentenced prisoners in state and federal institutions. The NPS reports are based on annual surveys of federal, state, and local institutions, prison admissions, and releases of prisoners sentenced to more than one year. The counts of inmate population at year-end are reported with some detailed breakdowns for specific types of admissions and releases. The data represent the number of transactions rather than the number of individual prisoners involved in such movements. Some discrepancies in this data source exist from one jurisdiction to another. But, they are considered not posing serious threat to the analyses in this study.

The new court commitments data approximate the number of total court dispositions by imprisonment. Not all defendants convicted and sentenced to incarceration are committed to state prisons. Jails are facilities for the confinement of convicted offenders sentenced to short-term imprisonment, usually less than a year, but sometimes used to house convicted felons due to overcrowded state facilities. These basic facts vary across jurisdictions. Using NPS new court commitments statistics means that our attention is focused mainly on relatively severe court dispositions. The analysis of these statistics can be thought of as consistent with the goal of evaluating the effects of criminal sentencing policies to increase the certainty and severity of criminal sanctions.

According to the NPS survey methodology, new court commitments include "all inmates who were admitted with all new sentences [and] probation violators entering prison for the first time on the probated offenses." This does not include the inmates readmitted for any sentences for which they had already served some prison time. Nor does it include parole violators with new sentences.[1]

The new court commitments data for the period from 1974 through 1984 were obtained from *Sourcebook of Criminal Justice Statistics* published annually by the Bureau of Justice Statistics since 1976. The earlier data were based on annual reports published in the *National Prisoner Statistics Bulletin*.[2] The data series runs from 1971 to 1984 for the pooled data set and from 1967 to 1984 for some selected states.

Data on the occupancy rate come from the same source that reports national surveys of state adult correctional facilities conducted in 1977, 1979, and 1983 (Flanagan et al. 1980; Flanagan and Jamieson 1988; Parisi et al. 1979). The occupancy rate of these three surveys is transformed into a cross-sectional indicator because these surveys were not conducted annually, and their full rated prison capacity used in calculating the occupancy rate for 1983 was redefined. With only three time points, this time series cannot be used in its raw form. By averaging the occupancy rate of these three years, the data are no longer time series but reflect only cross-sectional variation and should be treated as such. Treated as a cross-sectional variable, the series contains a constant value within each unit.

Prison crowding can be measured in several ways. The average square feet per inmate reflects population density in state prisons. Following the national standard, state prisons with average space

---

1. This definition is used in compiling admission statistics as reported by the U.S. Department of Justice, Bureau of Justice Statistics. For detailed explanatory notes pertaining to particular jurisdictions, see appendix 12 in *Sourcebook of Criminal Justice Statistics—1987* (Flanagan and Jamieson 1988).
2. The *NPS Bulletin* reports the totals of admissions to state institutions without subcategory breakdowns for 1971–73. The estimates of new court commitments are obtained by use of the average proportion of new court commitments among annual admissions for particular states during 1974–84 as a multiplier. The estimated new court commitments are computed by multiplying the reported total admissions with the multiplier obtained previously.

per inmate less than sixty square feet are considered as crowded. Another indicator, percent of rated capacity occupied, measures the extent to which inmates are housed in state facilities in terms of their capacity. The occupancy rate beyond full capacity shows the crowding condition and the occupancy rate below full capacity shows no crowding problem. The prison crowding variable used in this study has a zero value at a perfect equilibrium condition, 100 percent occupied. This variable is computed by subtracting 100 from the occupancy rate (percentage of rated full capacity occupied by the number of total inmates).

The Federal Bureau of Investigation Uniform Crime Report (UCR) publishes data on crimes cleared by arrests, broken down for adults and juveniles (eighteen years old and under). The totals of adult arrests are used in calculation of the rate of new court commitments to state prisons per ten thousand adult arrests. The adult arrests series are moving averaged over the three-year period.

Data on the four major crimes counted in the violent crime index—murder, rape, robbery, and aggravated assault—are also obtained from UCR. This publication does not report incidents of these offenses with breakdowns of the types of weapons used in the commission of the crimes.[3] The UCR series contains observations from 1959 to 1987. The population series used in calculating the crime rate comes from *Statistical Abstract of the United States: 1961, 1968, 1971, 1981, and 1987* published by Bureau of Census of the U.S. Department of Commerce. The crime rate is expressed as the number of officially reported incidents per one hundred thousand resident population.[4]

Finally, the rate of sentenced prisoners in state institutions at year-end per one hundred thousand civilian population is obtained from table 6.18 in *Sourcebook of Criminal Justice Statistics—1987*

---

3. Another data source, Inter-University Consortium for Political and Social Research (ICPSR), provides time-series information about weapons used in crimes known to police from 1967 to 1982. The ICPSR data were excluded from analysis because the series is too short.
4. Estimated resident population includes armed forces stationed in the area. Estimates are as of July 1, except those of decennial censuses are enumerated population as of April 1.

(Flanagan and Jamieson 1988, 487).[5] The rate of prisoners in state institutions is computed from the U.S. Department of Justice national prisoner statistics. Sentenced prisoners refer to those serving sentences of more than one year. The data for 1971–77 include those in the custody of state institutions and the data for 1978–86 represent those under the jurisdiction of state correctional authorities.

EVALUATION MODEL SPECIFICATION

The theory of criminal sentencing reform presents a conceptual framework that guides this evaluation study of sentencing reform impacts (see figure 1.1). A multi-equation system, with lagged endogenous variables, is employed. Using lagged variables, each equation incorporates a temporal sequence so that a reverse causal relationship is ruled out as an implausible argument. That is, variables at time $t+1$ cannot cause an effect in a variable at time t. The lagged endogenous variable system is not underidentified and does not require structural-equation statistical methods, such as two-stage least squares regression, which would be prohibitingly difficult in the context of a pooled time-series design. The statistical method used, generalized least squares regression, also controls for the autoregressive problem of lagged variable models.

This conceptual framework for evaluating sentencing reform impacts can be broken down into four components, each of which can be specified and estimated separately. The first model compares the effects of the five sentencing reform types on the incarceration rate. The second model explores the effects of prison crowding on the incarceration rate in addition to sentencing reform impacts. The third model examines the effects of the five sentencing reform types on the size of the prison population. The fourth model evaluates sentencing reform impacts on violent crime rates.

---

5. The rates for the period before 1980 are based on the civilian population (the resident population less the armed forces stationed in area). Since 1980 the rates are based on the total resident population.

Effect of Reform Type on the Incarceration Rate

This model hypothesizes that sentencing behavior is a function of the type of sentencing reform policy, controlling for previous violent crime rates. The five sentencing reform types are mandatory minimum sentencing laws, mandatory determinate sentencing laws, presumptive determinate sentencing laws, presumptive sentencing guidelines, and voluntary sentencing guidelines. This specification tests the sentencing reform hypothesis that control over sentencing decision will increase the certainty of punishment, measured as the rate of new court commitments to state institutions per ten thousand adult arrests charged with FBI indexed violent offenses or the incarceration rate thereafter.

This specification further explores whether reform type makes any difference in realizing this particular policy goal. There are two basic considerations regarding the likelihood of reform success. Since reform types vary by the degree of legislative control over sentencing decisions, it is probable that reform effects will also vary with reform type. In order to address this concern, sentencing reforms are differentiated as five intervention variables. By this differentiation, each reform type can be evaluated and reform effects can be compared with one another. This specification treats the reforms as five dichotomous variables, each reflecting the year of product of multiplication of the particular reform type's intervention in the time series.

Another consideration involves environmental influences that may affect the incarceration rate independently of the reform's effects. The violent crime rate of the previous year is a strong candidate for inclusion. This model addresses the confounding effects of factors other than the sentencing reform variables. The effects of previous crime rates are what Logan (1975) calls "system strain effect"; Geerken and Gove (1977) refer to these effects as "system overload." As a matter of fact, the system overload hypothesis is generally vague about the relationship between the crime rate and the incarceration rate, bypassing several key organizational variables. A basic argument favoring inclusion of this variable is that "police and judicial resources cannot easily expand to take account of rising crime rates, and thus the enforcement system is overloaded or strained beyond capacity. . . . [T]he ability to capture, convict, and imprison offenders is thus diminished by a rising crime rate," and the certainty of punishment declines (Geerken and Gove 1977, 429).

Taking into account the effect of the crime rate on the incarceration rate, the violent crime rate is introduced into the evaluation model with a one-year lag period. It is expected that each of the five types of sentencing reforms will increase the incarceration rate significantly, controlling for the violent crime rate in the states. The evaluation specification can be expressed as follows:

$$IR_{it} = f(RF1_{it}, RF2_{it}, RF3_{it}, RF4_{it}, RF5_{it}, VCR_{it-1})$$

where IR_{it} is the incarceration rate for the ith state at time t; $RF1_{it}$ through $RF5_{it}$ represent the five types of sentencing reform; and VCR_{it-1} denotes the violent crime rate per one hundred thousand civilians for the ith state at time $t-1$.

A lack of association between reform innovations and the incarceration rate indicates that the sentencing reform model fails to explain the actual implementation process. The absence of this postulated relationship further suggests the likelihood, as the court community model suggests, that internal resistance and adaptive responses are present. With this evaluation specification, the possible effect of the rising crime rate is controlled for in estimating the effects of sentencing reforms on the incarceration rate.

Reform Effects on the Incarceration Rate and the Degree of Prison Crowding

The second evaluation model specifies another component of sentencing reform impacts by differentiating states on the basis of the degree of their prison crowding problem. This model addresses two basic hypotheses. Sentencing reform models posit an increase in the incarceration rate in response to restrictions on sentencing discretion to use nonincarcerative alternatives. The court-community researchers argue that the use of incarceration will decline where correctional resources are scarce, particularly when prisons are crowded to or beyond capacity available to accommodate inflow of inmate admissions (Eisenstein and Jacob 1977, 57; Eisenstein et al. 1988, 301; Nardulli et al. 1988, 293; Rosett and Cressey 1976, 91). This argument predicts judicial responses to prison crowding by lowering the incarceration rate. If this prediction is accurate, the higher the degree of prison crowding, the lower the incarceration rate, other things being equal. The policy issue addressed here is whether prison crowding is a determinant of policy success in increasing the certainty of imprisonment.

Due to data limitations, the prison crowding measure requires special treatment. A value of this prison crowding measure, as noted above, is the occupancy rate above or below 100 percent; it is computed by subtracting 100 from the occupancy rate. Depending on the intervention dates of particular states, three observations (1977, 1979, and 1983) or less where applicable will be averaged to represent post-reform averaged prison crowding values. This averaged prison crowding measure reflects cross-sectional variation in prison crowding following the intervention. Thus, its regression coefficient should be interpreted as the cross-sectional effects of prison crowding beyond the direct effects of sentencing reforms on the incarceration rate.

This evaluation model specification suggests this relationship:

$$IR_{it} = f(RF_{it}, PC_{it}, VCR_{it-1})$$

where IR_{it} is the incarceration rate for the ith state at time t; RF_{it} is the intervention term for the ith state at time t; PC_{it} is the post-reform averaged prison crowding measure; and VCR_{it-1} denotes the violent crime rate per one hundred thousand civilians for the ith state at time $t-1$, serving as a control variable. The post-reform prison crowding measure is assigned a value of zero prior to the reforms, and takes its averaged actual value throughout the post-reform period.

Reform Impact on Prison Populations

Since the early 1970s prison populations in state institutions throughout the country grew at a rapid rate. The growth in prison populations can be attributed to variation in inmate admissions, lengths of inmate sentences, and early releases. These three variables reflect changes in the number of arrests and indictments and composition of cases processed in the criminal justice system. In addition to this linkage, criminal rules and procedures under the sentencing reforms also have an impact on sentencing outcomes and prison populations.

The policy effects on prison populations merit careful investigation because most state prisons have been operating beyond their rated capacities. In the era of tight budgets to run state prisons, the explosion of the prison population poses a major problem with crowding. Reluctant to expand prison capacity, some states adopt emergency parole release to acquire more space, while others encourage more probationary sentences for convicted felons (Blumstein et al. 1983, 225; Galvin 1983, 5; Petersilia et al. 1985, 1). Whether the rapid growth in inmate populations can be attributed to the policies is an empirical question to be tested with real data. This model evaluates effects of each of the five sentencing reform policies on prison populations. Both the incarceration rate and the crime rate are included in the model for control purposes. A lag period of one year is specified for delayed effects of all variables included in this model.

It seems conceptually sound to specify a one-year period for delayed effects. First, most reforms did not take effect in January of the intervention year. Second, case processing time from arrest to final disposition varies widely from one jurisdiction to another and also depends on the mode of disposition, which ranges from about one hundred days for a guilty plea to more than two hundred days for a trial (Boland et al. 1983, 22; Boland et al. 1987, 9; Boland et al. 1988, 8). Thus, at least one year is needed to allow the reform to produce its effects.

This evaluation model is specified as follows:

$$\text{IPR}_{it+1} = f(\text{RF1}_{it}, \text{RF2}_{it}, \text{RF3}_{it}, \text{RF4}_{it}, \text{RF5}_{it}, \text{IR}_{it}, \text{VCR}_{it})$$

where IPR_{it+1} is the rate of sentenced inmates per one hundred thousand population for the ith state at time $t+1$; RF1_{it} through RF5_{it} represent the five types of sentencing reform; IR_{it} is the incarceration rate for the ith state at time t; and VCR_{it} denotes the violent crime rate per one hundred thousand population for the ith state at time t.

Reform Impact on the Violent Crime Rate

Crime control was one of the major driving forces behind enactment of the new sentencing policies in the United States, particularly the mandatory and determinate sentencing laws. A clear legislative intent of these policies was to increase the certainty and severity of imprisonment. From an anticrime perspective, an increase in certainty and severity of punishment is expected to deter violent crime. The emphasis on deterrence is placed on violent offenses committed by persistent or habitual offenders or with the use of firearms and other dangerous weapons.

The sentencing reforms draw support from a deterrence theory that predicts reduced crime rates as incarceration increases and legal sanctions become harsher. Both the mandatory minimum and determinate sentencing laws modify criminal codes and procedures to require the use of incarcerative sentences for several classes of designated offenses while making actual prison time to be served before offenders are eligible for early parole release more predictable.

From the deterrence perspective, crime rates respond to variation in legal sanctions. Thus, evaluation of the reforms should include the incarceration rate. To rule out the alternate explanation based on the overload hypothesis, the incarceration rate reported for the previous calendar year is used. The model for crime reduction effects of the reforms can be specified as:

$$VCR_{it+1} = f(RF1_{it}, RF2_{it}, RF3_{it}, RF4_{it}, RF5_{it}, IR_{it})$$

where VCR_{it+1} is the violent crime rate per one hundred thousand population for the ith state at time $t+1$; $RF1_{it}$ through $RF5_{it}$ represent the five types of sentencing reform; IR_{it} is the incarceration rate for the ith state at time t.

This evaluation model can also examine each of the four major offense types, including murder, rape, robbery, and aggravated assault. The effects of the new laws may vary in some fashion with crime type. It is possible that some offenders switch from certain offenses carrying severe penalties to other offenses (Deutsch and Alt 1977; Loftin and McDowall 1981; Luckenbill 1984; Pierce and Bowers 1981). This argument can be evaluated by disaggregating the violent crime measure into the different crime types.

RESEARCH DESIGN

In laboratory settings, scientists conduct an experiment to explain and predict physical phenomena. In social sciences, scientists study social phenomena in field settings under which random assignment and experimental conditions are unattainable and well beyond control. In social research, scientists observe behavioral responses to treatment that are introduced to the subjects in their natural settings. Under certain circumstances, social evaluation is uninterpretable. In order to improve the quality of research in field settings, researchers turn to quasi-experiments that are both feasible and control for various threats to design validity.

In the evaluation process, researchers are confronted with a series of frequent threats to research validity. A good research design is one that rules out most plausible rival hypotheses. To determine the quality of research, attention should be paid to two basic validity questions. Internal validity concerns the interpretability of research results; external validity concerns the generalizability of research findings. As Campbell and Stanley describe:

> Internal validity is the basic minimum without which any experiment is uninterpretable: Did in fact the experimental treatments make a difference in this specific experimental instance? External validity asks the question of generalizability: To what populations, settings, treatment variables, and measurement variables can this effect be generalized? (1966, 5)

The extraneous factors that threaten evaluations of policies like sentencing reforms include "history" (other events coincident with the treatment), "maturation" (a process of behavioral changes due to the passage of time or growth), "instrumentation" (changes in the measurement instrument), "mortality" (loss of samples from the observed groups, plus interaction effects among treatment, subjects, and environments that could preclude generalization about evaluation results across cases and environments (Campbell and Stanley 1966, 5).

One of the quasi-experimental designs that have great potential to minimize threats to research validity is the multiple time-series design (Campbell and Stanley 1963, 55) or interrupted time-series with comparison groups design (Bingham and Felbinger 1989, 110; Cook and Campbell 1979, 214). Cook and Campbell argue that "The ability to test for the threat of history is the major strength of the control group time-series design. Local history (selection x history) can be problematic, though, if the groups differ from each other considerably; one group may well experience a set of unique events that the other does not" (1979, 215).

A statistical technique specially developed for this research design is what is known as interrupted time-series analysis or intervention analysis (Box and Tiao 1965, 1975; Glass 1968; Hibbs 1977; McCleary and Hay 1980). The design received wide acceptance in the areas of public policy studies. Examples of research that use this design are studies by Campbell and Ross (1968), Hilton (1984), Maxwell (1981), Ross et al. (1982), and Wagenaar (1983) in traffic safety; by Deutsch and Alt (1977), Flemming et al. (1980), Loftin and McDowall (1984), and McPhethers et al. (1984) in criminal justice; by Albritton (1979), Albritton and Bahry (1979), and Albritton and Witayapanyanon (1989) in social welfare; and by Lewis-Beck and Alford (1980), Moe (1982), Moran (1985), and Wood (1988) in federal regulatory policy.

In these studies, the interrupted time-series technique is applied to the treatment or experimental group and the control group(s). The statistical results for these respective groups are then compared for interpretation. To generalize evaluation results, one could increase the number of both groups. Since random assignment to groups is not feasible in most events, comparison results cannot be interpreted simply. If the groups respond to the treatment in a consistent fashion, the interaction effects between the treatment and the group environment are not present.

Within the same family of multiple time-series designs, the pooled time-series quasi-experimental design is the most powerful. This design may provide a universal model, but it also has a drawback. The pooled time-series design has both pros and cons. Pooling data across both case and time dimensions can be an extraordinarily robust research design that allows the investigation of causal dynamics across multiple cases and the potential cause over time in particular cases. Many of the methodological limitations are specific to either cross-sectional or time-serial design. Many such threats to valid generalization can be jointly controlled by incorporating both space and time into the analysis. Note that the pooled design is desirable but difficult to implement (Stimson 1985, 916). To date, most of these statistical problems remain unsolved. No computer software that allows sufficient flexibility in model specification to deal with all problems of the design has been written. Pooled time-series analysis computer software packages that are available impose severe restrictions on selection of alternative estimators. Making a choice between these competing models requires a basic understanding about their statistical assumptions. The use of this design has been discouraged by this methodological technicality and the lack of computer software.

Pooled time-series statistical analysis has its roots in econometrics. This econometric contribution to scientific research in general and evaluation methodology in particular receives much less attention in social sciences than it should. Since the works of Zellner (1962), who emphasized a system of time-series equations, and Balestra and Nerlove (1966), who emphasized cross-sectional equations of several panels, applications of pooled time-series analysis to research problems have been less than enthusiastic. Introducing both time and space into research complicates analysis, and some considerations preclude the use of pooled time-series analysis.

In the pooled time series, the emphasis is placed on the pattern of causal relationship for the full, pooled population, rather than on specific groups of population. The price one has to pay for the generalizability of research is the loss of detailed descriptions of specific subpopulations. There is a trade-off between the gain in external validity and the loss in internal validity. Moreover, a number of statistical problems remain unsolved in the use of pooled time-series analysis. The only good description of how to apply pooled time-series analysis outside econometrics circles is Stimson's 1985 article in the *American Journal of Political Science*. Stimson provides a general framework for applications of alternative estimators to a research problem. For Stimson, the choice of a situationally suitable estimator requires a basic understanding of the data structure and corresponding assumptions about statistical problems inherent in the pooled data. For instance, with a data structure that resembles multiwave panels of cross-sectional units with a few time points, one should pay attention to problems in the spatial domain, such as wide variance among cross-sectional units. With a data structure that has extended time-series observations of a few cross-sectional units, one should attend to time-series problems, such as autocorrelation over time.

More discussion on several aspects of pooled time-series analysis can be found in the literature, particularly in the works of Algina and Swaminathan (1979) and Simonton (1977) for analysis issues in cross-sectional, time-series quasi-experiments; Johnston (1984), Judge et al. (1982), and Kmenta (1971) for theoretical description; Fuller and Battese (1974), Hannan and Young (1977), Maddala (1971), Mundlak (1978), Nerlove (1971), and Wallace and Hussain (1969) for the use of error components models; Parks (1967) for the use of pooled time-series analysis in the presence of autoregressive and heteroscedastic errors; and Berk et al. (1979), Scholz and Wei (1986), Sirisumphand (1987), Sutton (1987), and Zuk and Thompson (1982) for research application. None of these cited works deals with problems present in both spatial and temporal domains of the data structure that has a large number of cross-sectional units measured at extended time points.

CONCLUSION

In this appendix, four analytical models were specified to evaluate the impacts of sentencing reform policies on courts, prisons, and crime in the United States. Taking into account other external influences, these model specifications can estimate more accurately the net effects of sentencing reforms on the respective outcome measures selected. When appropriately applied, the pooled time-series design will yield evaluation results from which researchers can generalize more accurately about policy performance and outcomes across virtually all jurisdictions in the United States.

A reason policy analysts draw back from implementing pooled time-series quasi-experiments is that pooled data can complicate statistical analysis. To address this methodological issue, this appendix identified three major statistical problems frequently encountered in analyzing pooled time-series data: unit effects, time-serial autocorrelation, and heteroscedasticity. The four-step least squares technique outlined above provided general procedures to diagnose and overcome these statistical problems. Depending on the structure of pooled data, certain steps may be omitted in these procedures. Determining whether the design is dominated by time, space, or both problem dimensions requires diagnoses of OLS residuals in the first step. When a particular statistical problem poses no threat to a certain regression assumption, data transformation is not required in that step. When confronted with all three problems, which will be common in studies of comparative public policy across a number of cases over a long time period, the four-step least squares technique appears to be an effective and efficient solution.

Interrupted time-series quasi-experiments are now common in the study of policy impacts. This evaluation approach is generally conducted on a case-by-case basis. Policy performance and outcomes are then generalized according to the evaluation results of particular cases. This preliminary approach provides detailed case-by-case evaluation results essential for further pooled time-series quasi-experiments, particularly when these results are ambiguous and thus difficult to generalize.

However, both interrupted time-series and pooled time-series experiments are complementary candidates for any study of comparative public policy, particularly for a comparative study of public policy in the American states. The pooled time-series quasi-experimental design offers statistical significance tests of policy impacts across jurisdictions evaluated. Thus, it maximizes generalizability. When both designs are combined, they enhance each other synergetically to provide both internal and external validity to evaluation conclusion.

APPENDIX B

Statistical Procedure

This appendix presents interrupted time-series analysis based on Box and Tiao's technique and pooled time-series analysis according to the four-step least squares technique. Diagnostic statistics obtained during the four-step least squares estimation are also provided.

INTERRUPTED TIME-SERIES ANALYSIS: BOX AND TIAO'S TECHNIQUE

In the initial phase of data analysis, individual states are evaluated by use of interrupted time-series technique. The results of individual states' case studies are then compared. If the results reveal a clear pattern of impacts the new policies have in the same direction, then we can proceed to pool these time series across jurisdictions for a significance test of the overall impact estimate. If the results are mixed with policy impacts of different directions and forms, a more complex conceptual model for evaluation must be developed. The process of model development will be discussed in the next section.

A basic difference exists between interrupted time-series and multiple regression models in policy evaluation research. The ordinary regression technique includes other relevant factors in the causal modeling process in determining policy impacts. By contrast, the interrupted time-series analysis evaluates policy effects by modeling the time-series process according to an autoregressive integrated moving average (ARIMA) model. Any measurable shift in a time series associated with the policy intervention may be thought of as a behavioral change in the target population in response to the new policy. The interrupted time-series analysis has been increasingly used in conjunction with quasi-experimental designs.

This analytical procedure as applied to policy evaluation research draws on the pioneering work of Box and Tiao (1965,

189

1975). Less theoretical discussion of the Box and Tiao procedure has appeared in social science circles (Glass et al. 1975; McCleary and Hay 1980). In the modeling routine, both autocorrelation and partial autocorrelation diagrams of time series are used to identify the so-called noise structure in terms of an ARIMA process. An appropriate ARIMA model that adequately fits the noise structure of time series requires a set of parameter estimates that satisfy diagnostic tests. The autoregressive parameters must be within the stationarity range. The moving average parameter must be invertible. A statistically adequate model is one with parameters that satisfy either stationarity or invertibility criteria, whichever is appropriate, and one whose residuals are random or white noise. The model adequacy test yields a Q statistic statistically insignificant when the residual series is reduced to a white noise process (Box and Jenkins 1976, 209).

The next step involves specification of policy impacts by adding the response component to the same equation. The same modeling routine reiterates with specification, estimation, and diagnosis. The specification of policy response enables us to evaluate competing patterns of policy effects. A temporary impact may be evaluated by specification of the *pulse* function. For a policy impact that is permanent, a *step* function may be specified. Finally, a change in slope model of policy impact can be specified as a *ramp* function. The dynamics of policy responses can be considered by adding the *delta* function to specification of the response component.

The evaluation model can be expressed with this algebraic relationship:

$$Y_t = I_t + N_t,$$

where Y_t is the time series of policy interest; I_t is a policy response or impact component to be specified as a function of δ (rate of change), ω (initial impact estimate), and P_t, S_t, or R_t; N_t represents a noise structure of the observed time series Y_t. When the permanent policy impact is postulated, I is specified as a step function (S_t). The term S_t takes a value of 0 prior to the intervention and a value of 1 throughout the implementation period. For a pulse function (P_t) of the temporary effect model where $I = P_t$, the term P_t takes a value of 1 at the intervention date and a value of 0 elsewhere. When the intervention changes the slope in the series

Y_t, I is specified as a ramp function (R_t). Prior to the intervention date, R_t is coded as 0 and as a time counter during the post-intervention period.

For illustration of a step function specification, the relationship

$$Y_t = \frac{\omega}{(1 - \delta_1 B)} S_t + \{C + \frac{1}{(1 - \phi_1 B)}\} a_t$$

can be used to evaluate a long-term policy impact on the time series of a first-order autoregressive process, AR(1). The noise component can be replaced by an appropriate ARIMA model. With the noise component adequately modeled, the impact estimate, ω, can be estimated from the data. Modeling policy impacts involves an iterative process in testing rival hypotheses of competing impact types (Albritton and Witayapanyanon 1989; Box and Tiao 1975; Hibbs 1977; McCleary and Hay 1980; McDowall et al. 1980).

POOLED TIME-SERIES ANALYSIS: FOUR-STEP LEAST SQUARES TECHNIQUE

To a political science audience, Stimson (1985) proposes a statistical framework of pooled time-series analysis as a guide in selecting one appropriate estimator among several alternatives. Stimson distinguishes two basic types of pooled data and several kinds of inherent statistical problems accompanying them. The distinction between the two types of pooled data explains the data structure as (1) space dominant when it contains a large number of cross-sectional units (N) relative to the number of observations over time (T), N > T, and (2) time dominant when it contains more observations over time than the number of cross-sectional units, T > N. Space dominance is a research situation in which one employs multiwave panels that contain only a few time points. On the other hand, time dominance is a situation in which one employs multiple time series drawn from only a few units. The first situation implies that the analysis is focused on causality in the spatial domain, and statistical problems may be inherent in the cross-sectional dimension. The second situation implies that the analysis is focused on causality in the temporal domain, and statistical problems may be inherent in the time-serial dimension.

From a methodological perspective, a good research design is one that contains a large number of observations in both time and space. This design emphasizes causality in both temporal and spatial domains, thereby introducing statistical problems that emanate from both time and space. Both cross-sectional and time-serial problems pose serious threats to the analysis of a study with N approximately equal to T. As a matter of fact, both time and space should receive equal attention in either of these two conditions: the multiwave panels design with T approaching N and the multiple time-series design with N approaching T.

From the statistical perspective, as both N and T become large and approach one another, a tendency toward statistical problems in both time and space domains becomes greater. While the design of this type is ideal for design validity, its analytical complication is a major drawback. Little has been done in pooled time-series literature to develop a method that can overcome statistical problems in both dimensions, particularly those encountered in this study. Stimson's technique imposes several assumptions that are restrictive and difficult to meet in practice.

Stimson admits that no appropriate estimator has yet been developed for this special case. In his example data, there are twenty-four annual observations from 1957 to 1980 for eight regions of the United States. The design is clearly time dominant with a manageable number of units. Following his decision rules, the time-serial generalized least squares procedure, GLS-ARMA with dummy variables to control for cross-sectional variance, is appropriate. The use of GLS-ARMA with dummy variables becomes more complicated as N approaches T.

In comparative analysis of public policy in the American states, if each state contains about the same length of study period, N becomes larger than T. While this design becomes a space dominant case, it does not mean that problems associated with time are superseded by cross-sectional influence. The 1971–84 period is long enough to be complicated by time-serial problems.

The works of Sirisumphand (1987) and Zuk and Thompson (1982) employ time-series data pooled across a large number of country samples, each of which covers extended periods under study. A combination of time and space problems is present in this kind of research design. The Zuk and Thompson study, for example, includes ten annual observations drawn from sixty-six countries. Similarly, the Sirisumphand study observes and evaluates public policy trade-off choices in thirty-eight less developing countries during a ten-year period. Both studies are space-dominant designs of multiwave panels. But with ten annual observations for each country, they resemble the multiple-time-series design that attempts to generalize about causality over time.

According to Stimson (1985, 929), when both unit effects and timewise autocorrelation are present in a cross-sectional-dominant case, there is no appropriate solution yet developed. Zuk and Thompson employ the GLS-ARMA procedure with lagged dependent variables. The use of lagged endogenous variables helps improve model prediction and also serves another purpose, reduction of unit effects. As a general rule, this solution to unit effects should be avoided because the lagged endogenous variable introduces multicollinearity to the analysis. Alternatively, one can use dummy variables to cope with unit effects in conjunction with the GLS-ARMA procedure. The use of dummy variables jeopardizes efficiency due to substantial loss in degrees of freedom and lack of model parsimony (including the least number of estimates possible).

Step 1: Residual Analysis of OLS Regression

In the initial step, the ordinary least squares (OLS) procedure is applied to pooled data under the assumption of random errors with constant variance. The OLS estimator is justifiable only when this restricted assumption holds. Under the random errors assumption, residual means are zero within units and time periods. This condition is satisfied when pooled data are homogenous in time-series level across units and in panel means over time. With homogeneity in the data, the model fits observations to a single regression line with a common intercept. When pooled data are heterogenous in time-series level across units, residual means of those units deviant from the norm are nonzero. This spatial heterogeneity is known as unit effects. When panels of cross-sectional observations change in their means over time, the OLS residuals contain nonzero means for different panels. This kind of temporal heterogeneity is known as time effects.

Under the assumption of constant variance, residual variances (RVAR) or standard deviation (RSTD) are equal among all units and time periods. The residuals are homoscedastic when RSTDs of the ith units and the tth time periods are approximately equal.

Stimson (1985, 940) uses the residual variance ratio, the ratio of actual variance to expected variance, as an indication of homoscedasticity. Similarly, the residual standard deviation ratio serves as a diagnostic indication of homoscedasticity. As the ith units contain residual variances approximate to the model residual variance, their residual standard deviation ratios approach unity. When residual standard deviation ratios are well above or below unity across units, cross-sectional heteroscedasticity is a problem. When residual variances become smaller or larger for the tth panels than the overall residual variance, temporal heteroscedasticity is a problem.

The OLS procedure can be expressed in algebraic form as follows:

$$Y_{it} = \beta_0 + \beta_k X_{k,it} + \varepsilon_{it} \tag{1}$$

where Y_{it} is a series that contains observations of the ith units at the tth time periods for the dependent variable; $X_{k,it}$ represents observations of the ith units at the tth time periods for the kth independent variables; β_0 is a common intercept; β_k is a set of the kth corresponding regression weights; ε_{it} is a series of residuals randomly distributed with zero mean and constant variance across units and time periods. This OLS specification is adequate when the assumption of random errors and constant variance holds.

Thus, the first step in the analysis begins with OLS specification and diagnoses of the residuals. For illustration, the incarceration rate model will be employed to explain this estimation process. There are six variables in this model: five types of criminal sentencing reform policies and the prior year's violent crime rate. A series of residuals is obtained from regression of the incarceration rate on these six variables using an OLS specification.

Table B.1 presents results of residuals analysis with simple diagnostic statistics based on OLS residuals. For each unit and time period, mean, standard deviation, and standard deviation ratio are computed for diagnoses. Nonzero means across all units suggest that cross-sectional heterogeneity or unit effects problems are present. There are thirty-two states with means below zero, ranging from -22 for Alaska to -1166 for Hawaii. These negative means indicate that these thirty-two states have their own regression lines because their time series are at levels well below the norm. These figures show how far their regression lines are below the common regression line. These negative residual means are offset by positive means, particularly those found in Kentucky (1,049), Mississippi (2,061), South Carolina (2,669), and South Dakota (1,673). These four states are those that have levels of incarceration rate well above the grand regression line and thus they require intercepts higher than the common intercept. More than two-thirds of the total states deviate widely from the norm over the period under study. That is, the American states are heterogenous in the use of incarceration, at least during 1971–84.

On the time dimension, residual means are nonzero for all years. The means are all positive, with decreasing values from 248 in 1971 to 50 in 1975. For five years since 1976 all means are negative, moving away from the regression line for three years and turning back toward the regression line. Since 1981 all means are positive and increase in size from 36 in 1981 to 120 in 1984. This pattern suggests positive serial correlation in the residual means. That is, on the average the model residuals are positively correlated within states. This particular problem will be explored more closely in step 3.

Another OLS assumption concerns constant variance in the residuals. When the OLS estimator produces equal residual variances across units and over time, the error structure is said to be homoscedastic. Table B.1 also displays RSTDs of the ith units and the tth time periods. From the OLS procedure, the overall RSTD is obtained by taking a square root of residual variance, 731,769.84, which amounts to 855.44. With this information, it is expected that each unit and time period would have an actual RSTD that is approximately equal to the overall RSTD. When the actual RSTD approaches the expected RSTD, according to the constant variance assumption, the RSTD ratio approaches unity. The RSTD ratios for the ith units indicate whether cross-sectional heteroscedasticity is a problem. Temporal heteroscedasticity is a problem when the RSTD ratios for the tth time periods are well above or below unity.

As shown in table B.1, the RSTDs vary widely across units within a broad range from 104.39 for Michigan to 2,906.87 for South Carolina. The range of corresponding RSTD ratios from 0.122 to 3.398 indicates that the residual structure is heteroscedastic in this dimension. In the time dimension, the RSTDs range from 578.82 for 1983 to 1364.95 for 1971. The corresponding RSTD ratios within the range between 0.677 and 1.596 show that

Table B.1

Diagnostic Statistics from OLS Regression on the Incarceration Rate:
Residual Analysis of Unit Effects and Heteroscedasticity

State/Year	Residual Mean	Residual Standard Deviation (RSTD)	Actual to Expected RSTD Ratio[a]
a) Unit-Based Diagnostic Statistics			
Alabama	649.58	900.37	1.05
Alaska	-22.13	473.98	0.55
Arizona	-461.86	494.67	0.58
Arkansas	125.32	378.65	0.44
California	-422.43	479.46	0.56
Colorado	-329.14	340.74	0.40
Connecticut	-152.31	290.02	0.34
Delaware	-697.89	713.58	0.83
Florida	-124.52	200.56	0.23
Hawaii	-1166.01	1173.51	1.37
Idaho	-51.92	199.94	0.23
Illinois	-392.52	586.98	0.69
Indiana	182.33	410.24	0.48
Iowa	-179.53	314.76	0.37
Kansas	-519.94	534.52	0.62
Kentucky	1048.50	1174.77	1.37
Louisiana	83.08	298.48	0.35
Maine	260.97	724.18	0.85
Maryland	761.41	937.25	1.10
Massachusetts	-624.92	639.38	0.75
Michigan	38.54	104.39	0.12
Minnesota	-586.86	688.32	0.80
Mississippi	2061.14	2423.05	2.83
Missouri	-408.42	424.12	0.50
Nebraska	-697.46	757.04	0.88
Nevada	-144.29	312.15	0.36

State/Year	Residual Mean	Residual Standard Deviation (RSTD)	Actual to Expected RSTD Ratio[a]
New Hampshire	-351.29	482.28	0.56
New Jersey	-477.29	570.78	0.67
New Mexico	-286.40	354.20	0.41
New York	-282.68	318.38	0.37
North Carolina	983.29	1048.81	1.23
North Dakota	-70.14	360.99	0.42
Ohio	-122.08	258.06	0.30
Oklahoma	534.15	617.70	0.72
Oregon	-340.20	372.03	0.43
Pennsylvania	-449.51	572.45	0.67
Rhode Island	-882.73	894.50	1.05
South Carolina	2669.02	2906.87	3.40
South Dakota	1673.34	1830.73	2.14
Tennessee	721.60	789.89	0.92
Texas	-127.33	214.20	0.25
Utah	-826.12	836.36	0.98
Virginia	-224.14	363.41	0.42
Washington	-554.53	558.26	0.65
West Virginia	784.57	1058.78	1.24
Wisconsin	-545.61	556.30	0.65
Wyoming	-54.64	218.27	0.26

b) Time-Based Diagnostic Statistics

71	305.49	1364.95	1.60
72	162.78	959.19	1.12
73	129.09	970.80	1.13
74	86.66	1022.86	1.20
75	94.10	1014.65	1.19
76	-146.51	827.76	0.97
77	-234.17	674.67	0.79

Table B.1 (continued)

State/Year	Residual Mean	Residual Standard Deviation (RSTD)	Actual to Expected RSTD Ratio[a]
78	-262.99	648.30	0.76
79	-195.26	691.89	0.81
80	-114.70	695.88	0.81
81	-5.26	767.71	0.90
82	65.87	735.82	0.86
83	46.71	578.82	0.68
84	68.19	587.33	0.69

[a]Expected RSTD for homoscedasticity = 855.44; range of unit-based RSTD ratios = 0.12–3.40; range of time-based RSTD ratios = 0.68–1.60.

temporal heteroscedasticity is also present. It is clear that residual variances are more unequal across units than over time. Based on this comparison, one can conclude that heteroscedasticity is more problematic in the cross-sectional dimension. The weighted least squares (WLS) procedure will be employed in step 4 to cope with cross-sectional heteroscedasticity.

Step 2: A Solution for Unit Effects

This step deals with the unit-effects problem caused by heterogeneity in time-series levels among units. There are two alternatives available: least squares with dummy variables (LSDV) and generalized least squares with error components (GLSE). The LSDV estimator treats unit effects as a series of "fixed" constants that can be estimated from the data. The other alternative, GLSE, treats unit effects as a "stochastic" or "random" process with a constant variance.

The distinction between the two alternatives is the assumption about the behavior of unit effects. With the LSDV procedure, nonzero residual means across units can be treated as a condition of the data without any assumption about their distribution. A set of N (without a constant term) or N-1 (with a constant term) dummy variables can be used to overcome the problem of nonzero residual means. The LSDV estimator fits N regression lines to the data to achieve zero residual means across units. The model contains N differential intercepts, one for each unit. The distance from the ith differential intercept to the intercept mean is approximate to the OLS residual mean for the ith unit. This solution yields the residuals series that is stationary around zero mean.

The GLSE solution assumes that differences between the ith intercept and the intercept mean are stochastic with some constant variance that can be estimated. With this assumption, the total OLS residual variance can be decomposed into two components: one due to errors and one due to unit effects. Using this information, the ratio of error variance to total variance, ρ, can be calculated for Aitken's generalized least squares procedure (Balestra and Nerlove 1966, 595; Johnston 1984, 401; Maddala 1971, 342; Stimson 1985, 924).

The estimation of GLSE can also be achieved by application of OLS on transformed data (Hausman 1978, 1262; Johnston 1984, 404; Judge et al. 1982, 494). This transformation relies on the estimates of the two variance components. In a general usage of the GLSE estimator, both unit and time effects can be modeled with estimates of variance components due to unit and time (Fuller and Battese 1974; Kmenta 1971; Wallace and Hussain 1969). This procedure is inappropriate when the model is mis-specified either due to omitted relevant variables or to serial correlation (Hausman 1978). The use of GLSE is also limited to the assumption of stochastic unit and time effects. Hausman provides a statistical test that evaluates the null hypothesis of no misspecification (1978, 1263). Rejection of this hypothesis means that treatment of unit effects as stochastic is inadequate.

Another solution to unit effects is proposed by Judge et al. (1982). This solution, FE-GLS, treats unit effects as fixed constants that can be removed from estimation. What makes this solution different from LSDV is how fixed effects are treated in the estimation process. While LSDV estimates the fixed effects through the use of dummy variables, FE-GLS removes them through data transformation. From the FE-GLS transformation approach, the problem is overcome by reducing time-series levels of all units to zero. As a result, the time series fluctuates around a constant mean of zero and becomes stationary across all units. The transformation by taking deviations from unit means yields a new series centered around the same level. In other words, homogeneity in a time-series level is achieved. Under this situation, all units share the same regression line with a zero intercept. Thus, residual means become zero for all units. This procedure yields equivalent results with smaller standard errors compared with LSDV results. Finally, this FE-GLS specification is more parsimonious than LSDV because it does not require the use of dummy variables (Judge et al. 1980, 329–31).

The FE-GLS procedure can be carried out through OLS regression on transformed data. The FE-GLS specification can be written as follows:

$$Y^*_{it} = \beta^*_0 + \beta^*_k X^*_{k,it} + e^*_{it} \tag{2}$$

where both dependent and independent variables are transformed in the form:

$$Y^*_{it} = Y_{it} - \overline{Y}_i$$

The new intercept reduces to zero because of transformation on a constant. The residuals series contains zero means across all units and becomes stationary with fluctuations around zero. One should note that the error structure remains serially correlated and heteroscedastic. With either FE-GLS or LSDV solution, within unit variance due to nonzero residual means are eliminated. Another source of unequal residual variance is within-unit variance due to serial correlation.

Among the three estimators considered, LSDV is the least efficient and both FE-GLS and GLSE are equally efficient. Both LSDV and FE-GLS are equivalent solutions to fixed unit effects. A solution to random unit effects, GLSE, can address the problem of nonzero residual means due to time, which is frequently encountered in multiwave panels. Because the problem with time encountered in this study is serial correlation, the GLSE solution is inadequate.

In order to demonstrate how fixed unit effects are treated, pooled time-series analysis is performed using the LSDV estimator in comparison with the FE-GLS procedure. As shown in table B.2, both procedures are identical in their regression estimates but LSDV, with more parameters to estimate in the model, produces larger standard errors and substantial degrees of freedom lost in computation. The LSDV specification can be written as follows:

$$Y_{it} = \beta_0 + \beta_k X_{k,it} + \mu_i + \varepsilon_{it} \tag{3}$$

Table B.2

Comparison of Estimation Efficiency between Fixed-Effects Generalized
Least Squares (FE-GLS) and Least Squares with Dummy Variables
(LSDV) Solutions to Unit Effects

	FE-GLS		LSDV	
	β	s.e.	β	s.e.
$RF1_t$	-113.773	48.227	-113.773	50.027
$RF2_t$	-348.233	98.376	-348.233	102.048
$RF3_t$	258.871	129.310	258.871	134.136
$RF4_t$	48.930	167.843	48.930	174.107
$RF5_t$	-186.746	103.456	-186.746	107.316
VCR_{t-1}	-52.396	25.211	-52.396	26.152

	FE-GLS	LSDV
Total Variables	6	6 + 47 = 53
Degrees of Freedom	651	604
M.S.E.	156,148.11	168,020.53

where μ_i is a series of constants that account for unit effects and β_0 is a common intercept, a mean of all N differential intercepts. The ith differential intercepts, $\beta_i = \beta_0 + \mu_i$, can be estimated through OLS with N unit dummy variables with no constant. This specification yields the residuals series, ε_{it}, with zero means within all units.

Table B.3 presents the estimates of β_i and μ_i with t tests against the null hypothesis of $\mu_i = 0$. It is found that variation in unique intercepts is substantial within the range between 394.6 for Hawaii and 4,167.3 for South Carolina with the mean of 1,446.8. That is, the incarceration rate in Hawaii is 1,052.2 lower than the norm and South Carolina's level is 2,720.5 higher than the overall average. The series of μ_i approximates to the series of within-unit residual means displayed in table B.3. There are 31 states with t statistics that are statistically significant at p <.05. Some 11 states are well above the average and another 20 states are below the norm. There are 16 states with the incarceration rate close to the overall average of all states in the model.

The results show that the incarceration rate in the United States is heterogenous in level across jurisdictions. This type of heterogeneity is labeled unit effects in the literature. Judge et al. (1982) suggest two

Table B.3
Least Squares with Dummy Variables (LSDV)
Solution to Problems with Unit Effects

State	$\beta_i = \beta_0 + \mu_i$	μ_i	t for H$_0$: $\mu_i = 0$
Alabama	2096.19	649.39	4.534*
Alaska	1402.38	-44.42	-0.281
Arizona	991.09	-455.71	-2.830*
Arkansas	1576.56	129.76	0.991
California	678.72	-768.08	-3.781*
Colorado	1162.03	-284.77	-1.696*
Connecticut	1294.92	-151.88	-1.120
Delaware	705.15	-741.65	-4.927*
Florida	1307.97	-138.83	-0.686
Hawaii	394.62	-1052.18	-8.773*
Idaho	1457.80	11.00	0.092
Illinois	1053.37	-393.43	-2.283*
Indiana	1384.96	-61.84	-0.435
Iowa	1366.40	-80.40	-0.705
Kansas	1022.23	-424.57	-3.335*
Kentucky	2619.33	1172.53	9.561*
Louisiana	1527.31	80.51	0.481
Maine	1811.50	364.70	2.835*
Maryland	2189.46	742.66	3.607*
Massachusetts	913.63	-533.17	-3.601*
Michigan	1476.28	29.48	0.159
Minnesota	550.80	-896.00	-6.674*
Mississippi	3584.84	2138.04	16.710*
Missouri	1035.19	-411.61	-2.637*
Nebraska	849.69	-597.11	-5.038*
Nevada	1356.44	-90.36	-0.483
New Hampshire	1150.98	-295.82	-2.641*

State	$\beta_i = \beta_0 + \mu_i$	μ_i	t for $H_0: \mu_i = 0$
New Jersey	969.29	-477.51	-3.101*
New Mexico	901.28	-545.52	-3.195*
New York	1073.87	-372.93	-1.558
North Carolina	2466.66	1019.86	6.369*
North Dakota	1551.94	105.14	0.925
Ohio	1430.42	-16.38	-0.117
Oklahoma	2065.94	619.14	4.676*
Oregon	1152.64	-294.16	-2.026*
Pennsylvania	767.05	-679.75	-4.885*
Rhode Island	516.11	-930.69	-6.813*
South Carolina	4167.33	2720.53	16.595*
South Dakota	3149.42	1702.62	13.688*
Tennessee	2135.37	688.57	4.800*
Texas	1360.63	-86.17	-0.581
Utah	625.58	-821.22	-6.237*
Virginia	1334.11	-112.69	-0.881
Washington	811.67	-635.13	-4.434*
West Virginia	2274.93	828.13	7.218*
Wisconsin	898.90	-547.90	-4.697*
Wyoming	1386.58	-60.22	-0.461

Note: $\beta_0 = 1446.8$; $\lambda = 2385$; *p < .05.

alternatives for hypothesis testing. A simple F test can be performed by evaluating whether reduction in residual variance due to the use of LSDV is statistically significant (Johnston 1984, 218; Judge et al. 1982, 484). If dummy variables account for a substantial proportion of residual variance, residual variance due to nonzero means within units will be sizable. Another alternative evaluates the null hypothesis of $\sigma^2 = 0$ on the basis of OLS residuals. Residual means are used in the calculation of the Lagrange multiplier statistic, λ, which is asymptotically distributed as chi-square with one degree of freedom. According to Judge et al. (1982, 495),

$$\lambda = \frac{NT}{2\,(T-1)}\left[\frac{A}{B}-1\right]^2$$

where A is residual means sum of squares and B is the OLS error sum of squares. The null hypothesis is rejected if λ exceeds chi-square with one degree of freedom. With $\lambda = 2{,}385$ obtained from OLS residuals, the null hypothesis of no unit effects can be rejected. This overall evaluation of unit effects yields results consistent with case-by-case diagnoses of nonzero residual means in table B.3. Residual analysis of the FE-GLS procedure leads to the third step in which within-unit serial correlation will be treated.

Step 3: A Solution to Time-Serial Autocorrelation

The diagnosis of residual means over time in the example model finds a pattern of nonzero means that are positively correlated. The pattern shows that, on the average, within-unit residuals are positively correlated. If residual means fluctuated with no systematic pattern associated with time sequence, one would consider the use of the GLSE estimator because time effects are present.

With a restricted assumption about the serial correlation structure, Stimson's solution, GLS-AR(1), imposes a common pattern of a first-order autoregressive error structure across all units. Stimson's GLS-AR(1) estimator should be employed with caution; if the assumption does not hold, this solution is inappropriate.

In his 1987 study Sirisumphand finds that when serial correlations vary in their pattern across units, the estimate of the pooled autoregressive parameter turns out to be nonsignificant. With the same order but different magnitude, the problem is not so serious as when the error structure is mixed with positive correlation in some units and negative correlation in others. With different orders of residual autoregression, the use of Stimson's restricted GLS-AR(1) estimator is problematic.

Box-Jenkins analysis of the FE-GLS residuals yields a set of autoregressive estimates that are different in magnitude, sign, and order. Table B.4 displays results of this analysis. Significant serial correlation is absent in four states—Michigan, North Carolina, North Dakota, and Oregon. More than half, twenty-five states, have first-order autoregression. A second-order autoregressive structure is found in the remaining eighteen states. Variation in the error structure across units makes the use of GLS-AR(1) an unjustifiable solution to the problem at hand.

In general usage, the time-serial GLS procedure can be carried out with unrestricted assumptions about the serial correlation problem. Parks (1967) and Kmenta (1971) propose the use of OLS on the transformed data, which seems suitable here. No data transformation is required in the four states having no significant serial correlation. For the twenty-five states with a first-order autoregressive structure, data transformation follows the form:

for $t = 1$, $$Y_{it}^{**} = Y_{it}^* - \sqrt{1 - \rho_{1i}^2}$$

for $t > 1$, $$Y_{it}^{**} = Y_{it}^* - \rho_{1i} Y_{it-1}^*$$

where ρ_{1i} is the first-order autoregressive coefficient (Parks 1967, 502). In the second-order autoregression situation, the following transformations are required:

for $t = 1$, $$Y_{it}^{**} = \alpha\, Y_{it}^*$$

for $t = 2$, $$Y_{it}^{**} = \gamma Y_{it}^* - \delta\, Y_{it-1}^*$$

for $t > 2$, $$Y_{it}^{**} = Y_{it}^* - \rho_{1i} Y_{it-1}^* - \rho_{2i} Y_{it-2}^*$$

where $$\alpha = \sqrt{\frac{(1 + \rho_{2i})\{(1 - \rho_{2i})^2 - \rho_{1i}^2\}}{(1 - \rho_{2i})}}$$

$$\gamma = \alpha \bigg/ \sqrt{1 - \left\{\frac{\rho_{1i}}{(1 - \rho_{2i})}\right\}^2}$$

$$\delta = \gamma \left\{\frac{\rho_{1i}}{(1 - \rho_{2i})}\right\}$$

and ρ_{1i} and ρ_{2i} are the first- and second-order autoregressive coefficients (Lempers and Kloek 1973, 72). Note that no observations are lost in data transformation. OLS is then applied on second-round transformed data.

Table B.4
ARIMA Analysis of Fixed-Effects Generalized Least Squares (FE-GLS)
Residuals by State

State	Autoregressive Order	ρ_1	ρ_2
Alabama	2	0.95	-0.31
Alaska	2	1.80	-0.81
Arizona	2	1.15	-0.17
Arkansas	1	0.67	0.00
California	1	0.79	0.00
Colorado	1	0.47	0.00
Connecticut	2	0.74	-0.28
Delaware	2	1.29	-0.55
Florida	2	1.17	-0.49
Hawaii	2	1.30	-0.60
Idaho	1	0.60	0.00
Illinois	1	*1.00*	0.00
Indiana	1	0.71	0.00
Iowa	1	0.44	0.00
Kansas	1	0.33	0.00
Kentucky	1	0.82	0.00
Louisiana	1	0.47	0.00
Maine	1	0.81	0.00
Maryland	1	0.79	0.00
Massachusetts	1	0.71	0.00
Michigan	0	0.00	0.00
Minnesota	2	0.62	-0.38
Mississippi	1	0.38	0.00
Missouri	2	1.23	-0.33
Nebraska	1	0.43	0.00
Nevada	1	*1.00*	0.00
New Hampshire	2	0.93	-0.37

State	Autoregressive Order	ρ_1	ρ_2
New Jersey	2	*1.00*	-0.38
New Mexico	2	1.26	-0.72
New York	1	0.91	0.00
North Carolina	0	0.00	0.00
North Dakota	0	0.00	0.00
Ohio	1	0.52	0.00
Oklahoma	1	0.74	0.00
Oregon	0	0.00	0.00
Pennsylvania	2	0.94	-0.43
Rhode Island	1	0.93	0.00
South Carolina	1	0.67	0.00
South Dakota	1	0.62	0.00
Tennessee	2	1.03	-0.37
Texas	2	1.33	-0.42
Utah	1	*1.00*	0.00
Virginia	1	0.47	0.00
Washington	2	0.95	-0.44
West Virginia	2	0.98	-0.33
Wisconsin	2	0.66	-0.41
Wyoming	1	0.76	0.00

Note: The underlined first-order autoregressive parameter whose estimated value is equal to 1 can be expressed as a first-order differencing model or ARIMA(0,1,0).

The generalized least squares procedure with unit effects and second-order autoregressive errors, FEGLS-AR(2), can be written as:

$$Y^{**}_{it} = \beta^{**}_0 + \beta^{**}_k X^{**}_{k,it} + \varepsilon^{**}_{it} \qquad (4)$$

With the FEGLS-AR(2) estimator, the residuals series, ε^{**}_{it}, is no longer serially correlated. The diagnosis of residual variances shows that the range of RSTD ratios from 0.21 to 3.79 across units is broader than the range from 0.58 to 1.90 across time periods. That is, residual variance remains heteroscedastic, with the problem more severe in the space dimension than in the time dimension. The weighted least squares (WLS) solution to heteroscedasticity is the subject of the next section.

Step 4: A Solution to Heteroscedasticity

A final potential threat to pooled time-series analysis that deserves special attention is the problem of heteroscedasticity. When the data are an extended time series, unequal residual variances within units deserves special attention. In the works of Parks (1967), Kmenta (1971), and Johnston (1984), emphasis is placed on cross-sectional heteroscedasticity over temporal heteroscedasticity. There are good reasons for this attention. The pooled model may predict better for one unit than another. More likely than not, errors in model prediction are more variant in one state than in another. However, the pooled model may also predict better for one time period than for another. In the latter case, errors in prediction are more variant in one time period than another.

In order to evaluate both rival arguments, residual variances are explored on the two dimensions. The data show that the error structure is heteroscedastic with a broader range of variance inequality across states than over time periods. As seen in table B.5, the smallest residual standard deviation is 165.8 in 1980 and the largest is 542.1 in 1971. Minnesota has the smallest standard deviation, only 61.1, whereas Mississippi has the largest estimated standard deviation, 1,079.8. The range of 1,018.7 between the smallest to the largest among states is much wider than the range among time periods, 376.3.

The ratios of actual RSTD to expected RSTD, shown in table B.5, indicate that Minnesota's RSTD is much smaller than expected, with a ratio of 0.21 to 1. Mississippi's RSTD is nearly four times the size expected, 3.79 to 1. The range of RSTD ratios over the study period is from 0.58 for 1980 to 1.90 for 1971. It is evident that discrepancies across units are much greater than discrepancies one can find on the time dimension.

Based on this diagnosis, weighted least squares is required to achieve homoscedasticity. The WLS procedure can be carried out using OLS regression on transformed data. Kmenta (1971, 511) suggests the use of the ith unit's RSTD to divide all observations of

Table B.5
Analysis of Residual Standard Deviation (RSTD)
before and after Weighted Least Squares (WLS)

State/Year	Before WLS		After WLS	
	RSTD	RSTD Ratio[a]	RSTD	RSTD Ratio[a]
a) Unit-Based Diagnostic Statistics[b]				
Alabama	441.20	1.55	282.10	1.03
Alaska	243.68	0.85	284.67	1.04
Arizona	82.75	0.29	236.81	0.86
Arkansas	199.66	0.70	299.55	1.09
California	91.74	0.32	235.18	0.86
Colorado	62.43	0.22	273.85	1.00
Connecticut	203.34	0.71	280.51	1.02
Delaware	94.13	0.33	233.42	0.85
Florida	95.24	0.33	219.01	0.80
Hawaii	77.19	0.27	235.28	0.86
Idaho	97.06	0.34	306.53	1.12
Illinois	292.40	1.03	266.58	0.97
Indiana	201.95	0.71	281.90	1.03
Iowa	182.63	0.64	297.12	1.08
Kansas	88.59	0.31	268.27	0.98
Kentucky	322.03	1.13	294.50	1.07
Louisiana	294.47	1.03	271.62	0.99
Maine	351.58	1.23	294.33	1.07
Maryland	250.16	0.88	293.66	1.07
Massachusetts	118.52	0.42	205.20	0.75
Michigan	86.26	0.30	218.20	0.80
Minnesota	61.14	0.21	298.92	1.09
Mississippi	1079.83	3.79	290.15	1.06
Missouri	62.86	0.22	245.71	0.90
Nebraska	189.75	0.67	294.23	1.07
Nevada	142.08	0.50	266.24	0.97

State/Year	Before WLS		After WLS	
	RSTD	RSTD Ratio[a]	RSTD	RSTD Ratio[a]
New Hampshire	216.24	0.76	279.72	1.02
New Jersey	141.91	0.50	297.37	1.09
New Mexico	103.71	0.36	294.21	1.07
New York	90.58	0.32	216.66	0.79
North Carolina	339.12	1.19	292.00	1.07
North Dakota	285.43	1.00	298.11	1.09
Ohio	206.49	0.72	285.68	1.04
Oklahoma	171.06	0.60	297.34	1.09
Oregon	137.47	0.48	251.30	0.92
Pennsylvania	82.77	0.29	274.60	1.00
Rhode Island	105.75	0.37	197.57	0.72
South Carolina	819.72	2.88	293.32	1.07
South Dakota	481.23	1.69	305.45	1.11
Tennessee	239.37	0.84	276.70	1.01
Texas	85.66	0.30	262.98	0.96
Utah	99.60	0.35	262.67	0.96
Virginia	173.10	0.61	293.05	1.07
Washington	46.70	0.16	286.28	1.04
West Virginia	396.41	1.39	286.02	1.04
Wisconsin	97.63	0.34	256.47	0.94
Wyoming	163.43	0.57	259.47	0.95

b) Time-Based Diagnostic Statistics[c]

71	542.11	1.90	390.61	1.43
72	298.62	1.05	285.30	1.04
73	214.08	0.75	257.22	0.94
74	218.67	0.77	262.12	0.96
75	297.67	1.04	236.77	0.86
76	304.84	1.07	351.68	1.28

State/Year	Before WLS		After WLS	
	RSTD	RSTD Ratio[a]	RSTD	RSTD Ratio[a]
77	394.40	1.38	277.28	1.01
78	185.97	0.65	219.48	0.80
79	168.09	0.59	205.63	0.75
80	165.80	0.58	215.04	0.78
81	212.01	0.74	226.58	0.83
82	185.39	0.65	231.74	0.85
83	237.61	0.83	256.22	0.94
84	292.32	1.03	327.20	1.19

[a] Actual to expected RSTD ratio: expected RSTD before WLS = 285.04; expected RSTD after WLS = 274.00.
[b] The unit-based RSTD ratio range before WLS = 0.21–3.79; the unit-based RSTD ratio range after WLS = 0.72–1.12.
[c] The time-based RSTD ratio range before WLS = 0.58–1.90; the time-based RSTD ratio range after WLS = 0.75–1.43.

the same unit on both sides of the equation. This weighting scheme makes it difficult to compare residual variances before and after WLS because the scale is reduced exponentially after transformation. An equivalent solution uses RSTD ratios as weighting denominators for the ith units. Improvement in residual variance can be easily evaluated because RSTDs are calculated in the same scale. Another advantage of this weighting transformation is that the residual sum of squares can be evaluated with reference in the same scale to total sum of squares based on the raw data. Thus, R^2 can be calculated for the proportion of original variance explained by the four-step regression model.

The WLS specification can be expressed in terms of the following transformed series:

$$Y_{it}^{***} = \beta_0^{***} + \beta_k^{***} X_{k,it}^{***} + \varepsilon_{it}^{***} \tag{5}$$

where all time series of the ith units are transformed in the form:

$$Y_{it}^{***} = \frac{Y_{it}^{**}}{\sigma_i / \sigma}$$

The error structure in ε_{it}^{***} is nonautoregressive and homoscedastic. Residual analysis in table B.5 shows substantial improvement with respect to residual variance. Comparison of RSTDs of the ith units before and after WLS indicates that each RSTD approaches closer to expected RSTD (274.0), with the narrower range of RSTD ratios from 0.72 to 1.12. On the time dimension, the RSTD ratios fall within the narrower range of 0.75 to 1.43 after WLS, as opposed to the range of 0.58 to 1.90 before WLS.

All in all, the four-step regression procedure is effective in treating a series of statistical problems, namely, fixed unit effects, serial correlation, and heteroscedasticity. With $R^2 = .90$, the model accounts for 90 percent of the total original variance.

REFERENCES

Albonetti, Celesta A. 1986. "Criminality, Prosecutorial Screening, and Uncertainty: Toward a Theory of Discretionary Decision Making in Felony Case Processings." *Criminology* 24:623–43.

Albritton, Robert B. 1979. "Measuring Public Policy: Impacts of the Supplemental Security Income Program." *American J of Political Science* 23:560–78.

Albritton, Robert B., and Donna Bahry. 1979. "Effects of Public and Private Sector Decisions on Health Care Costs." *Policy Studies J* 7:762–70.

Albritton, Robert B., and Tamasak Witayapanyanon. 1989. "Impacts of SSI: A Reanalysis of Federal Welfare Policy." In *Evaluation in Practice: A Methodological Approach.* Ed. Richard D. Bingham and Claire L. Felbinger. New York: Longman. 113–24.

Algina, James, and Hariharan Swaminathan. 1979. "Alternatives to Simonton's Analyses of the Interrupted and Multiple-Group Time-Series Designs." *Psychological Bulletin* 86:919–26.

Allen, Francis A. 1964. *The Borderland of Criminal Justice: Essays in Law and Criminology.* Chicago: U of Chicago P.

———. 1981. *The Decline of the Rehabilitative Ideal: Penal Policy and Social Purpose.* New Haven: Yale UP.

Alschuler, Albert W. 1979. "Plea Bargaining and Its History." *Law & Society Review* 13:211–46.

American Friends Service Committee. 1971. *Struggle for Justice.* New York: Hill and Wang.

Andenaes, Johannes. 1974. *Punishment and Deterrence.* Ann Arbor: U of Michigan P.

Anderson, Linda S. 1979. "The Deterrent Effect of Criminal Sanctions: Reviewing the Evidence." In *Structure, Law, and Power.* Ed. Paul J. Brantingham and Jack M. Kress. Beverly Hills: Sage. 120–34.

Anspach, Donald F., Peter H. Lehman, and John H. Kramer. 1983. "Maine Rejects Indeterminacy: A Case Study of Flat Sentencing and Parole Abolition." Unpublished manuscript prepared for the National Institute of Justice.

Aspen, Marvin E. 1978. "New Class X Sentencing Law: An Analysis." *Illinois Bar J* 66:344–51.

Balestra, Pietro, and Marc Nerlove. 1966. "Pooling Cross Section and Time Series Data in the Estimation of a Dynamic Model: The Demand for Natural Gas." *Econometrica* 34:585–612.

Barnes, Harry Elmer. 1968. *The Evolution of Penology in Pennsylvania: A Study in American Social History*. Montclair: Patterson Smith.

Beccaria, Cesare. 1777. *On Crimes and Punishments*. Trans. Henry Paolucci. Indianapolis: Bobbs-Merrill.

Becker, Gary S. 1968. "Crime and Punishment: An Economic Approach." *J of Political Economy* 76:169–217.

Beha, James A. 1977. "'And Nobody Can Get You Out'—the Impact of a Mandatory Prison Sentence for the Illegal Carrying of a Firearm on the Use of Firearms and on the Administration of Criminal Justice in Boston." *Boston University Law Review* 57:96–146, 289–333.

Berk, Richard A., Donnie M. Hoffman, Judith E. Maki, David Rauma, and Herbert Wong. 1979. "Estimation Procedures for Pooled Cross-Sectional and Time Series Data." *Evaluation Review* 3:385–410.

Bingham, Richard D., and Claire L. Felbinger, eds. 1989. *Evaluation in Practice: A Methodological Approach*. New York: Longman.

Blumberg, Abraham S. 1967. *Criminal Justice*. Chicago: Quadrangle.

Blumstein, Alfred, Jacqueline Cohen, Susan E. Martin, and Michael H. Tonry, eds. 1983. *Research on Sentencing: The Search for Reform*. Washington: National Acad. P.

Blumstein, Alfred, Jacqueline Cohen, and David Nagin, eds. 1978. *Deterrence and Incapacitation: Estimating the Effects of Criminal Sanctions on Crime Rates*. Washington: National Acad. of Sciences.

Boland, Barbara, Catherine H. Conly, Lynn Warner, Ronald Sones, and William Martin. 1988. *The Prosecution of Felony Arrests, 1986*. Washington: Abt.

Boland, Barbara, Elizabeth Brady, Herbert Tyson, and John Bassler. 1983. *The Prosecution of Felony Arrests, 1979*. Washington: INSLAW.

Boland, Barbara, Wayne Logan, Ronald Sones, and William Martin. 1987. *The Prosecution of Felony Arrests, 1982*. Washington: Abt.

Box, George E. P., and Gwilym M. Jenkins. 1976. *Time-Series Analysis: Forecasting and Control*. Rev. ed. Oakland: Holden-Day.

Box, George E. P., and George C. Tiao. 1965. "A Change in Level of a Non-Stationary Time Series." *Biometrika* 52:181–92.

Box, George E. P., and George C. Tiao. 1975. "Intervention Analysis with Applications to Economic and Environmental Problems." *J of the American Statistical Assn.* 70:70–79.

Bowler, M. Kenneth. 1974. *The Nixon Guaranteed Income Proposal: Substance and Process in Policy Change*. Cambridge: Ballinger.

Braybrooke, D., and Charles E. Lindblom. 1985. *The Strategy of Decision*. 2nd ed. New York: Free.

Brewer, D., G. E. Beckett, and N. Holt. 1980. *Determinate Sentencing in California: The First Year's Experience.* Chino: California Dept. of Correction.

California Board of Prison Terms. 1981. *Sentencing Practices: Determinate Sentencing Law.* Chino: Board of Prison Terms.

Campbell, Donald T., and H. Laurence Ross. 1968. "The Connecticut Crackdown on Speeding: Time-Series Data in Quasi-Experimental Analysis." *Law & Society Review* 3:33–53.

Campbell, Donald T., and Julian Stanley. 1966. *Experimental and Quasi-Experimental Designs for Research.* Boston: Houghton Mifflin.

Carlson, Kenneth. 1982. *Mandatory Sentencing: The Experience of Two States.* Washington: GPO.

Carrow, Deborah M., Judith Feins, Beverly N. W. Lee, and Lois Olinger. 1985. *Guidelines Without Force: An Evaluation of the Multijurisdictional Sentencing Guidelines Field Test.* Cambridge: Abt.

Carter, Lief H. 1974. *The Limits of Order.* Lexington: Heath.

Carter, Robert, and Leslie Wilkins. 1967. "Some Factors in Sentencing Policy." *J of Criminal Law, Criminology, and Police Science* 58:503–14.

Casper, Jonathan D. 1984. "Determinate Sentencing and Prison Crowding in Illinois." *U of Illinois Law Review* 1984:231–52.

Casper, Jonathan D., and David Brereton. 1984. "Evaluating Criminal Justice Reforms." *Law & Society Review* 18:121–44.

Casper, Jonathan D., David Brereton, and David Neal. 1982. *The Implementation of the California Determinate Sentencing Law.* Washington: GPO.

Church, Thomas, Jr. 1976. "Plea Bargains, Concessions, and the Courts: Analysis of a Quasi-Experiment." *Law & Society Review* 10:377–401.

Clarke, Stevens H. 1984. "North Carolina's Determinate Sentencing Legislation." *Judicature* 68:140–52.

Clarke, Stevens H., Susan Turner Kurtz, Glenn F. Lang, Kenneth L. Parker, Elizabeth W. Rubinsky, and Donna J. Schleicher. 1983. *North Carolina's Determinate Sentencing Legislation: An Evaluation of the First Year's Experience.* Chapel Hill: U of North Carolina Institute of Government.

Coffee, John C., and Michael H. Tonry. 1983. "Hard Choices: Critical Trade-Offs in the Implementation of Sentencing Reform through Guidelines." In *Reform and Punishment.* Ed. Michael H. Tonry and Franklin E. Zimring. Chicago: U of Chicago P. 155–203.

Cohen, Jacqueline, and Joan Helland. 1982. *Methodology for Evaluating the Impact of Sentencing Guidelines.* Boston: Carnegie-Mellon U Urban Systems Institute.

Cohen, Jacqueline, and Michael H. Tonry. 1983. "Sentencing Reforms and Their Effects." In *Research on Sentencing: The Search for Reform.* Ed. Alfred Blumstein, Jacqueline Cohen, Susan E. Martin, and Michael H. Tonry. Washington: National Acad. P. 305–459.

Cole, George F. 1973. *Politics and the Administration of Justice.* Beverly Hills: Sage.

Cook, Philip J. 1983. "The Influence of Gun Availability on Violent Crime Patterns." In *Crime and Justice.* Ed. Michael Tonry and Norval Morris. Chicago: U of Chicago P. 49–89.

Cook, Thomas D., and Donald T. Campbell. 1979. *Quasi-Experimentation: Design & Analysis Issues for Field Settings.* Boston: Houghton Mifflin.

Cressey, Donald R. 1980. "Sentencing: Legislative Rule versus Judicial Discretion." In *New Directions in Sentencing.* Ed. Brian A. Grosman. Toronto: Butterworths. 51–69.

Cullen, Francis T., and Karen E. Gilbert. 1982. *Reaffirming Rehabilitation.* Cincinnati: Anderson.

Currie, Elliott. 1985. *Confronting Crime: An American Challenge.* New York: Pantheon.

Cyert, Richard M., and James March. 1963. *A Behavioral Theory of the Firm.* Englewood Cliffs: Prentice-Hall.

Davis, Kenneth Culp. 1969. *Discretionary Justice: A Preliminary Inquiry.* Urbana: U of Illinois P.

Dershowitz, Alan M. 1976. "Backgroup Paper." *Fair and Certain Punishment.* Twentieth Century Fund Task Force on Criminal Sentencing. New York: McGraw-Hill.

Deutsch, Stuart J., and Francis B. Alt. 1977. "The Effect of Massachusetts' Gun Control Law on Gun-Related Crimes in the City of Boston." *Evaluation Quarterly* 1:543–67.

Edelman, Murray C. 1967. *The Symbolic Uses of Politics.* Urbana: U of Illinois P.

Ehrlich, Isaac. 1973. "Participation in Illegitimate Activities: A Theoretical and Empirical Investigation." *J of Political Economy* 81:521–65.

Eisenstein, James, Roy B. Flemming, and Peter F. Nardulli. 1988. *The Contours of Justice: Communities and Their Courts.* Boston: Little, Brown.

Eisenstein, James, and Herbert Jacob. 1977. *Felony Justice: An Organizational Analysis of Criminal Courts.* Boston: Little, Brown.

Fattah, E. A. 1977. "Deterrence: A Review of the Literature." *Canadian J of Criminology* 19:1–119.

Feeley, Malcolm M. 1979. *The Process Is the Punishment: Handling Cases in a Lower Criminal Court.* New York: Russell Sage Foundation.

———. 1983. *Court Reform on Trial: Why Simple Solutions Fail.* New York: Basic.

Feeley, Malcolm M., and Austin D. Sarat. 1980. *The Policy Dilemma: Federal Crime Policy and the Law Enforcement Assistance Administration, 1968–1978.* Minneapolis: U of Minnesota P.

Finckenauer, James O. 1978. "Crime as a National Political Issue: 1964–76: From Law and Order to Domestic Tranquility." *Crime & Delinquency* 24:13–27.

Flanagan, Timothy J., Michael J. Hindelang, and Michael R. Gottfredson, eds. 1980. *Sourcebook of Criminal Justice Statistics–1979.* Washington: GPO.

Flanagan, Timothy J., and Katherine M. Jamieson. 1988. *Sourcebook of Criminal Justice Statistics—1987.* Washington: GPO.

Flemming, Roy B., C. W. Kohfeld, and Thomas M. Uhlman. 1980. "The Limits of Bail Reform: A Quasi-Experimental Analysis." *Law & Society Review* 14:947–76.

Fogel, David. 1975. *". . . We Are the Living Proof . . ." The Justice Model for Corrections.* Cincinnati: Anderson.

Fogel, David, and Joe Hudson, eds. 1981. *Justice as Fairness: Perspectives on the Justice Model.* Cincinnati: Anderson.

Forrester, Jay W. 1971. "Counterintuitive Behavior of Social Systems." *Technology Review* 73:52–68.

Frankel, Marvin E. 1972. *Criminal Sentences: Law without Order.* New York: Hill and Wang.

Friedman, Lawrence M. 1979. "Plea Bargaining in Historical Perspective." *Law & Society Review* 13:247–59.

Fuller, Wayne A., and George E. Battese. 1974. "Estimation of Linear Models with Crossed-Error Structure." *J of Econometrics* 2:67–78.

Galvin, Jim. 1983. "Setting Prison Terms." *Bureau of Justice Statistics Bulletin,* August. Rockville: Bureau of Justice Statistics.

Gaylin, Willard. 1974. *Partial Justice: A Study of Bias in Sentencing.* New York: Knopf.

Geerken, Michael, and Walter R. Gove. 1977. "Deterrence, Overload, and Incapacitation: An Empirical Evaluation." *Social Forces* 56:424–47.

Gibbons, Don C. 1968. *Society, Crime, and Criminal Careers.* Englewood Cliffs: Prentice-Hall.

Gibbs, Jack P. 1975. *Crime, Punishment, and Deterrence.* New York: Elsevier.

Glass, Gene V. 1968. "Analysis of Data on the Connecticut Speeding Crackdown as a Time-Series Quasi-Experiment." *Law & Society Review* 3:55–76.

Glass, Gene V., Victor L. Willson, and John M. Gottman. 1975. *Design and Analysis of Time-Series Experiments.* Boulder: Colorado Assoc. UP.

Goldberg, Louis P., and Eleanore Levenson. 1970. *Lawless Judges*. New York: Da Capo P.

Goodstein, Lynne, and John R. Hepburn. 1985. *Determinate Sentencing and Imprisonment: A Failure of Reform*. Cincinnati: Anderson.

Gottfredson, Don M., Leslie T. Wilkins, and Peter B. Hoffman. 1978. *Guidelines for Parole and Sentencing: A Policy Control Method*. Lexington: Heath.

Grasmick, Harold G., and George J. Bryjak. 1980. "The Deterrent Effect of Perceived Severity of Punishment." *Social Forces* 59:471–91.

Greenberg, David F. 1975. "The Incapacitative Effect of Imprisonment: Some Estimates." *Law & Society Review* 9:541–80.

Greenberg, David F., and Drew Humphries. 1980. "The Cooptation of Fixed Sentencing Reform." *Crime & Delinquency* 26:206–25.

Hagan, John. 1985. *Modern Criminology: Crime, Criminal Behavior, and Its Control*. New York: McGraw-Hill.

Hamline Law Review. 1982. "Introduction to the Minnesota Sentencing Guidelines." *Hamline Law Review* 5:293–437.

Hannan, Michael T., and Alice A. Young. 1977. "Estimation in Panel Models: Results on Pooling Cross-Sections and Time Series." In *Sociological Methodology*. Ed. David R. Heise. San Francisco: Jossey-Bass. 52–83.

Hart, H. L. A. 1961. *The Concept of Law*. New York: Oxford UP.

———. 1968. *Punishment and Responsibility: Essays in the Philosophy of Law*. New York: Oxford UP.

Hausman, J. A. 1978. "Specification Tests in Econometrics." *Econometrica* 46:1251–70.

Hepburn, John R., and Lynne Goodstein. 1986. "Organizational Imperatives and Sentencing Reform Implementation: The Impacts of Prison Practices and Priorities on the Attainment of the Objective of Determinate Sentencing." *Crime & Delinquency* 32:339–65.

Heumann, Milton. 1978. *Plea Bargaining: The Experiences of Prosecutors, Judges, and Defense Attorneys*. Chicago: U of Chicago P.

Heumann, Milton, and Colin Loftin. 1979. "Mandatory Sentencing and the Abolition of Plea Bargaining: The Michigan Felony Firearm Statute." *Law & Society Review* 13:393–430.

Hibbs, Douglas A., Jr. 1977. "On Analyzing the Effects of Policy Interventions: Box-Jenkins vs. Structural Equation Models." In *Sociological Methodology*. Ed. D. R. Heise. San Francisco: Jossey-Bass. 137–79.

Hilton, Michael E. 1984. "The Impact of Recent Changes in California Drinking-Driving Laws on Fatal Accident Levels During the First Postintervention Year: An Interrupted Time Series Analysis." *Law & Society Review* 18:605–27.

Hogarth, John. 1971. *Sentencing as a Human Process*. Buffalo: U of Toronto P.

Hogwood, Brian W., and Lewis A. Gunn. 1984. *Policy Analysis for the Real World*. New York: Oxford UP.

Inciardi, James A. 1987. *Criminal Justice*. 2nd ed. San Diego: Harcourt Brace Jovanovich.

Inverarity, James M., Pat Lauderdale, and Barry C. Feld. 1983. *Law and Society: Sociological Perspectives on Criminal Law*. Boston: Little, Brown.

Jacob, Herbert. 1986. *The Frustration of Policy: Responses to Crime by American Cities*. Boston: Little, Brown.

Jamieson, Katherine M., and Timothy J. Flanagan, ed. 1989. *Sourcebook of Criminal Justice Statistics—1988*. U.S. Department of Justice, Bureau of Justice Statistics. Washington: GPO.

Johnston, J. 1984. *Econometric Methods*. 3rd ed. New York: McGraw-Hill.

Judge, George G., William E. Griffiths, R. Carter Hill, and Tsoung-Chao Lee. 1980. *The Theory and Practice of Econometrics*. New York: Wiley.

Judge, George G., R. Carter Hill, William E. Griffiths, Helmut Luetkepohl, and Tsoung-Chao Lee. 1982. *Introduction to the Theory and Practice of Econometrics*. New York: Wiley.

Katz, Daniel, and Robert L. Kahn. 1966. *The Social Psychology of Organizations*. New York: Wiley.

Kmenta, J. 1971. *Elements of Econometrics*. New York: Macmillan.

Knapp, Kay A. 1982. "Impact of the Minnesota Sentencing Guidelines on Sentencing Practices." *Hamline Law Review* 5:237–56.

———. 1984. *The Impact of the Minnesota Sentencing Guidelines—Three Year Evaluation*. St. Paul: Minnesota Sentencing Guidelines Commission.

———. 1987. "Implementation of the Minnesota Guidelines: Can the Innovative Spirit Be Preserved?" In *The Sentencing Commission and Its Guidelines*. Ed. Andrew von Hirsch, Kay A. Knapp, and Michael Tonry. Boston: Northeastern UP. 127–41.

Krislov, Samuel. 1979. "Debating on Bargaining: Comments from a Synthesizer." *Law & Society Review* 13:573–82.

Ku, R. 1980. "Case Studies of New Legislation Governing Sentencing and Release." *American Prions and Jails*. Vol. 5. Washington: GPO.

Lagoy, Stephen P., Frederick A. Hussey, and John H. Kramer. 1978. "A Comparative Assessment of Determinate Sentencing in the Four Pioneer States." *Crime & Delinquency* 24:385–400.

Langbein, Laura Irwin. 1980. *Discovering Whether Programs Work: A Guide to Statistical Methods for Program Evaluation*. Glenview: Scott.

Lempers, F. B., and T. Kloek. 1973. "On a Simple Transformation for Second-Order Autocorrelated Disturbances in Regression Analysis." *Statistica Neerlandica* 27:69–73.

Lewis-Beck, Michael S., and J. R. Alford. 1980. "Can Government Regulate Safety: The Coal Mine Example." *American Political Science Review* 74:745–56.

Lindblom, Charles E. 1959. "The Science of Muddling Through." *Public Administration Review* 19:79–88.

Lipson, A. J., and Mark A. Peterson. 1980. *California Justice under Determinate Sentencing: A Review and Agenda for Research*. Santa Monica: Rand.

Loftin, Colin, Milton Heumann, and David McDowall. 1983. "Mandatory Sentencing and Firearms Violence: Evaluating an Alternative to Gun Control." *Law & Society Review* 17:287–318.

Loftin, Colin, and David McDowall. 1981. "'One with a Gun Gets You Two': Mandatory Sentencing and Firearms Violence in Detroit." *The Annals of the Academy of Political and Social Science* 455:150–67.

———. 1984. "The Deterrent Effects of the Florida Felony Firearm Law." *J of Criminal Law & Criminology* 75:250–59.

Logan, C. 1975. "Arrest Rates and Deterrence." *Social Science Quarterly* 56:376–89.

Luckenbill, David F. 1984. "Character Coercion, Instrumental Coercion, and Gun Control." *J of Applied Behavioral Science* 20:181–92.

McCleary, Richard, and Richard A. Hay Jr. 1980. *Applied Time Series Analysis for the Social Sciences*. Beverly Hills: Sage.

McDowall, David, Richard McCleary, Errol E. Meidinger, and Richard A. Hay Jr. 1980. "Interrupted Time Series Analysis." Sage University Paper Series on Quantitative Applications in the Social Sciences, 07–021. Beverly Hills: Sage.

McPhethers, Lee R., Robert Mann, and Don Schlagenhauf. 1984. "Economic Response to a Crime Deterrence Program: Mandatory Sentencing for Robbery with a Firearm." *Economic Inquiry* 22:550–70.

Maddala, G. S. 1971. "The Use of Variance Components Models in Pooling Cross Section and Time Series Data." *Econometrica* 39:341–58.

Mannheim, Hermann, ed. 1973. *Pioneers in Criminology*. Montclair: Patterson Smith.

Mather, Lynn M. 1974. "Some Determinants of the Method of Case Disposition: Decision-Making by Public Defenders in Los Angeles." *Law & Society Review* 8:187–216.

———. 1979. *Plea Bargaining or Trial?: The Process of Criminal Case Disposition*. Lexington: Heath.

Maxwell, Delmas M. 1981. "Impact Analysis of the Raised Legal Drinking Age in Illinois." NHTSA Technical Report DOT HS–806–115, U.S. Department of Transportation.

Mazmanian, Daniel A., and Paul A. Sabatier. 1983. *Implementation and Public Policy*. Glenview: Scott.

Moe, Terry M. 1982. "Regulatory Performance and Presidential Administration." *American J of Politics* 26:197–224.

Moran, Garrett E. 1985. "Regulatory Strategies for Workplace Injury Reduction: A Program Evaluation." *Evaluation Review* 9:21–33.

Morris, Norval. 1974. *The Future of Imprisonment.* Chicago: U of Chicago P.

Mullen, Joan, Kenneth Carlson, and Bradford Smith. 1980. *American Prisons and Jails.* Washington: GPO.

Mundlak, Yair. 1978. "On the Pooling of Time Series and Cross Section Data." *Econometrica* 46:69–85.

Nagin, David. 1978. "General Deterrence: A Review of the Empirical Evidence." In *Deterrence and Incapacitation: Estimating the Effects of Criminal Sanctions on Crime Rates.* Ed. Alfred Blumstein, Jacqueline Cohen, and David Nagin. Washington: National Acad. of Sciences. 95–139.

Nardulli, Peter F., ed. 1979. *The Study of Criminal Courts: Political Perspectives.* Cambridge: Ballinger.

Nardulli, Peter F., James Eisenstein, and Roy B. Flemming. 1988. *The Tenor of Justice: Criminal Courts and the Guilty Plea Process.* Urbana: U of Illinois P.

National Advisory Commission on Criminal Justice Standards and Goals. 1973a. *A National Strategy to Reduce Crime.* Washington: GPO.

———. 1973b. *Criminal Justice System.* Washington: GPO.

———. 1973c. *Courts.* Washington: GPO.

———. 1973d. *Corrections.* Washington: GPO.

National Commission on the Causes and Prevention of Violence. 1970. *To Establish Justice, to Insure Domestic Tranquility: The Final Report of the National Commission on the Causes and Prevention of Violence.* New York: Praeger.

Nerlove, Marc. 1971. "Further Evidence on the Estimation of Dynamic Economic Relations from a Time Series of Cross Sections." *Econometrica* 39:359–81.

Neubauer, David W. 1979. *America's Courts and the Criminal Justice System.* Sacramento: Brooks.

Newman, Graeme. 1978. *The Punishment Response.* Philadelphia: Lippincott.

Nimmer, Raymond T. 1978. *The Nature of System Change: Reform Impact in the Criminal Courts.* Chicago: American Bar Foundation.

Packer, Herbert L. 1968. *The Limits of the Criminal Sanction.* Stanford: Stanford UP.

Parisi, Nicolette, Michael R. Gottfredson, Michael J. Hindelang, and Timothy J. Flanagan, eds. 1979. *Sourcebook of Criminal Justice Statistics–1978.* Washington: GPO.

222 SIMPLE THEORY, HARD REALITY

Parks, Richard W. 1967. "Efficient Estimation of a System of Regression Equations When Disturbances Are Both Serially and Contemporaneously Correlated." *J of the American Statistical Assn.* 62:500–509.

Paternoster, Raymond, L. E. Saltzman, G. P. Waldo, and T. G. Chiricos. 1983a. "Estimating Perceptual Stability and Deterrent Effects: The Role of Perceived Legal Punishment in the Inhibition of Criminal Involvement." *J of Criminal Law & Criminology* 74:270–97.

———. 1983b. "Perceived Risk and Social Control: Do Sanctions Really Deter?" *Law & Society Review* 17:457–79.

———. 1984. "Prosecutorial Discretion in Requesting the Death Penalty: A Case of Victim-Based Racial Discrimination." *Law & Society Review* 18:437–78.

Petersilia, Joan, and Peter W. Greenwood. 1978. "Mandatory Prison Sentences: Their Projected Effects on Crime and Prison Populations." *J of Criminal Law & Criminology* 69:604–15.

Petersilia, Joan, Susan Turner, James Kahan, and Joyce Peterson. 1985. *Granting Felons Probation: Public Risks and Alternatives.* Santamonica: Rand.

Phillips, L., and H. L. Votey. 1972. "An Economic Analysis of the Deterrent Effect of Law Enforcement on Criminal Activity." *J of Criminal Law, Criminology, and Police Science* 63:330–42.

Pierce, Glenn L., and William J. Bowers. 1981. "The Bartley-Fox Gun Law's Short-Term Impact on Crime in Boston." *Annals of the American Acad. of Political and Social Science* 455:120–37.

President's Commission on Law Enforcement and Administration of Justice. 1967a. *Commission Report: The Challenge of Crime in a Free Society.* Washington: GPO.

———. 1967b. *Task Force Report: The Courts.* Washington: GPO.

———. 1967c. *Task Force Report: Science and Technology.* Washington: GPO.

Rathke, Stephen C. 1982. "Plea Negotiating under the Sentencing Guidelines." *Hamline Law Review* 5:271–91.

Rawls, John. 1971. *A Theory of Justice.* Cambridge: Harvard UP.

Rich, William D., L. Paul Sutton, Todd D. Clear, and Michael J. Saks. 1981. *Sentencing Guidelines: Their Operation and Impact on the Courts.* Williamsburg: National Center for State Courts.

Rosett, Arthur, and Donald R. Cressey. 1976. *Justice by Consent: Plea Bargains in the American Courthouse.* Philadelphia: Lippincott.

Ross, H. Laurence. 1976. "The Neutralization of Severe Penalties: Some Traffic Law Studies." *Law & Society Review* 10:403–13.

Ross, H. Laurence, Richard McCleary, and Thomas Epperlein. 1982. "Deterrence of Drinking and Driving in France: An Evaluation of the Law of July 12, 1978." *Law & Society Review* 16:345–74.

Rossi, Peter H., and Howard E. Freeman. 1985. *Evaluation: A Systematic Approach.* 3rd ed. Beverly Hills: Sage.

Rossman, David, Paul Froyd, Glen L. Pierce, John McDevitt, and William J. Bowers. 1979. *The Impact of the Mandatory Gun Law in Massachusetts.* Washington: GPO.

Rothman, David J. 1971. *The Discovery of the Asylum: Social Order and Disorder in the New Republic.* Boston: Little, Brown.

——. 1980. *Conscience and Convenience: The Asylum and Its Alternatives in Progressive America.* Boston: Little, Brown.

Rutman, L. 1980. *Planning Useful Evaluations: Evaluability Assessment.* Beverly Hills: Sage.

Schein, Edgar H. 1985. *Organizational Culture and Leadership.* San Francisco: Jossey-Bass.

Scholz, John T., and Feng Heng Wei. 1986. "Regulatory Enforcement in a Federalist System." *American Political Science Review* 80:1249–70.

Schuwerk, Robert P. 1984. "Illinois' Experience with Determinate Sentencing: A Critical Reappraisal, Part 1: Efforts to Structure the Exercise of Discretion in Bargaining for, Imposing, and Serving Criminal Sentences." *DePaul Law Review* 33:631–740.

Selznick, Philip. 1949. *TVA and the Grass Roots.* Berkeley: U of California P.

Shane-DuBow, Sandra, Alice P. Brown, and Erik Olsen. 1985. *Sentencing Reform in the United States: History, Content, and Effect.* Washington: GPO.

Silberman, M. 1976. "Toward a Theory of Criminal Deterrence." *American Sociological Review* 41:442–61.

Simon, Herbert. 1947. *Administrative Behavior.* New York: Macmillan.

Simonton, Dean Keith. 1977. "Cross-Sectional Time-Series Experiments: Some Suggested Statistical Analyses." *Psychological Bulletin* 84:489–502.

Singer, Richard G. 1978. "In Favor of 'Presumptive Sentences' Set by a Sentencing Commission." *Crime & Delinquency* 24:401–27.

——. 1979. *Just Deserts: Sentencing Based on Equality and Desert.* Cambridge: Ballinger.

Sirisumphand, Thosaporn. 1987. "Public Policy Choices: Trade-Offs between National Defense and Economic Development Expenditures in Developing Countries." Diss. Northern Illinois U.

Sparks, Richard S. 1981. "Sentencing before and after DSL: Some Statistical Findings." In *Report on Strategies for Determinate Sentencing.* Ed. S. L. Messinger, Andrew von Hirsch, and Richard Sparks. A report to National Institute of Justice.

Spohn, Cassia, John Gruhl, and Susan Welch. 1981. "The Effect of Race on Sentencing: A Re-Examination of an Unsettled Question." *Law & Society Review* 16:71–88.

Stimson, James A. 1985. "Regression in Space and Time: A Statistical Essay." *American J of Political Science* 29:914–47.

Sudnow, David. 1965. "Normal Crimes: Sociological Features of the Penal Codes in a Public Defender Office." *Social Problems* 12:254–76.

Sutherland, Edwin H., and Donald R. Cressey. 1978. *Criminology*. 10th ed. Philadelphia: Lippincott.

Sutton, John R. 1987. "Doing Time: Dynamics of Imprisonment in the Reformist State." *American Sociological Review* 52:612–30.

Tappan, Paul W. 1960. *Crime, Justice and Correction*. New York: McGraw-Hill.

Teevan, James J., Jr. 1976. "Subjective Perception of Deterrence (continued)." *J of Research in Crime and Delinquency* 13:155–64.

Thomas, Charles W., and Donna M. Bishop. 1984. "The Effect of Formal and Informal Sanctions on Delinquency: A Longitudinal Comparison of Labeling and Deterrence Theories." *J of Criminal Law & Criminology* 75:1222–45.

Thompson, James D. 1967. *Organizations in Action*. New York: McGraw-Hill.

Tittle, Charles R. 1977. "Sanction Fear and the Maintenance of Social Order." *Social Forces* 5:579–96.

Tittle, Charles R., and Alan R. Rowe. 1973. "Moral Appeal, Sanction Threat, and Deviance: An Experimental Test." *Social Problems* 20:488–98.

Tonry, Michael. 1987. *Sentencing Reform Impacts*. Washington: GPO.

Twentieth-Century Fund Task Force on Criminal Sentencing. 1976. *Fair and Certain Punishment*. New York: McGraw-Hill.

United States Department of Commerce. Bureau of Census. *Statistical Abstract of the United States, 1969–89*. Washington: GPO.

United States Department of Justice. Federal Bureau of Investigation. *Uniform Crime Reports for the United States, 1959–87*. Washington: GPO.

———. Bureau of Justice Statistics. 1988. *Report to the Nation on Crime and Justice*. Washington: GPO.

Utz, Pamela J. 1978. *Settling the Facts: Discretion and Negotiation in Criminal Courts*. Lexington: Heath.

———. 1981. "Determinate Sentencing in Two California Courts." In *Report on Strategies for Determinate Sentencing*. Ed. S. L. Messinger, Andrew von Hirsch, and Richard Sparks. A report to National Institute of Justice.

van den Haag, Ernest. 1975. *Punishing Criminals: Concerning a Very Old and Painful Question*. New York: Basic.

Vold, George B., and Thomas J. Bernard. 1986. *Theoretical Criminology*. 3rd ed. New York: Oxford UP.

von Bertalanffy, Ludwig. 1951. "General Systems Theory: A New Approach to Unity of Science." *Human Biology* 23:303–61.

von Hirsch, Andrew. 1976. *Doing Justice: The Choice of Punishments.* New York: Hill and Wang.

von Hirsch, Andrew, and Kathleen J. Hanrahan. 1981. "Determinate Penalty Systems in America: An Overview." *Crime & Delinquency* 27:289–316.

von Hirsch, Andrew, Kay A. Knapp, and Michael Tonry. 1987. *The Sentencing Commission and Its Guidelines.* Boston: Northeastern UP.

Wagenaar, Alexander C. 1983. *Alcohol, Young Drivers, and Traffic Accidents: Effects of Minimum-Age Laws.* Lexington: Heath.

Waldo, Gordon P., and Theodore G. Chiricos. 1972. "Perceived Penal Sanctions and Self-Reported Criminality: A Neglected Approach to Deterrence Research." *Social Problems* 19:522–40.

Walker, Samuel. 1978. "Reexamining the President's Crime Commission: The Challenge of Crime in a Free Society after Ten Years." *Crime & Delinquency* 24:1–12.

———. 1980. *Popular Justice: A History of American Criminal Justice.* New York: Oxford UP.

Wallace, T. D., and Ashiq Hussain. 1969. "The Use of Error Components Models in Combining Cross Section with Time Series Data." *Econometrica* 37:55–72.

Washington Sentencing Guidelines Commission. 1985. *Sentencing Practices under the Sentencing Reform Act: A Preliminary Report.* Olympia: Washington Sentencing Guidelines Commission.

Weiner, Norbert. 1948. *Cybernatics.* Cambridge: MIT P.

Wilkins, Leslie T., Jack Kress, Donald Gottfredson, J. Calpin, and Arthur Gelman. 1978. *Sentencing Guidelines: Structuring Judicial Discretion.* Washington: GPO.

Williams, Kirk R., and Richard Hawkins. 1986. "Perceptual Research on General Deterrence: A Critical Review." *Law & Society Review* 20:545–72.

Wilson, James Q. 1975. *Thinking about Crime.* New York: Basic.

———. 1983. *Thinking about Crime.* Rev. ed. New York: Basic.

Winslow, Robert W., ed. 1973. *Crime in a Free Society.* 2nd ed. Encino: Dickenson.

Witayapanyanon, Tamasak. 1992. "Illinois' Mandatory Minimum and Determinate Sentence Law: Its Effects on Crime Rates and Judicial Dispositions." *Thai J of Development Administration* 32:112–41.

Wood, B. Dan. 1988. "Principles, Bureaucrats, and Responsiveness in Clean Air Enforcement." *American Political Science Review* 82:213–34.

Zellner, Arnold. 1962. "An Efficient Method of Estimating Seemingly Unrelated Regressions and Tests for Aggregation Bias." *J of American Statistical Assn.* 57:348–68.

Zimring, Franklin E. 1976. "Making the Punishment Fit the Crime: A Consumer's Guide to Sentencing Reform." *Hastings Center Report* 6:13–21.

———. 1983. "Sentencing Reform in the States: Lessons from the 1970s." In *Reform and Punishment: Essays on Criminal Sentencing.* Ed. Michael Tonry and Franklin E. Zimring. Chicago: U of Chicago P. 101–21.

———. 1985. "Violence and Firearms Policy." In *Criminal Violence and Public Policy: An Update of the National Commission on the Causes and Prevention of Violence.* Ed. Lynn A. Curtis. New Haven: Yale UP. 133–52.

Zimring, Franklin E., and Gordon J. Hawkins. 1973. *Deterrence.* Chicago: U of Chicago P.

Zuk, Gary, and William R. Thompson. 1982. "The Post-Coup Military Spending Question: A Pooled Cross-Sectional Time-Series Analysis." *American Political Science Review* 76:40–72.

INDEX